BEYOND VICTIM

YOU CAN OVERCOME
CHILDHOOD ABUSE —
EVEN SEXUAL ABUSE

PSYCHOTHERAPIST
MARTHA BALDWIN, M.S.S.W.

RAINBOW BOOKS

Library of Congress Cataloging-in-Publication Data

Baldwin, Martha, 1941-
    Beyond victim.

        Bibliography: p.
        1. Adult child abuse victim.   2. Sexually abused
children.   3. Psychotherapy.   I. Title.
RC569.5.C55B35   1988   616.85'83   88-4673
ISBN: 0-935834-68-0 (pbk.)

BEYOND VICTIM
BY MARTHA BALDWIN

Produced by Ratzlaff & Associates
Cover Design by Ann Boughton
Published by Rainbow Books
2299 Riverside Drive
Moore Haven, FL 33471

Retail Price: $16.95

Printed in the United States of America

DEDICATION

This book is dedicated
to you.

To your courage, your integrity, your strength, your
vulnerability; and to your darkest, most abused, abusing
side that cries out for your healing love.

Also by Martha Baldwin:

Nurture Yourself To Success
A Psychotherapist's Guide to Ending Self-Sabotage

CONTENTS

ACKNOWLEDGEMENTS

I am grateful to many people who have encouraged me and helped me through the experience of writing this book. My office manager, Peggy Bryant, has spent hours proofreading. Her suggestions and her support are valuable resources. Betty Wright, my editor, has given me the benefit of her wisdom and experience. Marilyn Ratzlaff has been a joy to work with on the production of the book. Debi Pettigrew has given me her loving support and encouragement for the past five years. Thanks to Ann Boughton who is responsible for the cover design.

Bill Davidson's writing expertise helped me improve mine. Brent Babcock and Warren Cremer read the manuscript and gave me their invaluable feedback. Linda Blackwood also lent her eagle-eye and editing expertise to proofreading. I am grateful to Beverly Rodgers for her ideas and her energetic support. And I appreciate Nancy Drisko's encouragement. Her delightful illustrations of the Saboteur and its cohorts finally gave form to the mental images I had of them but couldn't draw.

I also want to thank the members of the women's group whose sharing over the years has touched me deeply and taught me about the impact of childhood sexual abuse and the stages and steps involved in the healing process. I am especially grateful to the people who gave me permission to use parts of their stories for illustrative purposes. Their generosity and courage will light the way for others along the path to healing their lives.

I also am grateful to Barbara and Jim Allen and Michael Allen who are my adopted family. Jut and Elissa Meininger and Liz Holt are my friends who are always here for me.

Joan Bolmer's intelligence and clarity inspire and support me. Bill Brown is my good friend and a healing presence in my life. Gary Baldwin taught me to believe in myself and has encouraged me every step of the way. The presence and wisdom of my office family, Peggy Bryant, Katherine Wise, Sandy Morrison, Erik Dalton, Richard Fiske, and Joe LaRocca, provide a firm foundation for all I do.

My daughters, Lucie and Leigh, lived through my healing process with me. Their strength and integrity and their love and support are the most precious gifts of all.

FOREWORD

The pioneers who conquered the Western wilderness have become so mythologized in our time that we may have forgotten that they were people much like ourselves. The frontiersmen who led them have become Legends transcending mortality. Yet, "greenhorn" and seasoned wilderness scout alike for all the difference in their experience were subject to accident, illness and death on the journey that they shared.

Today we are facing the social wilderness that is not only unfamiliar to us but growing more chaotic and threatening each day. Social and institutional reforms continually fail, leaving us angry and frustrated — with no apparent solution in sight. Nor have we found a Legend in our time to lead the way.

Perhaps because we find our outer way blocked, we have turned inward to achieve some semblance of an orderly and harmonious life. A growing number of people are daring to risk a journey into the inner wilderness and with them has come a new kind of frontiersman — a new kind of therapist. No longer God-the-Doctor, aloof, detached, and antisceptically perfect (leading us with a vague sense of personal inadequacy and inner isolation), but the therapist as a human being with his or her personal adventure of growth — a fellow human being sharing our journey, often revealing his or her own struggle and risking an empathy that is at once both authentic and human.

Martha Baldwin, the author of this book, is such a therapist. She not only offers us guidance as our inner journey reveals dark woods and hidden ravines, but shares her person with us that we might know whatever fear or despair we may encounter we can survive the journey. It takes daring and measured courage to reveal inner struggle, but it bespeaks an integral confidence that we all share the struggle and can emerge from the journey whole and free. Martha Baldwin shows us that confidence. Dare we share it?

Warren P. Cremer

TO THE READER

One of the hardest parts of writing a book is ending it. My growth process continues to evolve rapidly. Each day, through working with myself in meditation and through working with my clients in therapy, I discover more and more about healing after childhood abuse, and especially after sexual abuse.

I also find that my commitment to this work becomes stronger and stronger. Local and national newscasts bring almost daily reports of family violence, mass murders, and murder-suicides. These tragedies reflect generations of suppressed pain in families where physical, emotional, and sexual abuse are the shameful secrets that abused, love-starved children have dared not reveal.

Violence has reached epidemic proportions in our culture. Acts of erupting rage leave scores of people dead and their survivors shackled with grief. It is easy to blame these tragedies on external factors that impact the life of the one who perpetrates the crime. No doubt, these externals are relevant; economic stress, divorce, custody battles, personal losses, bad weather, the holidays, and hundreds of other challenges force people to call upon their deepest resources to cope with changes they don't control.

But stressful changes themselves are not the causes of violence. Violence emerges when inner resources for coping are blocked by emotional chaos, confused thinking, repressed rage and sorrow, and feelings of helplessness and futility. Those determining inner realities have their roots in the experiences of childhood.

When children are physically, emotionally, or sexually abused, they have no choice but to suppress their feelings.

They cannot let themselves recognize the pathology of an abusive parent's behavior, nor can they gain his understanding. Yet they know their survival depends upon him. They learn to suppress their feelings to survive in a world that ignores their needs, their dignity, and their humanness. They grow up depressed, defeated, and filled with buried rage and sorrow.

As adults, their behavior is a direct reflection of how they were treated as children. As long as emotions are held in and suppressed, adult behavior repeats what was experienced when the adult was young and vulnerable. If he was threatened, he will use threats to try to control others. If he was lectured, he will lecture. If he was abused, physically, emotionally, or sexually, he will abuse. If his psyche was destroyed, he will kill.

When as an adult, he encounters the vulnerability of his own children, he is vividly reminded of his own childhood helplessness which he cannot bear to remember. In the face of this powerful emotional loop-back to his buried pain, he unconsciously re-enacts the abuse he endured. He denies his children's vulnerability and preys upon them. They are like extensions of him, without separate needs and feelings of their own. Their boundaries are violated repeatedly and when they become adults, they will carry on the abusive family tradition.

Consequently, an escalating drama of abuse and violence moves through the generations within a family, unnoticed by outsiders until it finally erupts so powerfully that the rest of the world is forced to see. But we don't like to look too closely. We are afraid of what we'll find if we really examine the problem. For if we go to its core, we have to face the inner reaches of our own psyches and encounter what we've buried inside, too.

But it is in that looking and facing and feeling that we can heal ourselves and our culture. We can stop the potential violence that brews inside when we deny our feelings and unconsciously repeat what we once suffered and tried to forget. It is time we recognize the price we are paying for the physical, emotional, and sexually abusive behavior we have ignored for generations. We have created a culture that encourages denial, overlooks lying, controls and manipulates with fear, and promotes addictions to drugs, alcohol, sex, money, work, food, and exercise.

Our challenge is to stop denying reality, to tell the truth, and to learn how to relate to ourselves and others through love rather than through fear, threats, and abuse. We must develop a sane understanding of how to nurture children successfully and teach young people how to be loving, effective parents when they become adults.

Those of us who suffered abuse as children must heal our lives and stop the chain of destructive behavior that culminated in our pain. We must commit ourselves to a continual growth process, using the tools we develop to help ourselves evolve to realize our fullest creative potential. We must recognize and embrace the daily discipline of the on-going process of healing our lives and helping to heal the culture we share.

If you were abused as a child, now is the time to heal your life. I have written this book to address the specific issue of healing after sexual abuse. But the healing principles involved are relevant for emotional and physical abuse as well. You will want to read this book whether or not you think you may have been sexually abused as a child. You can follow the healing process that is presented and work with the issues that are relevant for you. In the process, you will gain a much deeper understanding and acceptance of yourself and of others as well. As you heal your life, you help heal our world.

So set your intention and make your commitment to yourself. It's time to move beyond victim and violence to create a world that is both safe and sane for all of us, especially our children. You have your part to do. I have mine. When we join hands and work together, the synergy we create will generate miracles for the new millenium.

INTRODUCTION

You can heal your life after experiencing incest/sexual abuse. *BEYOND VICTIM* is a step-by-step guide through the stages of the healing process as I lived it myself and have shared it with my psychotherapy clients. This book is not a substitute for therapy. Working with a competent therapist who is skilled in dealing with these issues is an essential part of the healing process. A therapist provides perspective, confrontation, feedback, healthy boundaries, support and encouragement for you on this sometimes discouraging, but intensely challenging path.

As you clear your life from the ravages of sexual abuse, your therapist also can help you spot your Internal Saboteur. Your Saboteur is the negative, fearful-thinking part of you who accompanies you every step of the way. Its mission is to fill your mind with suggestions designed to persuade or con you into stopping short of completely healing your life. You may notice its activity now, because chances are it will object to your buying and reading this book. As you will discover, your Internal Saboteur is dedicated to your self-punishment, self-sabotage, and eventual self-destruction. It doesn't like books or therapists that blow its cover.

If you are still with me, here is a map of the path that lies ahead. Section I of *BEYOND VICTIM* is an overview of the issues involved in dealing with incest/sexual abuse. It includes a description of twenty-three patterns of thought, feeling, and behavior that are common in the lives of women who were sexually abused as children or adolescents. In addition, there are seven payoffs for keeping the abuse secret and refusing to resolve it. All these patterns, translated to their masculine counterparts, are also evident in men who were abused sexually. Though I have addressed this book to women because incest/sexual abuse is so prevalent in their lives. I believe it is much more frequent among men than existing reports indicate. The healing process I describe is just as revelant for men as it is for women. However, the constraints of the English language make it simpler to direct the book to one sex. I hope male readers will be willing to make the necessary translations from she to he.

Section II of this book is the story of my own healing experiences. Writing it was an important part of releasing and forgiving my parents and myself for what happened in our family. Section III begins with an outline of the stages and steps involved in healing your life after sexual abuse. This portion of the book describes each stage of the healing process. It also introduces you to the members of a women's therapy group, which meets once a week to deal with these issues. You will share their experiences as they acknowledge the presence of abuse patterns in their lives and remember and express their intense feelings about incest/sexual abuse and its impact on them. We will explore the fundamental elements that are crucial to healing after sexual abuse. You will be part of the entire process as we work our way through forgiveness and confrontation to transformation, the ultimate healing and release.

My incest memories were blocked until I was forty-one years old. At that time, I had been married and divorced twice. When my memories returned, I gradually realized that before I was four years old, I had had sexual experiences with both my father and my mother. Mother stopped her abuse of me after her brother's death. My father continued to have sexual encounters with me until I was nine and he suffered an emotional breakdown.

During the break-up of my first marriage, I sought healing for the pain I had always known. I searched in every way I could find to understand myself. I undertook and completed eight years of psychoanalytically oriented therapy, attended a wide variety of workshops and conferences, and worked with Transactional Analysis, Gestalt Therapy, Neurolinguistic Programming and Transformational Therapy. Despite all my searching, I still couldn't understand how I could be so successful in many areas of my life and not be able to have what I wanted most: a normal, happy, sane relationship with a man I loved who also loved me.

My male psychoanalytic therapist kept strict boundaries in place throughout my work with him. He was adamant on the subject of limits and their importance. Through our work together, I experienced sane boundaries in a relationship with a man. When I left that relationship with those boundaries between us intact, I was ready to face the violation of boundaries that had occurred with my father. Less than two weeks after ending therapy, I began having fleeting visual images of sexual contacts with my father.

At this time, I was deeply involved in a relationship with a man who was eighteen years older than I. It was a wonderfully exciting experience. I loved him and was overjoyed with our relationship. But, outside my conscious awareness, I was recreating the dynamics in my relationship with my father. Being with Jason felt familiar. He loved me in the same overwhelming, smothering, sometimes irrational way my father had. I was either extremely happy with him or devastated by his latest blaming rage when I failed to satisfy his expectations. I was addicted to the relationship, though my better judgment told me to be careful and protect myself. Despite my knowledge and capacity to see how destructive the patterns between us were, I was drawn to him in a way that defied reason. So I used my well-developed capacity to disassociate in order to ignore the dark side of our relationship and cling to the part I craved. With Jason in my life, I relived what I had hidden from myself for more than thirty years.

When my memories of sexual experiences with my father returned to consciousness, I was both enraged and relieved to find the missing pieces in the puzzle of my life. Now I understood why all my previous therapy had not been complete. The vulnerability, pain, and confusion I had experienced in relationships with men made sense. I knew I no longer had to resign myself to believing I was somehow defective in a way I did not understand. As painful as it was, I welcomed this opening that I knew would allow me finally to complete my healing. I was not sure how I would work my way through my memories and feelings, but I knew I would find the way now that I had discovered the pieces to the puzzle that I had blocked from consciousness for so long.

The path I followed unfolded in numerous ways and opened unexpected doors. Along the way I worked with many men and women who had similar experiences. Their sharing enhanced my own growth and healing as we moved together beyond being the "victims" of incest. Giving up my old, familiar "victim" posture wasn't easy. But gradually, by learning to nurture and encourage myself, I grew up, let go of my pain and anger, and found healing and forgiveness. I reclaimed my self-esteem by extricating myself from the labyrinth of emotional pain and confusing behavior I had endured and accepted as inevitable since childhood.

I have made peace with myself and with my parents and transformed my old destructive behavior into creative activity. When my writing and my work as a therapist help others heal their lives, the pain and hurt I experienced have a larger purpose. Now, from a deep sense of the beauty and meaning in every facet of life's unfolding, I open my heart to share with you what I have discovered through my journey to this point in my life.

CHAPTER I

INCEST/SEXUAL ABUSE: AN OVERVIEW

Sexual abuse occurs when an adult takes sexual liberties and crosses sexual boundaries with a child. It includes fondling and touching the child's breasts or genitals as well as actual oral, genital, or anal intercourse. If the abuser is a family member, the sexual experiences are incestuous and more emotionally damaging to the child than abuse by a stranger, who is not so closely tied to the child's emerging identity. Sexual experiences between older and younger siblings, cousins, or neighborhood children, where the older child or adolescent knows that he is violating the younger child's innocence and vulnerability, are also abusive and destructive. Where this occurs, the older abusing child may have been abused by an adult himself. Sexual play among young children who are peers is normal. Such early sexual experiences are not harmful unless parents' reactions are violent, abusive, and guilt producing.

If a child reports sexual abuse to a parent, or to another trusted adult, that adult's response to her sharing has a powerful impact on the abused child. If the adult believes the child, takes her needs seriously, and sees that she gets help, the healing process can begin. If, however, the adult discounts what the child tells him, implies that she must be mistaken or imagining things, or accuses the child of lying and responds in an angry, abusive way, the child is devastated and buries her secret as deeply as she can. Chances are she won't risk telling anyone and being doubted again.

Sexual abuse occurs far too frequently in our culture. The American Humane Association, Denver, Colorado,

notes that two million children per year are reported
through agencies and therapists as being abused. The Mass-
achusetts Committee for Children and Youth finds that
1/5 to 1/3 of the adult female population and 3% to 9%
of the male population were sexually abused as children.
Both men and women abuse both girls and boys. While
father-daughter, older male-younger female abuse appears
to be the most common occurrence, boys also are abused
by both older men and women, and girls are abused by
their mothers, too. Abused children suffer pain and confusion that follow them into adulthood and distort their lives
and relationships. Unresolved sexual abuse experiences
bear their painful fruit for years after the final sexual act
has ended. They gestate in the darkest reaches of the
psyche, expressing themselves in patterns of thought, feeling, and behavior that create pain, confusion, guilt, and
self-punishment. These patterns dominate the lives of
those who were sexually abused until they are ready to face
their childhood sexual experiences and acknowledge,
express, and release the deeply buried rage, sorrow, guilt
and fear they have hidden and suppressed for years.

In treating sexual abuse in my therapy practice, I have
worked with many women and female teenagers who were
sexually abused as children. Some of these women were
sexually abused by both their parents. Others were abused
by only one parent. Abuse-by-mother issues are much
more confusing, deeply buried, and difficult to face than
abuse by father usually is. Obviously, the damage to a
woman's life is even more severe if her trust was betrayed
by both her parents.

I have also worked with a number of male clients who
were sexually abused. The recovery process and the issues
to be faced are similar for both sexes. In discussing the
healing process in the remainder of this book, I will focus
on women who were abused by their fathers, step-fathers,
grandfathers, uncles, older brothers, or older men who
were not relatives. In our therapy group for these women,

you also will meet members who were sexually abused by both their mothers and their fathers. Again, I hope men will make the necessary translations and be aware that similar behavioral patterns and stages of healing are applicable in their lives as well.

Patterns of self-sacrifice and self-abuse are common in the lives of women who were sexually abused as children or adolescents. The abused child's feelings and her physical body are violated to satisfy someone else's sexual desires. Frequently this someone else is an adult who occupies a position of trust and authority in the child's life. If he is her father, he is someone whose love she craves and needs for emotional support. This may also be true with step-fathers, grandfathers, uncles, and cousins.

The sexually abused child learns that the price of "love" is self-sacrifice; unconsciously, she accepts abuse as an inevitable part of life. She learns not to trust other people. She experiences little power over what happens to her. She feels guilty and different from other children. Unless she brings her abuse experiences into conscious awareness and works through the stages of the healing process, she will continue repeating patterns of self-sacrifice and self-abuse, and perpetuating her life position as a victim.

I have identified twenty-three patterns that frequently emerge in the lives of women who were sexually abused as children. Not all patterns are present in every woman, nor does the presence of four or five patterns necessarily indicate you are a sexual abuse victim. Some of these patterns reflect emotional, physical, and/or sexual abuse, but not necessarily all three. They are marked "e/p/s" in the list below. Other patterns are more directly related to sexual abuse though they also include elements of physical and emotional abuse. They are marked, "e/p/S". A few of the patterns are strongly indicative of sexual abuse and are marked "S". Recognizing that ten or more of the patterns from these three categories are operating in your life gives a strong indication that sexual abuse may have occurred even though you may not remember it. Seeing these patterns and understanding how they may relate to childhood abuse experiences will help you free yourself from the compulsive re-enactment and re-experiencing of the pain, isolation, and vulnerability you felt as a child.

PATTERNS THAT INDICATE POSSIBLE CHILDHOOD SEXUAL ABUSE

1. *There were serious emotional problems in your family when you were a child. (e/p/s)*

If your parents were blatantly dysfunctional and you trusted your own perception of their behavior, you are aware of the pain you experienced growing-up in such a crippling environment. But, if you learned not to trust your own perceptions, you may have misperceived the situation in your family and believed it was normal, even "wonderful." You learned to disassociate yourself from your painful experiences and erased them from your memory in order not to notice the double standards, double messages, and parental abuses of power you faced. Yours may have been a "nice" family, respected in the community. You assumed that what was wrong was with you, not your parents. They supported this assumption, often blaming you and attributing power to you that you did not possess.

Alcohol and drug abuse are common in families where sexual abuse occurs. Compulsive behavior like overworking, overeating, excessive spending, constant dieting, and obsessive cleanliness are also common. Rigid ideas about religion, politics, sex, and the ways children should behave are prevalent. Physical abuse and constant arguing may be the family norm. Other abusive families may appear to be tranquil on the surface until massive fits of rage erupt. Frightened family members walk on eggshells, trying to keep the peace and avoid the next explosion.

2. *As an adult, you become extremely vulnerable to and dependent upon your sexual partner. (e/p/s)*

Your needs for security and stability were not met when you were a child. You long to feel safe in your relationship, but your deep-seated fears keep you terrified that your partner may abandon you. Consequently, you experience childlike feelings of helplessness at the prospect of a conflict with him. You are blindly devoted to him and feel that you could not survive without his love and continued presence in your life. You overlook his negative behavior and hold onto the possibilities you see for what your man can become if only you are able to nurture him to mental health and success through the magic of your love.

3. *You are strongly attracted to men who are destructive, insensitive, infantile, and self-centered. They mirror similar tendencies which are hard for you to see in yourself. (e/p/s)*

Destructive, emotionally unavailable men are stand-ins for your parents whose love you craved but didn't receive. Now you devote yourself to trying to get love from a man who is similarly unable to give it to you. You are trying to work through your childhood pain by means of your relationship with him. He is trying to bolster his shaky self-esteem with the feelings of power he experiences in the relationship with you. He exploits your devotion and childlike attitude of helplessness.

4. *You may be a high achiever who is driven, but quite successful professionally. (e/p/s)*

You are driven to earn the right to be happy and to purge yourself of the deep guilt you feel. If you were sexually abused by your father, you also may have felt unconsciously empowered by him; you are his special girl and you can do and be whatever you choose (as long as you don't replace daddy with a new man in your life with whom you can be truly intimate). Your troubled relationships with men present a sharp contrast to other areas of your life.

5. *Unconsciously, you are hostile toward men, especially your mate. (e/p/s)*

Your hostility is expressed directly in crazy, destructive outbursts of rage that occur when events in the present trigger buried rage from the past. Your hostility also is expressed covertly through exaggerated helplessness (being a burden), illnesses that interfere with life and pleasure, alcohol and drug abuse, and sexual inhibition. You try to control your man through attempts to help him or save him. When these efforts fail, you are enraged and see him as responsible for the buried pain and unhappiness you have carried inside yourself since childhood.

6. *You do not trust men. (e/p/S)*

You hear yourself make statements like, "You can't trust men," or "I don't trust any man I meet." You expect the worst from men and usually you get it. You don't trust yourself either. Your self-esteem is low, and you don't believe you deserve or ever will find genuine, lasting happiness.

7. *You are afraid of closeness with men and avoid a complete, whole relationship that includes a healthy sexual relationship. (e/p/S)*

You may establish a stable marriage based on friendship with very little sex or very volatile love-hate relationships with passionate sex. Or you may choose not to marry. The net result is unconscious loyalty to your original incestuous marriage to father (or the man who abused you).

8. *You have no sense of the boundaries between what is appropriate and inappropriate in a relationship with a man. (e/p/S)*

You are confused about what love is, and you accept destructive, negative behavior from men as an inevitable price for their affection.

9. *You have difficulty saying "no" to men and maintaining your autonomy and self-direction when you are dealing with a man. (S)*

This is particularly true once you establish a sexual relationship. But even before becoming sexually intimate, you may feel that you can't refuse his advances even though you don't like him and are not attracted to him.

10. *You feel powerless in important relationships and are terrified of honest confrontations. Yet you try to control and manipulate other people. (e/p/S)*

The adults in your life when you were a child abused their power with you. Now you tend to alternate between feeling powerless and becoming abusive yourself in stressful situations. Under stress, you become confused, helpless, and demanding, like a child looking for comfort, love and support from a nurturing adult. Because of the confusion of boundaries that took place in your family, you confuse boundaries, too. You play martyr, discounting yourself and others, trying to hold other people responsible for meeting your needs, and ignoring the pain you cause them with your controlling behavior, your demands, and your suffering.

11. *Your capacity to nurture and protect yourself adequately is severely impaired. Instead you nurture others, giving them what you long to receive but don't know how to give yourself. Unconcsiously, you hope they will become dependent on you and never abandon you. Yet you secretly resent their insensitivity to your feelings and play martyr, laying guilt trips on those you serve and sometimes becoming enraged with them for their lack of regard for you. (e/p/S)*

You live for other people, sacrificing yourself and your personal needs in an effort to take care of those whose love seems necessary for your survival. You are insensitive to your own needs and feelings while being acutely attuned to subtle nuances of feelings in others. You project your needs onto them and take care of them while rejecting yourself. Your rejected self is enraged and expresses itself in distorted ways that create pain for you and for others. As a child, you may have functioned as a parent for your immature parents, taking on major responsibilities and emotional burdens that were overwhelming and inappropriate for a child.

12. *You may be afraid of money and money matters, exhibit*

*helplessness about money, and long for a man to take care of you
financially. (e/p/S)*

You may have careless, childlike, and impulsive spending habits and try to use money and material items as a
substitute for love. Your father (or other abuser) may have
given you money and material advantages to allay his guilt
for his sexual activity with you.

13. *You may engage in promiscuous, impulsive sexual
behavior, which often is coupled with alcohol and drug abuse,
and is extremely dangerous and self-destructive. (S)*

You may have frequent sexual liasons with men who are
not available for anything more than sex with you (affairs
with married men, for example). Or you may frequent
bars, drink heavily, and pick up strange men for sexual
encounters. You may lead a double life. Your night-life
might shock people who know you as responsible and successful professionally. In extreme cases, you may disassociate completely from different aspects of yourself and
manifest multiple personalities.

14. *You may experience various degrees of sexual dysfunction, from vaginismus, where intercourse is extremely painful or
impossible, to lack of interest in and desire for sex, or extreme
fear of any kind of sexual activity. (S)*

15. *You may engage in prostitution and experience your sexuality as your only attribute. (S)*

16. *There are powerful blocks to the free flow of energy in
your body, especially in the thighs, hips, and genitals. (S)*

You may keep your pelvic muscles tensed so that
feeling in your genitals is blocked. (Rolfing is very helpful in releasing these blocks and the accompanying
memories and feelings.)

17. *You may eat compulsively and use food as a weapon
against yourself. (e/p/S)*

You believe that eating is bad. This reflects your belief
that you are bad and guilty and therefore don't deserve to
be nurtured and fed. You alternate starving yourself with
binge eating. You may be anorexic or extremely obese.

Both are ways of hiding your sexuality, which you fear and seek to disown.

18. *You are sometimes depressed and suicidal, plagued by anxiety attacks, and overwhelmed by feelings of helplessness, confusion, guilt, and futility. (e/p/S)*

You doubt you will ever be healthy, happy, and well, and live dreading your next painful episode of anxiety and depression. You may be addicted to tranquilizers or antidepressant medications that have been prescribed for you to treat your emotional pain.

19. *You may have experienced psychosis precipitated by a threat to your blocked memory of sexual abuse. (S)*

For example, a psychotic episode occurs in response to an affair with an older man who relates to you as your father did, and taps into deeply buried childhood feelings of pain, rage, and confusion. You are terrified and retreat into psychosis to avoid the near return of blocked memories. Psychosis also may be triggered by rejection and abandonment by a mate or lover.

20. *You may experience recurrent nightmares or compulsive recurrent mental images. You also may be afraid of the dark. (e/p/S)*

Sexual imagery is common in your dreams as are bathroom scenes, sewers, and toilets that need flushing. You also may have memory pictures that haunt you because they are like still-movie shots that have no scene that precedes or follows them. As your memory returns, you may find that the scenes that precede and follow these isolated still pictures are abuse experiences you hid from yourself.

21. *Fear and guilt are dominant forces in your life. (e/p/S)*

You engage in repeated efforts to make your life worthwhile despite your deep inner feelings of worthlessness and despair. Yet you are afraid of success and expect to lose whatever you gain, anticipating eternal punishment for your childhood sins.

22. *"My father was perfect. My mother was nuts." (e/p/S)*

You over-idealize your father and fail to see his destructive side while seeing the negative side of your mother and ignoring her positive attributes. Consequently, you overvalue and misperceive men while devaluing and discounting women. (Or you may over-idealize your mother and see your father as totally bad. This pattern is common with men who were sexually abused by either their mothers or their fathers.)

23. *Your thinking is impaired when you try to analyze your relationships with others. (e/p/S)*

You tend to see things as you want them to be rather than as they actually are. You refuse to consider the consequences of what you are ignoring, going against your own better judgment and setting yourself up to be victim time after time.

DID YOU EXPERIENCE SEXUAL ABUSE?

Various reports indicate that more than 36% of all women seeking treatment at all kinds of mental health facilities know they were sexually abused as children. Many have been in therapy repeatedly and have never told a therapist what happened to them as children. They are embarrassed and ashamed to reveal their guilty secret. Because it is a difficult subject for many people to discuss, I routinely ask my clients if they experienced any kind of sexual abuse as children.

Even if their honest answer is "no" when I make this inquiry, the possibility that abuse occurred still exists. Many women have blocked their memories of sexual encounters, especially if those encounters were with their natural fathers. Women are more likely to remember sexual abuse when the abuser was a grandfather, step-father, uncle, brother, or cousin. Though some women do remember being sexually abused by their natural fathers, many have blocked their memory completely. In these instances, the presence of the behavioral patterns I have described above may be the only available clue to the underlying cause of the woman's difficulty.

If you remember and know that you were sexually abused as a child, you will benefit from identifying the sexual abuse patterns that are relevant in your life. By recognizing and taking responsibility for these patterns in your behavior, you create new choices for yourself for healing, health, and successful relationships. You also will want to enter a therapy program for assistance and support as you work through the stages of the recovery process.

If you have no memory of sexual abuse, but a number of these sexual abuse patterns are present in your life, you also will want to enter a therapy program. As you read about these patterns and identify them in yourself, notice your reaction to allowing yourself even to entertain the possibility that you might have experienced sexual abuse that you have blocked from your conscious memory. If you are heavily invested in denying the possibility, you may be expressing the strength of your desire to keep the abuse secret hidden in order to protect your abuser and yourself from facing what happened.

When this occurs with a client I am working with in therapy, I do not push her, but simply maintain that I see this as a possibility she may want to consider, and give her time and space to integrate what I have said. Since I ask my clients to keep a dream journal, we can watch her dreams and notice what her unconscious mind is communicating. Sometimes, several months later, she may have a particularly vivid dream or she may remember some incident that surprises her and again suggests the possibility we have discussed.Other memories and dreams may emerge gradually. Or she may continue to deny the possibility that abuse occurred and concentrate on other issues in her life. If her difficulties persist, I again may suggest that she consider the possibility that she has blocked her memory of events in her childhood that are causing her pain in the present.

If my client is open to the possibility that sexual abuse

might have occurred, but upon reflection and consideration, concludes that it simply doesn't fit with her experience, I assume that she is correct and that abuse probably did not occur. If she has no other strong reactions like illness, acting out, intense anger, or missed sessions, and if she makes progress in her therapy, feels better, and is more successful in her life and her relationships, the possibility that sexual abuse might have occurred is dismissed.

If, however, she is drawn to the possibility, has dreams that appear to confirm it, continues her therapy, and begins to feel better after talking about the abuse issue, she may begin to remember as we proceed. Hypnotic regression can be very helpful, though usually a gradual process is necessary. In a relaxed state of consciousness, I invite her unconscious mind and her higher self to take her back in time and space to whatever earlier time in her life she needs to remember and take into account in order to heal her life. This suggestion honors whatever pace she sets as she approaches her memories, sees partial pictures, blocks the next step, and gradually readies herself to see the whole of what she experienced. It is crucial that she not be pushed to go too quickly, but simply be assured that if abuse did occur she will remember as she is ready to handle those memories and the feelings that accompany them.

Remembering the incest secret is like recognizing that daddy had a dark, crazy side. When the secret is blocked from memory, daughter is able to keep an idealized memory of her father intact. She does this at great cost to herself, because she will find the rejected aspects of her father in the men she attracts. She will be surprised and confused when her lover/husband shows his dark side and will be angry, hurt, and outraged by his behavior. "How can he do this to me?" As long as she keeps her illusion of her father's perfection, she will be drawn into relationships with men that are painful and destructive and that mirror the crazy father she has hidden from herself, inside herself.

Blocked memory of the incest secret also keeps her

from seeing the whole picture of her mother. She sees her mother as bad, crazy, weak, helpless, and jealous. She is alienated from her mother and sees the dark side of her quite clearly. But she misses the good mother, the nurturing mother, the side of mother that may have been bright, light, and beautiful. And she cannot incorporate this blocked side of her mother within herself.

Missing this valuable, nurturing energy is also enormously costly to her. She feels inadequate to care for herself and nurture herself. Instead she nurtures others, and then expects that they will reciprocate, nurturing her in return. She looks for this essential nurturing energy especially in the man she loves. She projects the disowned good, nurturing mother onto her lover/husband and feels that her survival depends upon his presence in her life. This creates a massive dilemma. She sees her nurturing as coming from her man. At the same time, she disowns the dark-sided crazy father in herself and sees it in this same lover-husband. As long as she continues to split herself in this way, she is doomed to survive by ignoring the crazy, hurtful side of both herself and her husband/lover in order to have the nurturing mother energy disowned in herself and projected onto him.

He is engaged in the complimentary side of this projection. He is attracted to the good, strong father in her, often having had a cold, distant, alcoholic, isolated father himself. He sees his father as bad and troubled; a poor model for him as a male. He views his mother as his savior, the one who took care of him despite his father's bad treatment of her. He fails to see the dark side of mother and instead finds that in his lover/wife. She manifests the crazy mother he fails to see and the strong father he missed as well. Their positions are complimentary. He plays crazy father to her crazy mother and good mother to her good father. He may have been sexually abused as a child, also.

In relationships like this, both partners are challenged to see, claim, accept, and express their feelings about both their parents. At the same time, they must develop healthy, nurturing parent parts within themselves to care for the hurt, damaged child parts within each of them. Only then can they forgive the whole of both their parents in order to heal their own lives. Once they become whole and healed as individuals, they can relate to each other in a healthy, centered, loving energy rather than from the abusive, fearful energy they incorporated from their parents.

THE INCEST/ABUSE SECRET AND THE PAYOFFS FOR KEEPING IT

The incest/abuse secret is a burden that destroys the one who clings to it, either because of blocked memory, or after memory returns, because of fear of releasing the self-sabotaging payoffs that derive from its hold on her life. As long as she holds onto the secret, the woman who was sexually abused as a child remains a victim, sabotaging her life, and clinging to destructive payoffs like these:

1. The incest/abuse victim feels special and different from others. She may feel that she has a special mission that sets her apart from others, or she may feel hopelessly isolated and helpless.

2. She may be driven to achieve by the powerful energy of the guilt she carries, or she may be addicted to repeated failures and guilty, suicidal fantasies. Often, she is a workaholic, exhausting herself by taking care of others but resenting them for letting her.

3. She is addicted to being a victim, a tragic figure with all the attendant pain, drama, and excitement a martyr generates. She cherishes pain and illness and clings to it, using it to abuse and manipulate other people whose presence she thinks she needs in order to survive.

4. She avoids growing up and instead continues to blame her problems on others, especially the man in her life and her children.

5. She fears her power (because she is afraid of being

abusive herself and doesn't like to notice the subtle, indirect ways she hurts others) and blocks her creativity. She fascinates others with what she might do if she ever owned her strengths and resources.

6. She spends her energy trying to fix others while refusing to face herself.

7. She clings to relationships that are destructive and debilitating rather than finding the strength to face herself and risk losing the relationship if it cannot survive her healing.

Letting go of the incest/abuse secret means letting go of these payoffs. It further includes redeciding about one's identity, which has been tied to keeping the secret. It is a big step and a process that requires time, patience, and a treatment program that assists the abuse survivor in cleansing her beliefs, her thinking, her emotions, her behavior, and her physical body from the aftermath of childhood sexual abuse.

Where sexual abuse was incestuous, the overriding issue that makes letting go of the secret such a challenge is control. An incestuous relationship is a vehicle for controlling the life of a child. The injunctions from father to daughter are, "Don't be separate from me. Let me control your life in return for my loving/abusing you." And, "Don't ever tell our secret."

Father also gives his child a message about her mother. "Don't upset your mother" implies that mother, and therefore females in general, are weak and need protection in order to survive. All these injunctions are attempts to hold the child in an alliance with her father that assures the secrecy of their sexual activities and teaches her that she, like mother, is weak, helpless, and needs a protector: the one who also abuses her, her dad.

She also learns that she is supposed to care for her parents, protect them, and be acutely sensitive to their needs and feelings. Often she functions as a child/parent in her home, performing tasks that are her parents' responsibilities. This teaches her to be a superb caretaker for others. But she also learns to ignore her needs and feelings, just as her father did, when he used her for his sexual pleasure. She has great difficulty caring for herself adequately. She will put up with endless provocations from others, especially the men in her life, and remain more concerned about them than she is interested in caring adequately for herself. She sets herself up to be victim again and again, reinforcing her experience as a victim of sexual abuse, and forwarding her self-destructive life script.

This self-destructive script is founded on the injunction from her father, "Don't be separate from me (let me control your life)." He reinforces this message with, "Don't dare tell anyone our secret . . . ever," and "Don't upset your mother." His counter-injunction to her is, "Be perfect." Her mother's injunction is a strong, "Don't be (my rival)." This is countered by, "Be my mother."

Breaking out of this destructive life script requires seeing these patterns clearly and redeciding about remaining a victim in order to buy pseudo-nurturing and the feeling of being important because of being needed by others. Redeciding the victim position means looking squarely at yourself and claiming all of who you are. It also requires breaking the injunction to keep the secret. Ultimately your challenge is to confront your father and your mother; or, if they are no longer living, to talk with surviving family members about what actually happened during your growing-up years. Preparing for the confrontation helps to surface the deep reservoir of feelings you have to face, accept, express, and release as you move through the stages of the healing process.

With this overview of the issues involved in facing sexual abuse, I invite you to join me on the journey I made through the healing process. In my personal sharing, I have changed some names and identifying details to respect the privacy of those who were my teachers and companions along the way.

CHAPTER 1i

CHILD OF ALABAMA

I was a child of Alabama, but being a Southerner didn't make sense to me. I knew our Southern heritage was supposed to mean our family was special in some mysterious way I didn't understand. I couldn't figure it out, and I was baffled by the inconsistencies I noticed all around me.

As a child, I remember asking lots of questions about what I noticed and did not understand. "Why does that water fountain say 'colored?' Why do they have different restrooms?" I wondered.

These things were confusing. Black women took care of me and seemed to love me. They cleaned our home and cooked meals for us. Surely they must have used our bathroom. Surely they drank the same water we did. Why was it different when we went downtown?

I wondered what it meant when I heard people at church saying the beautiful words of the Episcopal Prayer Book, confessing their sins, asking for forgiveness, and praising God. Then, only moments after church was over, these same people gathered in small clusters outside, criticizing, judging, and saying cruel things about those who weren't present to hear. How could that be? Why didn't church work better than that?

Contradictions like these made no sense to me. Neither did the answers I got to my questions, when I got any answers at all. Sometimes I was admonished not to be impudent by asking about such things. I was told that when I grew up I would understand why black people were different. They were supposed to be dirty somehow. But they cleaned our house. How could that be possible? I just knew they liked me and I liked them.

I noticed contradictions like these all around me. My curiosity created a profound dilemma for me. Was I to decide that I saw more clearly than the adults who sometimes answered and sometimes refused to answer my questions? Or did they know something that was beyond my grasp? My survival need for these adults led me to conclude that surely they must be right! I must be mistaken somehow. There must be something children couldn't see or understand.

And so I decided not to trust my own perceptions. My solution was to disconnect one reality from another. I began to disassociate.

Learning to disassociate solved another, even more perplexing and painful problem for me. By disassociating, I made sure I kept the terrible secret I held deep inside me. The good girl in me didn't know the bad, guilty girl who played doctor with Daddy in his workshop. He always locked the door after the good girl skipped happily across the backyard to "help" him out there. She didn't know what happened after the lock clicked shut. Only the bad, guilty girl knew about the rest. It was years before they discovered each other.

Though my capacity to disassociate helped me avoid this confrontation for many years, I paid a huge price for the secret I protected by forgetting. In the meantime, other incidents reinforced the costly choice I made not to trust my own perceptions of my own experience. I learned that children were to be seen, not heard. I translated this to mean that children must have nothing to say worth hearing. Their thoughts, their feelings, their ideas obviously did not count. Children didn't count; I didn't count. What I experienced, said, or thought wasn't important.

It was also strange to me that adults were careful not to say anything nice about a child when the child could hear what the adult had to say. That was supposed to keep children from thinking too highly of themselves. In practice it meant that criticism was OK, but praise and affirmation were suspect. Fear was in charge.

In those days, the South was afraid of its children; afraid of a new generation; afraid of the future; and afraid of change. Its glory was in the past when plantations were plantations and slaves were slaves. In those golden days, people lucky enough to come from "good families" enjoyed a lifestyle that Yankees finally destroyed with their foreign, evil ideas, and their cruel generals like Sherman.

Everyone knew Southerners were the only ones who really loved Negroes. After all, they looked after their faithful servants. They gave them their leftovers and old clothes; they gave them a ride to town in the back seat of the car after they'd cleaned house, cooked lunch, washed, and ironed, earning $2.00 a day.

Why "colored" people were so different bothered me; but I was a child and my status sometimes felt similar to theirs. The idea seemed to be that children existed to meet their parents' needs, just as blacks apparently existed to take care of white people. Sometimes I'd ask myself how I got so lucky to be white instead of black. Yet when we rode through "colored town" on a Saturday or Sunday, I got the distinct impression that the colored children were having lots of fun, jumping, dancing around, and getting to eat catfish cooked on street corners by old black men who seemed to be enjoying themselves, too. They looked lots happier than I felt.

For mine was a fearful world. We talked about love, but lived in fear. There was fear of the future, fear of blacks, fear of change, fear of children, fear of other people (especially what they thought and might say), fear of illness, fear of Yankees, fear of ideas, fear of another Great Depression, fear of money, fear of death. There was fear of just about everything. And fear is a painful energy.

Fortunately for me, my first seven years also taught me a lot about love. My mother adored me, though she too crossed sexual boundaries with me. Those experiences I carefully blanked out and assigned to the bad, dark, guilty child in me. The good girl helped Mother with chores, listened to her marvelous stories, played school with her, and learned to read. She even brought my goldfish, Lucky and Silver, back to life when we found them floating on top of the fishbowl. She was magic. She was everything in my eyes.

My father was happier during my early years, too. World War II was raging. He was too old to enlist, but he had a victory garden. Sometimes he let me help pick vegetables. I was "Daddy's Little Girl." We adored each other. I sat on the curb everyday at lunch time waiting to catch the first glimpse of his car rounding the corner, bringing him back to my world for a little while.

Mealtimes were happy times. Mother, and the cook when she was there, started early in the morning, cooking vegetables for lunch. When we sat down at the dining room table at noon, there was a wonderful array of fresh tomatoes, turnip greens, beans, fried corn, salads, and on very special days, sweet potato pie for dessert. We had tall glasses of iced tea with lemon. I loved the fun of stirring in sugar that never dissolved completely, but floated to the bottom of the glass and sat there inviting me to stir some more and play cook at the same time.

I had two grandmothers, a grandfather, two uncles and aunts, and one first cousin, who was adored by everyone. He was a boy. I knew that was important. I'd never be quite as special as he. But he was fourteen years older than I, and I thought he was wonderful, too. His occasional visits when he would play with me, bring me presents, and call me "Muffin" were highlights of my growing-up years.

When I was four years old, the challenges of tragedy and death confronted our family. No one seemed to know how to cope with grief. And no one was there to help us learn what we all needed to know about living through such difficult times.

The first tragedy was the death of my uncle, my mother's only brother, in an automobile accident. Mother was devastated by her grief. She cried, she was ill, she suffered. Nothing seemed to comfort her. She was overwhelmed with guilt and stopped her sexual activities with me.

The following year, my father's mother died. I saw my father "break down" only once. It was at the hospital when he was told that she had breast cancer. After that he buried his pain deep inside as men who were "real men" were supposed to do.

Eventually, Mother made a partial recovery from her grief because her parents needed her. My grandmother had several slight strokes but was not physically impaired. My grandfather was becoming more deaf and senile. They moved from Tennessee to Alabama to live with us. Their presence gave Mother a purpose. She could express her love for them and deal with her guilt while sublimating her grief for her brother.

And now I had "Nanny" all the time. I was her namesake, and we adored each other. She was my only grandmother after Mom, Daddy's mother died. Nanny was the center of my new world after all these changes. She was my first spiritual teacher. I learned to say the Episcopal creed. She made sure I was standing, even if it was in the middle of my bed at naptime, when I recited those sacred words. She taught me to read from her New Testament that had great big letters she could see with her aging eyes and I could follow with my young ones. I shared her devotionals every day.

Nanny talked to me about death. She hoped she'd die healthy and suddenly one day when the Lord was ready to receive her spirit. She also prepared me for her death, for what she taught me to read was the 14th Chapter of John's Gospel. *"Let not your hearts be troubled. Ye believe in God, believe also in Me. I go to prepare a place for you . . . I will come again to bring you unto Me . . . In My Father's house are many mansions . . .''*

But I knew she'd never leave me. Death just couldn't happen to her. It couldn't happen to my Nanny.

One day when I was seven, I told her goodbye after breakfast. As I went out the door, I turned to wave to her once more. She was sitting at the table, on the edge of her chair as she always was, full of energy to begin her day. I knew she would be helping Mother with the house, doing her share of the work.

Three hours later, a friend's mother brought me home for lunch. An ambulance was parked in front of our house, its back doors gaping open. Daddy met me in the front yard. I saw Mother's friend, Sara, on the front porch. Granddaddy was sitting in a chair on the lawn, beneath my favorite tree. I knew something terrible had happened.

"Nanny has gone away to live with God." I heard what Daddy said. But, I was dumbfounded. I looked at Granddaddy. How could he possibly be just sitting there like nothing had happened, like this was a normal day? And where was God? How could He be so mean and so selfish? Didn't He know how much I needed Nanny here with me? This must be some terrible punishment for me. God must be punishing me for all the times I had been bad. This couldn't really be happening.

Mother was inside the house, overwhelmed with grief. She sat in front of her dresser mirror, sobbing. Her tears were terrifying to me. Everyone was trying to comfort her. Her world was shattered; her brother, and now her mother were gone. She was left with her deaf, already senile father. Somehow the fact that she still had Daddy and me didn't seem to matter. I always knew that the bond between my parents was not strong enough to fill her needs. I was not enough either. She was desolate. And she never fully recovered from her grief.

Twenty-nine years later, during my first therapy session, I finally was able to cry for Nanny myself. In 1948, no one around me realized children grieve, too. Instead of crying, I became a straight A student. I got lots of strokes from adults for being smart, and I wanted to be sure I didn't upset Mother anymore than she already was. I also wanted to make up to Daddy for not being the son I was sure he wished he'd had. In my child's mind, I interpreted his sexual doctor games with me as an effort to make me like him; a male, instead of the female I am.

Yet, the love I experienced in those first seven years was stronger than all the fear, hurt, and sexual abuse that were also there. Love, woven through the pain, gave me the foundation I needed to survive the fearful years of unresolved rage and sorrow I faced in the future. That powerful love I absorbed early in my life kept me going, kept me seeking ways to cope, kept me active, even though I also experienced severe depression and battled physical illness. The energy of love carried me through until, as a woman in my 30's, I learned that through love and lots of dedicated work with myself, I could heal my life.

Ultimately I became the therapist-teacher I'd needed as a child. In learning to help myself and others, I've found that life is incredibly beautiful and precious. The inner peace I know now is more beautiful than anything I'd ever dared dream was possible. I've learned to live in love. I feel as safe and special again as the little girl, Muffin, was, snuggled close to Nanny, reading those beautiful words.

"Let not your hearts be troubled . . ."

Only now I also have the depth and strength that come with meeting life and its challenges head on . . .

CHAPTER III

THE SUMMER OF MY FATHER'S DEATH

The turning point in my life came in March, 1980, on a mountain in the Mohave desert. I was part of a two-week workshop with a doctor named Brugh Joy. A year earlier, Virginia Satir had mentioned him to me. She told me she planned to attend one of his conferences. I immediately set out to get a copy of his book, *Joy's Way*. If Virginia Satir, one of the finest therapists in the world, thought he was a teacher, I wanted to know what he had to say.

I read *Joy's Way* in March of 1979. In it, Brugh describes his transformational journey and talks about the energy of unconditional love. I responded to his teaching with every fiber of my being. My inner guidance was clear: "You must work with this man." I knew I had been seeking this message of love all my life.

My husband, Dean, and I called to request places in a June conference with Brugh. There was not space available for both of us then so we enrolled in a session scheduled for the following March. I was frustrated to have to wait so many months, but it wasn't long before I discovered why my desert experience was delayed.

There were issues I had to confront before I made my desert sojourn. As it turned out, June, 1979, marked the beginning of the wrenching summer of my father's death. The depth of understanding I found in *Joy's Way* helped me face and survive that experience. Journal writing sustained me through making the most challenging choice I had yet encountered. All of this was necessary before I was ready to encounter Brugh.

At that time, I still had no memory of childhood sexual experiences with my father. In the light of what I now remember, my conflict that summer was even deeper than I realized as I lived through it. I was not only facing my father's death, I was also grappling with my buried rage and guilt, my emotional dependence on him, and my secret shame. While it was happening, I only knew that the intensity of my pain seemed much greater than a father's death should cause.

The ordeal began on a Thursday afternoon. Feeling clear and good after a session with my therapist, I went by for a visit with my parents who shared a room at the nursing center. They were both helpless invalids.

My mother was senile; my father was paralyzed on his right side and unable to speak. He had his first massive stroke in November, 1976, less than six months after he and I put Mother into a nursing home in Alabama when he was no longer able to care for her at home. After his stroke, when I was faced with the responsibility for two invalid parents, I decided to move them from Alabama to Oklahoma where I could supervise their care. In December, 1976, the three of us made the trip by air ambulance, and I settled them in a nursing home in Oklahoma City.

After this move, I was torn between the needs of my family, the demands of my business, and the terrible responsibility I felt for them. I made endless trips to the nursing home, trying to cheer them and help them adjust to their situation. Mother seemed reasonably content, but Daddy was miserable. I tried every possibility I could conceive to amuse him and help him develop some way to communicate. Nothing worked. He grew more and more frustrated, and I tried harder and harder. I realized I was exhausting myself and accomplishing nothing. I also saw that I had to come to terms with my relationship with both my parents, but especially with my father. The emotional hold he had on me was powerful. My life revolved around trying to make him happy.

Through therapy, I recognized that I needed to separate my life from his and stop allowing his demands to control me. My older daughter was busy taking charge of her life and setting limits with me. Her determination woke me up to the fact that I had protected my parents far too long from the fact that I had grown up, too. I had a life of my own, separate from theirs, and other responsibilities that were just as important as the obligation I felt to them.

Gradually, I began breaking the emotional bonds. I struggled with my guilt, which I knew was really rage. I felt like a robot, making endless trips to the nursing home, bringing ice cream and trying to comfort them. Nothing I did seemed to help. Eventually, I began to release them and to resign myself to the fact that I wasn't responsible for Daddy's unhappiness.

On this particular Thursday afternoon in early June, 1979, they greeted me warmly as I entered their room. Mother was seated in her chair, content in the privacy of the child's world she occupied. Daddy was watching TV, his only occupation, trapped as he was with a body that no longer worked and a mind that was still alert but didn't allow him to speak. I hugged them both and then talked with Daddy, who, though he couldn't respond verbally, was able to communicate with me by nodding his head.

Quite spontaneously, I shared with him my growing awareness that I wanted to spend more time with my family that summer. "I need relief from the pressure I put on myself to be at the nursing home whenever I have time off from work. My children are growing up (at that time they were 15 and 10), and I want to enjoy these precious years while they're still at home," I told him. I assured him that I would see him regularly during the week, but I would be spending weekends at our lake home. I knew he wouldn't like this change, and I struggled with my guilt at disappointing him. But he seemed to understand; he nodded his head, agreeing with me. I felt very close to him and accepted by him. It was one of the most honest conversations we ever had. Instead of trying to please and placate him as I usually did, I was sharing with him how I really felt and what my needs were. And he seemed to understand and even encourage me!

I was elated when I left the nursing home after putting him to bed and tucking him in for the night. I felt a whole new level of understanding in our relationship and was excited to share my good news with my family when I got home. The next day we'd be heading out for a weekend at the lake.

But, the next morning, the phone call came. It was 7:00 A.M. "A massive stroke! the ambulance is on its way; come at once." Dazed, my older daughter, Lucie, and Dean and I drove to the nursing home and followed the ambulance to the hospital. I was churning inside. So this was his real response to my honesty with him.

Always he had clung to me. When I was nineteen, he had stood before me with his shotgun, threatening to kill himself if I married the young man I loved. I chose Daddy, not my fiance. It was a costly mistake, although at the time I didn't even see it as a choice. It never occurred to me that my father was bluffing. His hold over me was so strong the only thing I could conceive of doing was to believe him and feel responsible for his life.

Frequently he would say he felt a heart attack coming on (though he never had one) if I crossed him or got angry with him. Now he'd finally done it; he'd managed to have his stroke and timed it perfectly so I could feel guilty if I chose to feel responsible for his life and death as I'd done so many times before. I had hurt him with my words, he seemed to be telling me, hurt him so badly he wouldn't survive.

My head and my heart told me this was his choice and his responsibility just as it was my choice to honor my needs and my family's needs. But the Frightened Child in me knew this was his way of punishing me for daring to put my needs ahead of his. I struggled with the opposing energies within me. My internal, Frightened Child was devastated, sure she'd finally killed Daddy by daring to claim her right to her own life. The newly developed nurturing Parent within me assured the Child this was not her doing. She didn't hold the power of life and death over this man. It was his choice. The Child was not convinced, but the healthy, Grown-up me took charge and dealt with the emergency at hand.

The truth was, I knew he was ready to die. The therapist I had engaged to see him regularly had told me Daddy was thinking about dying. Just a few weeks before, when he came to dinner at my home, arriving by Medi-Van in his wheel chair, he had motioned and signaled frantically, insisting that he communicate something to Dean and me. Finally Dean understood him; he wanted to be sure I had the deed to his cemetery lots in Alabama. He wanted to be buried there. It was an enormous relief to him when Dean finally understood what he was trying to tell us. He reached for Dean with gratitude in what was one of the few moments of real connection the two of them ever shared.

So I knew he was ready. And perhaps dying was his way of trying to give me my freedom. I'm sure in many ways it was. Yet what I'd always wanted, and never had, was my life, clear and free for me, and a relationship with my parents that was a grown-up, adult one. I wanted to have my life and have my father alive, too.

That was not to be. The bond between us was too deep, too complex, too guilty for either of us to remember, acknowledge, and face with each other. It was a secret buried in me and hidden even from myself. Whether he remembered or not, I'll never know.

When we arrived at the hospital, I told his doctor that I knew he was ready to die. I asked that no extraordinary measures be taken to prolong his life. For three-and-a-half years, he had lived in a wheelchair, paralyzed and trapped in a body he could no longer use, without even speech to allow him some control over his existence. Now he was even worse, but he didn't die.

He was weakened terribly by this latest stroke, which had left new paralysis on his left side. But by Sunday afternoon, on my 38th birthday, he was able to watch golf matches on TV. He seemed interested, though his responses were much more feeble than before. I stayed with him as much as I could and visited him each morning before going to my office.

By Wednesday morning I was exhausted. Instead of going to the hospital, which involved an hour's driving time round trip, I called and asked the nurses to tell him I would be there later that afternoon. About 2:00 P.M., I was working with a family in my office, when an emergency phone call rang through my answering service. "Come at once. He's had another stroke and he's dying."

I raced to the hospital, my heart pounding. Once again, I had neglected Daddy to take care of myself. Now he was really going to do it. The Frightened Child in me clutched at the pit of my stomach. My nurturing, Grown-up Self comforted her, reminding her that she did not control his living or his dying. Again this was his choice, the outcome of his life, his responsibility, not mine or hers. But the Child, locked in the horror of her secret, unremembered shame and the threats of, "If you ever tell, I'll have to kill us both." knew better. Though she settled down and relaxed her grip, she wasn't healed or about to go away. She simply retreated, burying herself a little deeper, so the strong me could face what had to be faced.

The final devastation of this latest stroke left him with only Cheyne-Stokes breathing. Each breath, sounding like his last gasp for air, was followed by a pause so long I knew it had to be final; then, another gasp continued the cycle. I stood beside his bed, holding his hand. His gasping went on and on, punctuated by the long, still pauses that seemed like death. He was gone, yet his body breathed. And kept breathing. A nun came in, dressed in white. In my dazed state, she looked and felt like an angel. The conflict inside me raged. "Please help him die; please let him live." I felt relief and despair with each fresh gasp he made. How long could this last?

The afternoon wore on. Dean joined me, lovingly aware of my pain and offering his support. My friend, Liz, the therapist who had been working with Daddy, came in the room. No one had called her. She simply knew she should come. After she left, it seemed clear that this might go on for quite a while. Finally, I went out of the room, keeping my ears tuned into the breathing sounds I could hear even from the hall. Day turned into night. I went home, exhausted, but too keyed up to sleep. I wrote in my journal, finding relief in putting words on paper, honoring my feelings and my experience in that way. Eventually I meditated.

As I became quiet, letting my breath flow, releasing my thoughts, centering myself, I felt tremendous peace surrounding me and filling my body. I continued to breathe deeply, embracing this wondrous serenity. Gradually I became aware of a familiar presence there beside me. My grandmother's face appeared, an experience I had never had before in meditation. She reminded me of the 14th Chapter of St. John. *Let not your heart be troubled.* She assured me that she was with me and that she was there to welcome my father to the other side. She let me know there were others waiting to receive him, too. *There is nothing to fear. We are here to help him. You can let him go. We are with you, too.*

In this state of deep peace, comforted by her presence, I fell asleep and slept soundly. I knew all was well and I knew I had the strength to live through what was coming.

What I didn't know was how long this process would last. On Saturday, I called a Catholic priest, Bill Ross, who was a close friend of mine, and asked him to come to the hospital. Together we stood beside Daddy's bed. I talked to Daddy, telling him how I loved him, what I appreciated about him, and what I had resented, following the Gestalt

process for saying goodbye. Bill prayed with us. I told
Daddy about my experience with Nanny and assured him
there was nothing to fear. I knew I was ready to release
him. I told him it was OK to go.

Still he continued to breathe. I sat beside his bed. I read
Elizabeth Kubler-Ross's *On Death and Dying*. I reflected on
my life. I asked myself what I wanted to do with myself and
the precious time that is mine to live. "When it's my turn
to die, what will I wish I had done when I was 38 years
old?" I realized that I want to be able to look back and say,
"I'm glad I did that. I'm glad I took that risk. I'm glad I
used the time I had."

I didn't want to waste another moment of my life. I
knew I wanted to write. I would write, whether anyone else
ever read what I wrote; I would write and explore my
creativity. I would enjoy my children. I would love and be
loved. I would become a better and better therapist. I
would grow. I would love life. I would live in love. I would
find the teachers I knew I needed. I would find the teacher
inside myself. I would embrace every moment of every day.
I would celebrate. I marveled that I could feel so wonderful
while living through the experience I had dreaded and
feared all my life: my father's death.

But still he didn't die.

By the following Wednesday, I was told he could no
longer remain in the hospital. I made arrangements to
take him back to the nursing home. When I arrived at the
hospital to check him out, I encountered for the first time
the innocent-looking device that became the focus of a
dilemma I thought I had already arranged to avoid.

"What's that tube in his nose," I asked the nurse when I
entered his room.

"Oh, that's just a feeding tube."

"Does it keep him alive?"

"Oh, no, it just keeps him comfortable and hydrated."

"Oh — oh." That seemed reasonable enough.

He returned to the nursing home, back to the room he

shared with Mother. I explained to her again that Daddy had had another stroke. She seemed to understand and accept his condition. She was loving with me. Even though she couldn't speak coherently, I knew she was aware of what was unfolding.

The nursing home staff took beautiful care of him. He was like an infant, lovingly and gently attended. Mother sat in her chair, gazing at the television and keeping her private vigil by his side. The weeks crept by. Day after day I sat beside him, too. His gasping breath continued.

Gradually it became clearer and clearer that the innocent-looking feeding tube did more than keep him comfortable. It must be keeping him alive.

I asked my therapist, a medical doctor and a psychiatrist, to see Daddy and evaluate his situation. It was several days before he responded after making his visit to the nursing home. I got the call at my office on a Monday, between sessions with clients.

"I've thought about this all weekend," he said. "If it were my father, I would remove the feeding tube."

I thanked him and hung up. As I released the phone, the full import of my dilemma flooded my consciousness. My therapist, my father; my father, myself; God, why do I have to face this one?

I had already planned two weeks at the lake to give myself a break. I decided to take this time to reflect and seek spiritual guidance before I made any decision.

Those two weeks were wonderful and awful. I experienced the depths of grief, sadness, anger, and despair. And I also found myself having more fun than ever before. Water skiing was a new adventure that summer. Gliding along in the bright Oklahoma sunshine, I cut back and forth crossing the boat's wake, daring to take chances and ski as my daughters did. I gave myself to the experience and felt freedom flowing through me. I began to know the meaning of release.

I was discovering that a choice like the one I faced

was larger than logic and reason. Logic and reason couldn't begin to encompass the web of mystery that shrouded my relationship with my father through his life and at his death. How would I ever reach a decision and live with my choice?

On the 6th of July, I wrote in my journal:

One month today since Daddy had the second stroke — gone since then, but still breathing. What to do or not do about the feeding tube? Perhaps this time is allowing him some experience somewhere that is important for him or perhaps it's just artificially holding him back from the natural experience of dying. Can I live with me no matter which decision I make — letting go of him and the decision once it is made? I can — must do that — live in peace with my choice — trusting myself and the process I am going through to make the decision.

I wrote a poem sitting on the deck, looking at the lake, enjoying a storm.

> *Tonight's storm came*
> *Showing us how it is*
> *With this planet and its people.*
>
> *There is no controlling the winds,*
> *No holding back the rain,*
> *No resisting what is.*
>
> *But you can unfurl your sails,*
> *Make windmills.*
> *Embrace your power and fly.*
>
> *Let rage rumble, crackle, and flash,*
> *Tears rain gently or come splattering down,*
> *Always joy's patch of blue appears.*
>
> *Transforming the storm.*

As the days moved by, I lived with my ears tuned to approaching cars, hoping and dreading that a message might come that he had died on his own. But no message came. In fact, when I called the nursing home, I learned that he had opened his eyes. Now there was a breathing corpse with open eyes; my father, my child.

At the lake I wrote and wrote. I was looking for a way out of my dilemma, a way to avoid the decision I faced. I knew I did not want to remove the feeding tube and feel responsible for his dying. On the other hand, I didn't want to prolong his life artificially if he were lying there wanting to die. Was I holding onto him because of my fear of his death? Or, was I caring for him in a loving way by feeding him formula through a tube? Gradually, I concluded that perhaps this time was some kind of spiritual healing experience for him. Perhaps it was time he needed, time to be totally cared for, totally helpless, totally in the world of spirit. After all, he had cared for Mother for years as she became progressively more senile. Now it was his turn. I would not deprive him. I would not make the death choice for him.

I also faced the issue this choice raised between me and my therapist. I wouldn't just do as he suggested. I had to find my own way. I had to find my own choice, not follow his advice in an effort to please and impress him rather than being true to myself. I had to live with myself after this was over. But would it ever end?

I returned from the lake and told my therapist I had decided not to remove the tube. I attempted to return to life as usual; as usual, that is, as I could make it with my consciousness always aware of that nursing home room filled with my two invalid parents, one senile, one comatose, both dependent on me.

The weeks moved on. I rested with my choice. He would have to die on his own.

One evening when I came into his room, I found him with no feeding tube. I was astounded. His Catholic doctor had told me that once the tube was in, removing it would constitute murder. And he had let me know he would never remove that tube. So why was it out now?

I found his nurse, a lovely young woman I liked and had talked with many times before. She told me the tube was out because she was changing it. That was the first time it dawned on me that it had to be changed. I had assumed it was a permanent fixture after what the doctor had told me.

In the nursing home hall, punctuated by the sounds of dying people and the smell of incontinence, I told the nurse about my dilemma. I told her how I struggled with what to do. I told her what the doctor said and what my therapist said. I told her how torn I was. She told me how the physical vestige of a patient can last for years with those tubes, the body deteriorating into sores that won't heal; sores that smell so badly of decay that entering the room becomes a dreaded ordeal for a nurse.

We talked and shared. I felt a oneness and connection with her that soothed the pain inside me. When I left that evening, the tube was still out.

The next day a call came from the Catholic doctor. "I understand you told the nurse not to replace the feeding tube," he said, in an accusing tone. "No, I did not tell her any such thing. I know only doctors can give such orders," I replied. Then he said that maybe since it was out, he could just leave it out for a while and see if Daddy could take enough nourishment by mouth. Enough for what, I wondered. But I seized the opportunity this turn of events created. Now, no one had to feel responsible for actually removing the tube. The doctor could handle it this way, and I would be spared the same burden of responsibility. And if he could take enough by mouth, we would know he could still live on his own.

I was elated, delivered from my dilemma. If Daddy could survive without the tube, obviously he meant to stay alive. If not, then truly his life was over, and he and I would be released from our separate struggles.

Four days later, I entered his room. The tube was in again. This time I was enraged. "Why?" I asked another nurse. "He wasn't getting enough food. Doctor's orders."

"Doctor's orders!" I muttered through clenched teeth. "There was no effort to even communicate with me about this choice."

I was propelled by my rage. Everything seemed clear now. The tube had to go. I had to release this father I loved so much. I had to see that he was allowed to die. I had to give him protection from the conscience of the Catholic doctor (and my own, projected onto him). This frightened conscience so feared death that it would opt for life like this, life, no matter what the cost. Not for my father; no longer. I knew with all my being that this was it.

I got into my car and drove to a nearby bookstore, a source for me of books and nourishment. I did not know why I went there. I just knew I had to go.

There I found my friend, the owner of the store, whose husband had died recently after a long battle with cancer. He, too, had been in a wheelchair for years. I knew she could help me. I told her what was happening. She told me of her fights with hospitals and doctors to allow her husband the release of death which he had been ready to welcome. As we opened our hearts to each other, I felt deep healing love surrounding me; love for my father and love to release him; love to allow him to go on to the only next step possible for him. Love, no longer fear, filled my heart. Only fear of death, fear of letting him go, could keep me hanging onto him as I had been doing; only fear of taking responsibility for saying death is nothing to fear.

Another close friend suddenly appeared in the bookstore. She joined us and lovingly affirmed the choice I was making. I left them there and drove straight to my therapist's office. My timing was perfect. It was Friday afternoon, and he had just finished his last appointment.

I was face to face with Dr. Porter as I entered his office suite. "He put the tube back in without telling me. I've got to take it out." Without a word, Dr. Porter picked up his phone. I heard him tell the Catholic doctor that at my request, he was taking over my father's treatment.

We left his office together. Dr. Porter drove his car. I drove mine. We met at the nursing home and entered together. I explained to the charge nurse that I had decided to remove the feeding tube. She assisted as Dr. Porter told my father what was happening. I stood at the foot of the bed, praying for strength. The tube removed, he turned to me and we held each other. "We can do this because we know we are not murderers," he said. And then we parted.

I knew what to expect. In a week to ten days, my father would die of pneumonia.

For hours that night I sat beside his bed. His eyes were open. He looked at me. For the first time in weeks, he seemed to really be present behind those eyes. I looked at him. What was going through his mind? What did he know? Was he afraid? I was frightened. I imagined he was, too. Was he afraid to die? Could death possibly be worse than this? I held his shriveled hand. I loved him so. He wouldn't close his eyes. I couldn't leave with those eyes fixed on me. Did he think he would die if he closed them? Could he think at all? How would I live through the next week?

I worked, I prayed, I meditated, I listened. On the following Tuesday morning, during meditation, the releasing came. I knew within me that that day was the point of no return. If putting the tube back in would save him, it had to be done then. As I relaxed, a deep calm and certainty filled my heart. After that meditation, I had no more doubt. I released my father, and I released myself from responsibility for his living or dying: responsibility that was never really mine. It was a relic of our troubled past that I still didn't remember.

Over the weekend, he began running a temperature. Just as I had been told to expect, he was developing pneumonia. This was the beginning of the end. I wanted to be with him when he died, and was relieved whenever I entered his room and heard his still loud, Cheyne-Stokes breathing. He was there.

On Monday night, I sat by his bed, waiting, listening, trying to prepare myself for the final goodbye. In the darkness, I heard my mother stir in her bed on the other side of the room. Suddenly, she spoke, as clearly and coherently as she would have years before when her mind and her speech were still connected. "I've loved you all my life," she said. "Now you're going and I can't go. You just go on now. It's time to go. You're OK."

I was astounded! Mother was there. She knew what was happening. She was trying to reassure him. Perhaps he heard and understood, too. Perhaps this was the final release he needed.

I went out of the room, shaken by what had just happened. In the light of the nursing home's reception area, I took out my journal, but words wouldn't come. All I knew was that I was not with him, not facing this with him. I had to go back.

And so I sat with my hand on his head, counting his breaths, trying to comfort him with my touch. Late that night I kissed him goodbye and told Mother goodnight. I was exhausted, and I knew there was no guessing when death would come.

From my journal:

8-21-79   *Ten minutes till six — the phone rings. It's Dr. Porter. Daddy died.*

8-22-79   *Daddy — my father — my dad — He is dead. He died. He's gone. I'll never feel his warmth again. I can't cry — nothing comes out. I can't sleep — nothing lets go. I can't conceive that he's gone — not my father.*

The phone rang. I knew. It was/is inconceivable and inevitable.

Words don't come.

That morning I drove to the nursing home to see my mother. As I entered the now half-empty room, she was sitting in her chair, with her breakfast tray in front of her. She reached out her arms to me and said, "No one in the world could have been better to him. You were wonderful and you loved him so much."

I was dumbfounded. Once again she was coherent and appropriate. She knew exactly what had happened. I didn't have to tell her. Instead she told me the one thing I most needed to hear that morning. She came through to comfort me. Finally my mother was there when I needed her. I hugged her and sat with her, talking with her as I had never been able to when I was younger and she was still well. It dawned on me that now she and I were alone without Daddy. Perhaps there was hope for our relationship yet.

Later that morning, Dean went with me to begin making funeral arrangements. I asked two close friends of mine to visit Mother at the time of Daddy's funeral on Thursday and bring her ice cream, the treat she loved like a child. I wanted her to have some way to mark such an important event in her life, and I wanted her to be connected with us as we buried Daddy in Alabama.

On Wednesday, we flew to Alabama, arriving late in the afternoon. Before having dinner with a close friend, we made our trek to the local funeral home to select a casket. We'd decided in Oklahoma that it made sense to buy the casket in Alabama.

Unfortunately, we had looked at the selection that was available in the elegant funeral home in Oklahoma City. What we found here was a different matter. Suddenly I became obsessed with finding a casket that Daddy would have liked. He had always been extremely sensitive about wearing proper clothes and doing what was in "good taste." Now the one thing left that I could do for him was to be sure he was buried in a casket he would have approved. I went around and around the room. Nothing was suitable. I knew he would have hated them all.

My daughters were there, too. We all agreed that these caskets were terrible. It was incredible. Here we were, shopping for a casket as if this were a matter of the utmost importance. It was like trying to find the right dress for an important party. We were completely absorbed in the process. It was a wonderful diversion from our grief.

The funeral home attendant seemed to be a sensitive young man. When we walked upstairs to the casket room, he told me that this had been a tough week. He had helped bury a child who was the same age as one of his own children. I noticed that he was very distressed. But, he sensed our plight trying to find a casket we liked, and remembered one that was available in a small town about thirty miles away. He graciously offered to drive there while we went to dinner and bring the casket back for us to see later that evening. Relieved with this solution to our quest, we left.

About nine-thirty, the girls and I returned. We had dropped Dean off at the motel. The stress was beginning to get to him, and he didn't want to face the funeral home scene again. I had long since given up on trying to force him to do anything he didn't want to do.

As we three trooped up the funeral home stairs once more, I noticed that our young attendant was having trouble keeping his balance. By the time we arrived in the casket room, it was obvious that he was in really bad shape. But he was proud of the casket he had found for us. And indeed he had come up with just what I wanted; beautifully finished wood with brass handles and an unadorned satin lining inside. I thanked him and suggested that we complete the arrangements since it was getting late and we were all tired.

We went back downstairs and into his office. He took out his forms and tried to ask me questions. But, by this time, he was having difficulty talking; his speech was slurred, and he was barely able to hold up his head. There was no one else there that night to help us, he told me when I asked. The manager was still at the airport trying to find my father's body which, I now discovered, had not arrived on schedule and was currently lost.

When I finally was able to understand his words and realized what he was telling me, I stole a glance at my 10-

and 15-year-old daughters, as the humor in our situation
struck us all. There we were, alone in a funeral home with a
man who was so drugged that he was beyond functioning,
trying to buy a casket for Daddy's body that was lost. We
got the giggles.

Again, I was struck by the fact that here I was, tending
to a responsibility I had feared and dreaded all my life, and
it would make a great scene for a soap opera. Here we were
laughing, and I hadn't even been able to have a good cry
yet. To top it all off, I realized I was going to have to take
charge and get the papers filled out since the funeral was
scheduled for the next afternoon, and we had no time to
waste. (I assumed they would find Daddy.) Once again, as
was typical in my life, I was the responsible one in a situation where I might have expected to be cared for and comforted by others.

Just as I finished filling out the papers, figuring the final
price of the casket, and writing the obituary notice for the
newspaper, the manager returned. He stuck his head into
the room where we were, to tell us he had found Daddy.
One glance showed him what had happened while he was
away. Apologizing profusely, he escorted us to our car and
assured us that everything would be taken care of beautifully by tomorrow.

I didn't sleep a wink that night. Still I couldn't cry.
Instead I planned the funeral service and wrote a tribute to
my father for the minister to read. When morning finally
came, I hurried to the florist to arrange for flowers and
then drove to the funeral home for my own private
encounter with my father's body.

As soon as I saw him dead, my tears came, releasing the
terrible tightness I had in my chest. I sobbed and sobbed,
relieved to feel the finality of his death at last. He was not
there, not in his body. I touched his face and knew, knew
in that touch what no other experience had taught me
before. His body was dead; no longer him in that body.
This was not my father. He was gone, released from this

body that had ceased to serve him long ago. I could bury him in peace. *The peace that passes all understanding, be amongst you and remain with you always. Amen.*

When I returned to join Dean and my daughters, they were dressed and ready for the funeral. Dean was his most beautiful self that day, exquisitely sensitive to them and their needs and feelings. He had appointed Leigh in charge of Kleenex for everyone, and she was happy having a job to do. They were all there to support me and comfort me. I was blessed with the kind of family I had always wanted at the time I needed it most.

I didn't try to protect Lucie and Leigh from their grief as my parents had protected me when I was a child. I wanted them to do their grieving then and release their grandfather, not carry their pain buried inside them for years as I had when my grandmother died.

When we arrived at the funeral home, they had their first direct experience with death. I left them free to look at his body, or touch him if they chose to. I was composed and peaceful now, able to attend to them and support them in their pain. One of Lucie's tears fell on Daddy's forehead when she kissed him goodbye. She stood beside me, the artist in her struck by the contrast between the warmth of her tear and the cold touch of his skin, as she pointed out to me the beauty she found in that moment. Leigh chose not to touch him, but sobbed freely. She went to the side of the room and sat on a small sofa. Later she told me she had seen her grandfather's spirit, and he had sat beside her and comforted her. In subsequent weeks, she had several other visual encounters with him. She accepted these experiences calmly and was reassured by them.

After greeting family friends, we left the funeral home. Thirty minutes later, we were enjoying lunch in the wonderful, warm home of a friend of my parents, whom I have known since childhood. Surrounded by marvelous dolls, wood carvings, plants, pictures, china treasures, and handmade items from all over the world, we celebrated

Daddy's life with his long-time friend, who was now 73 years old and going strong. She has lived her life her own way, not daunted by the opinions of others. Unlike most Southern women of her generation, she was her own person. I loved her and respected her. During lunch, she presented me with a beautiful cross Daddy had made for her from wood that was a relic from the college she had attended.

Fortified and nourished, we left for the funeral. A week later I wrote in my journal:

I wrote about Daddy for his funeral. I chose all the scriptures; I used the new Liturgy. We sang the Doxology. I stood straight and tall; my father's daughter. "Praise God from whom all blessings flow."

We walked behind his casket. I was so proud to be his child. "Daddy's Little Girl" grown up now. The love, the marvelous, mysterious love we shared when he brought me the record of "Daddy's Little Girl" so long ago (I must have been six or so), has been infinitely enriched by all the years since. And yet it is still the same. It is the warmest love, like sunlight and life and pure joy.

I was in love with my father as I had never been free to love any other man. In my heart there was no room for any other. I see that now, but at the time I didn't realize the toll this secret marriage was taking on my life. It was seven years more before I divorced myself from him and released my life from his. He took our secret to his grave. But now I was ready to begin unraveling the mystery that I sensed in our relationship, but had not yet begun to fathom.

CHAPTER IV

SKY HI RANCH — MY TURNING POINT

It was a grandiose illusion; my feeling of responsibility
for my father's living and dying. When I was a child he
invaded my life so completely that I lost the sense of myself
as a separate being. As an adult I was afraid to acknowledge
the boundaries that existed between his life and mine. I
thought I couldn't live without his presence in my life. I
imagined that my actions and decisions determined the
outcome of his life. I was afraid I couldn't exist apart from
him. He possessed me. I clung to him.

His dying taught me to face my own living. His death
forced me to confront my fears. I thought it was my father
who held me in his grip. I discovered that fear was the
culprit. And I was the one who embraced that dark energy
with a desperation born of years of not knowing any other
way to live.

The experience of unconditional love and the teaching
of Brugh Joy opened new realms of possibility for me. I
realized that love accepts what is with another person. It
does not possess another. Rather love releases the loved
one and honors the free will he possesses to shape and
form his own life.

*Unconditional love does not judge. Nor does it compare one
person's life with another's. The need for intellectual understanding is suspended. Unconditional love exists in the absence
of fear.*

Gradually, as I experienced this healing, releasing love
energy, I awakened to the realization that my father had
chosen and directed his own life. His hurts and disap-

pointments, triumphs and successes, were his very own. I had made none of his choices.

But my own choices are mine to claim. My life belongs to me. My sorrows, successes, mistakes, and accomplishments are mine. I choose my path. He chose his.

Seeing the outcome of the choices he had made convinced me that I must become fully conscious of the choices I was making, moment by moment, every day of my life. I knew that it was time to move ahead with my life. I knew I must dare to take risks. I knew I must shake off the mantle of fear I had used to deny the potential I possessed. I wanted to embrace my life fully and responsibly. When I die I want to look back and say, "I'm glad I did that. I'm glad I took that risk. No matter what the outcome, I'm glad I reached for my dreams . . ."

While my new and growing spiritual awareness sustained me, fear still held me in a constant battle to dominate my mind. My Internal Saboteur argued that I had killed my father. I was bad, guilty, a murderer. I deserved to suffer. My Nurturing-Enabling Self reminded me that I had not killed him. I simply had allowed him to die. His death was inevitable; his choice, not mine. In my quiet moments of spiritual attunement, I knew this was true. In my frightened moments, when I identified with my Saboteur, I tried and convicted myself. Why did I feel such guilt and pain about my father? The answer to that question was three more years in coming. Forgiving both of us completely took even longer.

My healing process, which required six years, began at Sky Hi Ranch in March of 1980. Just a year after my first reading of Joy's Way, my second husband, Dean, and I were participants in one of Brugh Joy's conference retreats. For two weeks we were away from our usual world. There were no phone calls, radios, televisions, or newspapers. Brugh insisted that each conference participant put aside his ordinary concerns and enter a quiet space where deep spiritual awakening was a possibility.

During the two weeks, there were three days of fasting and silence. By the time the fast began, at the beginning of the second week, each of us had learned from Brugh that we were to seek our own Inner Teacher through meditation, music, hikes in the desert, quiet communion with rocks, plants, and animals, and our dreams and encounters with others, in both waking and sleeping states of consciousness. Again and again, Brugh refused to give us answers to our questions. Instead he urged us to look more deeply inside ourselves and to trust the teaching of our own experience.

During the first week of the conference I had an experience which taught me more powerfully than words or books could ever do. Early in the first week Brugh announced that a schedule was posted for energy balancing sessions which he and his assistant, Chuck, would be giving. Three people were scheduled early each morning during the meditation period before breakfast and three in the late afternoon. We were to select the music we wanted to hear during our energy balancing experience. And we were not to talk about this experience in our group sessions until everyone had completed his own process and all the balancing sessions were done.

I had studied the illustrations in Joy's Way of the system of energy centers that link the physical body with its etheric counterpart. These energy centers, called chakras, spiral out from the physical body at specific points on the body's surface. Chakra is a Sanskrit word which means "wheel." Some people are able to see these rotating fields of energy which radiate from the body and form visual patterns that look like wheels or disks.

Chakras can be felt by passing a hand through the energy field. If you want to experiment with how this chakra energy feels to you, have a friend imagine that he is holding a ball of energy between the palms of his hands. His hands should be six to twelve inches apart as he visualizes the chakras radiating from the palms of each of his hands and connecting in the space between them. When he is able to feel this ball of energy, let your hand slice through it. You may feel warmth, or coolness, or a pulsing vibration as your hand passes through the energy field. Different people feel energy differently. Discover how it feels to you. You will find that this exercise is easy to do if you are relaxed and centered in unconditional love. Let go of your logical mind and simply allow yourself to experience what is present in a dimension of consciousness that is beyond what you usually allow yourself to feel.

Chakras have been recognized for centuries in various Eastern traditions. These traditions usually identify seven different chakras; the root, at the base of the spine; the sexual chakra, just above the genitals; the solar plexus, above the navel; the heart, in the center of the chest; the throat; the brow, just above and between the eyes; and the crown chakra, at the top of the head. Brugh found through his energy scanning of the human body, a number of additional chakras which he includes in his illustrations. To the traditional seven chakras, he adds energy centers at the midchest, midway between the heart and the throat; at the spleen, about midway on the left side of the body; and at the transpersonal point, twelve to twenty-four inches above the crown. There are also chakras at the shoulders, hips, elbows, knees, palms of the hands, the feet, and extending from the tips of the fingers and toes. (See *Joy's Way*, pp. 155-177.)

Brugh describes his energy balancing process in *Joy's Way*. As I watched others during their sessions, I saw Brugh on the right side of the large wooden balancing table and Chuck on the left. The person receiving the balancing lay quietly on the table with his shoes removed. When the musical selection began, Brugh placed his right hand over the heart chakra as he focused and channeled love energy through his body and out through the palms of his hands.

In my mind's eye, I could see a brilliant beam of white light streaming down, entering his head through the crown chakra, then moving down and filling his heart, spreading through his whole body and flowing out through his hands into the energy field of the person lying on the table. As he leaned gently into the table, his body slightly stooped, I saw Brugh, the doctor, practicing his ancient healing art. It seemed so natural, so peaceful; a complete and perfect expression of one human being's sharing with another. I knew that this energy was much larger than Brugh himself. It was not that he presented himself as a miracle maker. It was simply that he allowed himself to be an instrument for healing, releasing the person receiving this love energy to use it for himself as he himself chose to do.

His hands moved in a spiral pattern that began at the heart chakra in the center of the chest. The spiral moved outward from the heart down to the solar plexus, then up to the midchest, and down again to the spleen area on the left side of the body. The next focus point was the sexual chakra, then his hands moved up again to the throat chakra at the base of the neck and from there, down to the root chakra in the genital area. The third eye, in the center of the forehead and just above the eyes, was next. Then he moved to the left elbow, the left knee, the right knee, the right elbow, then up again to the crown of the head. From the crown chakra he went to the left hand, left foot, right foot, and right hand. Finally the outward spiral culminated at the transpersonal point, twelve or more inches above the crown and away from the physical body.

There followed a period of connecting work. Using both hands now, Brugh moved energy from his right hand to his left as he placed his right hand on the right foot, his left hand on the right knee. On the other side of the table, Chuck's movements mirrored his. They moved up the body, connecting the energy flow between the chakras now. Where there was a block in the free flow of energy, they paused, giving that area time to open completely.

Once the connecting work and their intuitive work were completed, the opening spiral energy pattern was reversed. Working back from the transpersonal point above the crown chakra in reverse order, Brugh and Chuck moved their hands counterclockwise, touching each chakra point again, as they closed the spiral pattern, ending where it began, at the heart.

The large meditation room where our group members gathered to share this wordless experiencing of love and healing was filled with light. Though dawn was just breaking outside, radiant light flooded the room. Music played softly in the background, interrupted only by the click of the tape player when Brugh changed tapes between balancing sessions.

When my turn finally came, early in the morning on Wednesday, I lay on the table and did my best to center myself and relax as my music, Bach's Greatest Hits, began. I felt a powerful warmth and a strong vibration penetrating my heart as Brugh held his hands slightly above my body. With my eyes closed, I felt each chakra opening and expanding as he focused and channeled energy through it. I felt enormously blessed and completely peaceful. Never had I experienced such harmony within myself. Time was suspended; minutes felt like hours while the whole process also seemed instantaneous.

After he completed his work and moved on to another person, I rested on the table, totally relaxed and released. Suddenly, I felt myself outside my body, way above my body, though still attached to it. I felt as if my body were the gondola basket of an enormous hot-air balloon. I knew I was much larger than my body, much freer than my body. My body was only an insignificant part of the total of my being. Instantly I understood the meaning of Brugh's words, "You are not inside your body. Your body is inside you." I realized I am much more than this body that I am so attached to and dependent upon. I knew that death is nothing to fear, that my consciousness transcends this physical dimension I love so much. I knew I exist above and beyond the body I occupy.

I understood that the key to the meaning of my life lies within me. No one else, no teacher, parent, child, friend or mate holds that key. Nor can anyone else find it for me. I saw that my responsibility is to express myself as fully and as honestly as I can; that the key to my life is taking hold of the talents I possess and using them to make my contribution to this world I love. I am complete and whole and connected with God.

This experience was a major step for me in consciously releasing the issue of having removed the feeding tube from my father. For now I knew that his death was simply the severing of his connection with his physical body. I had severed an artificial connection that served to bind him to his body when he no longer could sustain his own connection with that body. I knew I had only freed him to complete his dying process and to emerge unencumbered on the other side.

Beyond this recognition and release, my out-of-body experience changed the direction of my life. It opened new dimensions of growth and challenge for me while it also relieved me of my fear of death. I felt ready to take risks and live as fully as I could. I knew I had the power and strength within the larger self I had experienced to solve my problems and set and meet new goals for myself.

My first major challenge came within forty-eight hours. Friday morning I awoke filled with terror. It was as if all the emotional pain I had ever known had emerged for me to face. I felt rage, immense sadness, overwhelming helplessness, gaping emptiness, and frantic anxiety. I wanted someone to take this all away while at the same time I knew I had to be alone. My husband let me know he loved me but wisely resisted any attempt to rescue me. I stayed in my room that morning and missed the group session.

The cleansing, healing love I had experienced in the balancing session brought up all the emotional demons I needed to face and clear away. Even while I was torn with fear and pain, I felt in the center of myself a deep knowing that I was all right, that I would come through this torture. But at the outer levels of my being, I was terrified. These were the fears and pains that had haunted me and ruled my life. The question seemed to be, "Should I die; should I end my life?"

From my perspective now, six years later, I think the question really was, "Can I allow myself to live in joy and love? Can I allow this marvelous new dimension of love and peace I have uncovered to enter my life fully? Can I forgive myself completely for my mistakes, release my past, and move ahead into what I know will be totally new territory?" "Must I punish myself now for the pleasure and bliss I had felt on Wednesday and Thursday?"

I climbed a mountain while the rest of the group was in session. At the top I perched on a rock and viewed the desert below. Sitting quietly at that place, I asked for help and for strength. I made myself be still. I said "no" to my urges to run, to jump, to hurt myself. I sat and I waited.

I wondered if there were snakes lurking under my rock, waiting to bite me. I wondered how I could ever get beyond these feelings I had fought for so long. I wondered how I had gotten this far. I marveled that I had been able to help other people through their pain when there was so much left in me.

Finally, I wept, surrendering to my tears, welcoming the purging they gave me. I cried and cried, allowing my hurt and pain to engulf me. Eventually, when I had exhausted my tears, I felt peace and calm gradually soothing me. I was filled with a deep knowing that suicide was never a choice I could allow myself. For the first time in my life, I had been able to embrace the vulnerable, abused Child in me with love, acceptance, and compassion and allow her to feel her pain without fear. It was no longer necessary to imagine that the only solution for her unhappiness was to destroy her. I knew I would be all right, no matter what I encountered. I knew I had work to do, a purpose to accomplish, and the pleasures of life to experience.

I knew now that the energy of unconditional love was always available for me. It was as if the balancing session had opened a door deep within me, a door that I had closed when I was very young. Behind this door I found an infinite reservoir of love, mine to claim, to experience, to express and to share.

With this healing source within me, there is nothing to fear. I can allow joy in my life. There is no pain I cannot face. There is no guilt; no punishment to fear. There is simply me, connected at the deepest level through this love energy, with the energy that activates the universe, the love of God.

I stayed on my mountaintop perch for a long time, grateful and humbled by my experience. When I decided to come down to rejoin the group, I felt shaken and shy about sharing what I had experienced. The critic in me was worried that I would be judged for my absence. Even though I knew the whole workshop was about unconditional love, the parts of me that aren't very loving imagined that others might be as hard on me as I was accustomed to being with myself.

When the evening session began, I was relieved that Brugh chose not to notice that I had missed the morning gathering. I was thirsty for the deep level of acceptance I felt from him and from the rest of the group. I didn't have to account to anyone for choosing to be alone. My newly evolving nurturing self learned a valuable lesson. For the first time in my life, I knew I was free to choose for myself without having to satisfy or account to anyone else. Nor did I have to listen to my own internal critic. What a relief!

Brugh told us the story of the three injunctions: *Make no judgments; Make no comparisons; Delete your need to understand.* (See Joy's Way, p.58-66.) These admonitions were given to a woman who had never before had any sort of spiritual awakening or heightened consciousness.

During a walk at sunset on the beach at Santa Monica, this woman saw a brilliant display of light emanating from her feet and transforming the waves as she looked out at the ocean. Dazzled by the beauty of the light and color, she heard a powerful voice proclaiming, "There are three injunctions for you. Pay attention to them. Make no comparisons; make no comparisons. Make no judgments; make no judgments. Delete your need to understand; delete your need to understand."

She had no preparation for such an experience and no context for assimilating it. She was filled with wonder, but decided that this experience must have been a momentary lapse into insanity. She put the experience out of her mind and forgot about it.

When this same woman consulted Brugh three years after this experience, she wanted to get rid of the expanded psychic awareness that had opened for her quite suddenly, eighteen months after her walk on the Santa Monica beach. At first she had relished the new intuitive knowing she possessed. But, when she came to Brugh for help, she was disturbed and frightened by tragic events she foresaw. She wanted to stop the process.

When she told Brugh about her dilemma, she suddenly remembered her experience on the beach. In a flash of understanding, she realized that it had been her preparation for the sudden onset of psychic awareness that had come to her a year and a half later. The injunctions were given to her as guideposts for shifting her consciousness into the energy of unconditional love where she could experience her psychic awareness without fear and self-torture about what she saw.

From the perspective of unconditional love, her psychic awareness simply was what it was. There was no need to judge what she saw, to compare what she saw in one situation with what she saw in another, or to find any kind of intellectual understanding of why she saw what she saw. The challenge was to accept what she experienced and realize that even tragedies serve a larger purpose in the lives of the people who experience them.

When she told him her story, Brugh recognized that these three injunctions are requisites for the experience of unconditional love. He spoke to us about the contrast between the energy of the heart chakra, which is the energy of unconditional love, and the energy of the solar plexus chakra, which is power consciousness. At the power level, judgment, comparison, and the need for intellectual understanding are of paramount importance. This is the level of duality, right and wrong, good and bad, black and white. It is the level of consciousness that is the common denominator of our culture.

He invited us to notice when we were engaged in judging, comparing ourselves with others, or needing to figure things out. As soon as we noticed ourselves engaged in any of these processes, we could choose whether or not to continue energizing that state of mind.

As I hiked in the desert later that day, I watched my own internal mental process. To my amazement I realized that I was consistently engaged in one of these three activities. And I discovered that uncomfortable feelings inevitably followed as I judged myself or others, declared this to be right and that to be wrong, compared myself favorably or unfavorably with others, or tried to control my experiencing through intellectualizing rather than allowing it to be whatever it happened to be.

Seeing my process clearly allowed me the choice of shifting my perspective by consciously focusing my awareness at the level of my heart chakra. I explored lifting my mental focus from the solar plexus level to my heart and feeling into the energy of unconditional love. Immediately I could feel the deep peace and calm that I was beginning to realize is always and consistently available within me when I choose to access it. The *"peace that passes all understanding"* is the essence of my being. That wonderful phrase that I had repeated with yearning in church for so many years was becoming a reality in my own experience. With this capacity to shift consciousness at will, I sensed a deep knowing emerging within me that I would find complete healing for myself. Though I still didn't consciously recognize the source of my internal pain, confusion, fear, and self-destructive tendencies, I knew this energy of love was stronger than any turmoil my mind and emotions could create.

Brugh spoke about the necessity for working at both the psychological and spiritual levels in order to transform one's life. He used the analogy of a child's pounding toy. Working only at the psychological level is like pounding pegs with the toy hammer from one side of the object to the other. For the moment it looks as if a change has occurred. But when the toy is turned over, there are the same pegs waiting to be pounded through to the other side once again. Real transformation requires that the spiritual dimension of unconditional love, deep release, and complete forgiveness be part of the healing process. Instead of just pounding away without any real penetration occurring, transformation means allowing the force of unconditional love to permeate consciousness with its healing, accepting, enabling energy. This is like a real nail being driven into real wood so a lasting connection and stable structure are created.

Finally resolving my feelings about my father's death was a major focus for me during the conference. When I spoke in the group about what I had experienced the previous summer, I couldn't do so without tears. Despite all my efforts to let go of the guilt and responsibility I felt for his death, it was clear that I was still carrying a load of stones on my back, punishing myself and holding myself prisoner for the crime I thought I had committed. As Brugh and the group listened to me, I felt their energy, empathy and support surrounding me.

When I finished my story, I expected that Brugh would offer me some way to work through my grief at the psychological level. Perhaps he would suggest that I speak directly to my father as if he were present, following the Gestalt

tradition for grief work. Instead he lead me in a whole new
direction that affected me profoundly. He simply asked me
to tell my story again, but this time to center myself and
shift my awareness to heart level so I could share my experience from the perspective of unconditional love.

My immediate response was to doubt that I could do
this. I was so filled with emotion that I couldn't imagine
being able to make such a shift so quickly. Nevertheless I
took myself in hand, did my best to center myself, and
shifted my level of awareness. My words began to flow, and
I heard myself retelling my experience in a totally different
way. Viewed from this perspective, I felt peace and calm as
I shared what had happened. The elements of tragedy and
despair that had filled my earlier account were missing
now. The whole experience seemed perfect in its own way.
Of course, I realized, this was simply how it was. There is
nothing to judge, nothing to understand, nothing to struggle about. I was filled with love and a feeling of gratitude
for the richness of the experience I had had. It was no
longer overwhelming or emotionally charged. By sharing in
this way, I felt no fear about what had happened. It simply
was what it was.

When I finished my second account, I felt free of my
father for the first time in months. I realized that I had
done the best for him that I knew how to do and that that
was all I could ever ask from myself. There was nothing
more to be done but to put down my load of stones and
move on with my own life. By bringing the spiritual level of
consciousness to my experience of grief, Brugh taught me
how to heal my pain. Now I knew what he meant when he
talked about the necessity for working at both the psychological and spiritual levels in order to experience transformation. I had felt the contrast between the two levels of
awareness in a way that taught me the power and importance of both dimensions in the healing process.

I knew that the truth of this experience eventually
would help me free myself from the cycles of pain and

depression I had always known. I also realized that I was
about to make a profound shift in the way I worked with
my clients in therapy. Somehow I would discover how to
incorporate what I was learning and experiencing into my
practice. I remember thinking that this would be easy to do
if I worked in California where people are open to almost
anything. I imagined that Oklahoma was so different that I
would have trouble ever sharing or teaching what I now
knew from my own direct experience.

To my surprise when I returned to my practice, I found
I had a natural facility for sharing with my clients and
incorporating the spiritual dimension into our work. I also
discovered that everyone seemed to know deep within
them that what I was saying about unconditional love and
heart-level energy matched their own intuitive sense about
the essence of life and love. I have yet to have anyone reject
what I share when I allow myself to speak with them from
heart-level awareness and share what simply comes to me
without any conscious effort at all. What I say when I work
in this way comes from a source much higher than my own
conscious mind can comprehend. In the desert I found the
capacity to release my conscious mind so that my expression can flow from this higher source without my trying to
control and direct the process with my outer mind.

Releasing myself to express in this way seemed to relate
to having set an intention for my life during my conference
experience. When Brugh talked about setting an intention
for our lives, I realized I already knew my intention for
myself though I never before had articulated it. It is to
realize my potential to express love and help bring healing
self-acceptance into the hearts and minds of as many people as I am able to teach and work with during my life time.
I had no idea at that time what form this would take except
through my practice as a therapist, which I had already
begun. Since that time, doors have opened for me in directions I had never even dreamed.

In teaching us about setting an intention, Brugh

emphasized that the key is releasing that intention once it is set. He told us that once we are clear about our intention, we must release it, thereby getting our conscious minds out of the way so we can be open to the guidance and direction of our Inner Teacher. The conscious mind cannot see from a broad enough perspective to lead us to realizing our intention for our lives. Our Inner Teacher has the necessary breadth and depth of perspective and knows where we are going. The Inner Teacher knows how to direct us, step by step, toward the fulfillment of our purpose. All we can do at any moment in time is to take the next single step which presents itself to our consciousness. At this moment, I know all I have to do is write the next word, the next line, and complete this paragraph. For I know that writing this book is part of what I am guided to do for whatever useful purpose it may serve.

In 1980, I knew that the intention I set for myself was going to require some major changes in my life. Intuitively I realized I could not approach my potential for service unless I made some profound corrections.

Dean and I were two-and-a-half years into our marriage. Though the time he and I shared there in the desert was probably the closest experience of our eight-year relationship, I knew deep in my heart that the intention I had set for myself meant I would have to leave that marriage. I knew I had learned a great deal through the ups and downs of the years he and I had shared. I also knew that the marriage drained me and kept my energies focused on sheer emotional survival. In such a situation, I knew I could not grow as I now intended to do. By the following March, he and I had separated and were in the process of divorce.

My relationship with my older daughter was also painful and difficult at that time. One afternoon during the conference, I sat beside my desert teacher, a giant cactus, and concentrated on channeling unconditional love to Lucie. During that meditation, I realized that I wanted to give her a

16th birthday party that included all the people who loved her and had shared in her growing up. I would invite her father and her step-mother, her father's parents, and Elizabeth, who had been our housekeeper during her younger years. I wanted to show her that these adults could join hands in celebrating her coming of age and put aside the pain and differences that had led to my first divorce and had lain smoldering in the years since. I knew during that meditation that she needed to see our love for her expressed in a very concrete, visual way so she could begin to heal the battle that had raged inside her since her father and I were divorced when she was eight years old.

The 16th birthday dinner party took place in May and was a complete surprise for her. She was delighted to see us all together to honor her growing up. It was as if seeing her parents able to cooperate to celebrate her life meant that eventually she could make peace inside herself with the masculine and feminine energies she was struggling to encompass and integrate.

I also found that since my desert meditation I was able to let go of her in a way that previously had eluded me. I no longer felt that I had to make her into the person I imagined she ought to be. I didn't have my old feelings of discomfort when I saw her saying or doing something that I judged as less than optimal. I realized that she, too, would have to work through her own issues just as I knew I had to work through mine. I no longer had to fancy myself a perfect parent raising a perfect child. As I accepted myself at a deeper level, I could accept my daughter, too. I could let her be and appreciate that she is the perfect expression of her own essence and her own experiencing.

And as I released her, she began to let go of me, too. Just before Christmas, she decided to live with her father for a while, a step I had known in my heart she would have to take, and a step I dreaded and resisted. The child in me was devastated. I felt abandoned and deserted. I grieved and cried and hurt. At the same time, the grown-up in me realized that she and I needed this separation. And in some ways, I was relieved to have her father take over her parenting and give me a break. I also realized there was a message to me in her leaving about the necessity for ending my rapidly deteriorating second marriage.

Letting go of her in December, and then letting go of my husband in February, brought another enormous wave of healing to my life. Painful as those times were, and they were truly awful, I knew, as I went through the separation from my daughter and from the man I loved deeply and had pinned so many hopes and dreams on, that my pain was simply what I had to live through to reach a new place in my life that would be much better for me and for everyone else.

Another of my life-changing experiences at Sky Hi Ranch taught me about the value of the difficult periods in my life. On the next-to-last morning of the conference, I lay on the floor of the large group room listening to the magnificent selection from Wagner that Brugh played for that session. As I felt into the energy of the music, I saw my life played back before my eyes in the kind of experience often reported as a part of dying. I saw with absolute clarity that the great failures of my life, the events and experiences I most hated to remember, had all been essential to the path I had followed. I saw that without those mistakes, I could not have come to the place I had reached by that time in 1980. I saw that those mistakes, those failings, had pushed me on to new growth, new learning, new directions. I saw this especially with my first divorce, an experience I still believed was the greatest failure of my life. I realized in those moments of brilliant awareness, that the painful experience of losing my first husband, had set in motion the soul-searching and personal growth that were absolutely necessary for me and for the intention I now had set for myself.

This experience during the music that morning probably lasted less than five minutes. For the first time, I saw my life from the perspective of unconditional love, without judging myself, without comparing myself with any other person, without having to understand logically or intellectually. I simply saw through the eyes and energy of love how my Inner Teacher had guided me along a path more perfectly suited for my purpose than any path my outer mind could have created. I also realized how my Inner Teacher was the only possible guide for my life. I never could have chosen those steps had I also known the painful experiences the path would take me through. Yet the pain was as important as the triumphs. There was a wisdom and love in charge that was much greater than my outer mind could grasp. Just as I now knew that my physical body is only a tiny part of the whole of who I am, I also knew that my outer, conscious mind is only the tip of the iceberg in terms of the resources and wisdom available to me to guide my life.

This experience taught me that my challenge is to trust, to let go, and to let God; to allow the wisdom of my Inner Teacher to guide my steps while I use my physical, mental, and emotional resources to continue taking the next single step to be taken. I realized that this challenge means taking that next step, trusting that it is part of the unfolding process of reaching my intention, even when that step seems outrageous or too difficult or too risky to my outer mind.

Since that time six years ago, I've taken many steps that have led me in exciting new directions I didn't dream possible then. I've uncovered the source of the emotional pain that haunted me and healed my life. I've explored television production and developed a weekly radio therapy program. I write a newspaper column. I've published my first book. I've found a speciality within my therapy work by developing a treatment process for people who were sexually abused as children. I've found new joy in relationships and especially with my daughters. I've found peace within myself. As I release my life to the spiritual guidance of my Inner Teacher, each day I live becomes richer, more beautiful, and more rewarding.

CHAPTER V

BEGINNING TO REMEMBER

After my experiences at Sky Hi Ranch in 1980, I continued my healing process, learning and remembering more and more about my personal history and about how my childhood and adolescence affected me as an adult. My work with Brugh taught me to rely on myself and trust my Inner Teacher. Though I continued to see Dr. Porter regularly for two and half more years, I began reclaiming the authority I had projected onto him. The more responsibility I took for my growth, the more I discovered and understood. I realized that I had programmed myself to live out my previously unacknowledged beliefs that life and love hurt, that I was guilty and didn't deserve love, and that my life should be a sacrifice for others. The martyrhood and victim consciousness that I evolved from these beliefs kept me in a vicious circle of pain and suffering.

I felt the victim in difficult situations. In areas where I was successful, I was clear that I had earned my triumphs. But in areas that were painful and disappointing, I often felt that I had no part in creating what I experienced. It was easy to feel helpless myself and blame someone else for being thoughtless or abusive to me.

I realize now that my victim consciousness was a relic from my childhood. As a child I was a victim; a victim of emotional, sexual, and physical abuse. When I was a child, I didn't know there was any other way to be. My family was my world, and I assumed that this was the way the world is. Acknowledging my vulnerability and seeing myself as a victim of parental abuse of power were beyond my comprehension. Instead I believed that I was responsible for my parents' unhappiness. If I could just figure out how to be better, accomplish more, and make them proud of me, then maybe they would feel better, and I would feel safer and more loved.

Yet I knew my parents loved me. They told me so. They told me I was the most important person in the world to them. I was their "pride and joy."

My mother told me wonderful adventure stories about her travels before she and Daddy were married. She baked fragrant oatmeal cookies for after-school snacks. She prepared delicious meals. The three of us took exciting vacation trips together every year.

My father was proud of me. I was "Daddy's little girl." He brought me presents when I was sick. He tried to help me with my homework when I had trouble understanding my math. He let me help him with his woodworking projects in his backyard workshop. He wanted me to have the education and professional career he had missed. He wanted me to be just the way he wanted me to be.

And that was where the confusion began. There seemed to be no way my life could be separate from my parents'. They looked to me to create the meaning for their lives. They expected me to be their fulfillment. I was their possession. I would look after them in their old age. I would make them proud. Somehow I would satisfy their needs.

Beyond this confusion about the boundaries that separated my life from theirs, there was another dimension to life in my family. In that dimension my boundaries were actively violated by both my mother and my father. This was the dark side of our lives which couldn't be seen by anyone outside. It was the dark side that I couldn't let myself see either. This was the side that contradicted everything else. My mind wouldn't encompass the two realities. So I blotted out the dark, destructive part that didn't fit the rest. It was more than thirty years before I let myself see the whole of what I had experienced as a child.

I was 41 years old when I began to remember what I had hidden from myself. Yet I had many hints about those blocked memories over the years. When I read *Absalom! Absalom!* in college, I was mesmerized by the incestuous tale Faulkner tells. Fascinated by that book, I wrote three of my best academic papers about it. I understood Quentin Compson when he committed suicide, drowning himself in the Charles River while a senior at Harvard. I had come close to suicide many times during my college years. Still I could not see the direct connection with my own life.

My memory returned only after I had experienced profound healing in many areas of my life. Finally when I felt safe and secure enough within myself, I was ready to face that dark side of my experience. My father had been dead for three years. I had been married and divorced twice. It was two and a half years since the conference at Sky Hi Ranch with Brugh Joy.

I was involved with Jason, and he had just given me an engagement ring. I knew he loved me as I had never felt loved before. But I also knew there was something strangely familiar about the way I felt close to him. He loved me as my father had. He adored me, and yet in the flash of a moment's shift of feeling, he could turn on me in an abusive rage. I was terrified of his anger and mystified by it. Little did I realize at the time that the power of his rage was a perfect mirror for me of the depth of my own anger, which I had denied all my life. I did think it was strange that I could ignore and completely forget his rages when they were over. But, that also mirrored the way I ignored my own anger and disassociated myself from it.

Now, I see that unconsciously I was recreating important aspects of my relationship with my father. It was as if I had to relive a parallel situation in order to remember what I had forgotten and ultimately to resolve what I never before had been able to face. As my relationship with Jason unfolded, I found myself back in the nightmare of love and abuse that I had lived as a child. And, at the same time, I began having clearer and clearer visual memories of sexual experiences I had with my father when I was very young.

The more I remembered about my childhood, the more I felt I needed the relationship with Jason. Sometimes he was supportive and wonderfully understanding as the deep pain, hurt, confusion and anger I had buried inside me for all those years came up for me to experience and release. Sometimes he attacked me with what I had shared with him, called me a whore, and re-created the kind of verbal abuse my father sometimes showered me with after the sex was over and he tried to relieve his guilt by blaming me for his perversion.

But now I was an adult. Intellectually, I knew I didn't deserve these attacks. I couldn't understand why I didn't just leave Jason and put an end to what I knew was becoming a disaster. Yet, the child in me clung to him with the tenacity of one whose survival depended upon his love and approval. I lived for the periods when we were happy, and the world seemed more fun and more beautiful than I had ever known before. But the more I remembered of my childhood, the less able I was to block out and forget the abusive times in the present. The first memories that returned came while we were having sex. I was shocked and didn't believe the visual images I was seeing. As my former therapist discounted my mentioning any kind of sexual issue with my father, so I dismissed these memories as the kind of sexual fantasy that Freud said all female children have about their fathers.

But the images persisted and became stronger and more vivid. We were in Atlanta when the first memories emerged. I was close to the town in Alabama where I lived as a child. It was less than a week since Jason had given me an engagement ring for Christmas. I had ended therapy with Dr. Porter two weeks before. All these factors combined to jog my memory and allow my sexual experiences with my father finally to come into my conscious awareness.

I was in the South again, back where I always feel deeply connected with my early years. I was with Jason. We shared a powerful bond of love, and I felt a deep emotional dependence on him. It was just after Christmas, and I was wearing a beautiful engagement ring, a ring that was remarkably like one I treasured briefly during the Christmas holidays in 1960.

That year I was 19 years old, a sophomore in college, and in love. Kenny had graduated from Harvard the previous spring. He was a fine young man; a Naval officer, stationed in Georgia. We had shared one beautiful year; my freshman year at Wellesley, his senior year in Cambridge. When I came back to Alabama for Christmas in 1960, he gave me the engagement ring I had always dreamed of having. I was ecstatic. I loved him with all my heart. But I was worried about sharing my wonderful news with my parents. I didn't know how they would react.

When I mustered my courage and told them that Kenny and I wanted to be married, they were devastated. Though I had been apprehensive about sharing this with them, I wasn't prepared for the intensity of their reactions. They told me I would be throwing my life away, throwing my education away; they knew I wouldn't finish college if I married; they were determined to stop me from making such a horrible mistake. My mother went to bed, ill, because I had an engagement ring. My father stood before me with a shot gun in his hand and threatened to kill himself if I married this young man I loved.

I ran crying to my best friend's house. What was I to do? I was on the phone talking with Kenny when my father rang her doorbell. He rushed into her house, wearing his pajamas under a coat. He grabbed the phone away from me and threatened to kill Kenny, too, if he didn't get out of my life. This was behavior he never allowed anyone outside our family to see. I was horrified and enraged. And I felt completely helpless.

I still can't remember returning the ring to Kenny. I can

remember the last time I ever saw him on Christmas day of 1960. We made tentative plans that he would visit me in Boston at the end of January, during exam break. But, in my heart, I think I knew I never would see him again.

Just three days later, I was a bridesmaid for one of my best friends. My heart was breaking. I was like a robot. My mother arranged for a young man I had dated briefly in junior high school to escort me for the wedding activities. I was dead inside.

I had allowed my parents to control me with their hysterical dramatics and their threats. I was overwhelmed. My life no longer seemed to belong to me. I was a puppet and they were my masters, dictating, directing, telling me how to feel and whether or not I could love anyone but them.

I chose to protect them and honor their fears rather than protecting myself, my feelings, my life, and the love I shared with another worthy human being. I did not find the courage to simply leave them and assert my own will for my own life. I chose the passive route. I chose to assume I was responsible for keeping my father from killing himself rather than seeing that this was his choice and only his choice. And I chose not to be responsible for my own life, my own happiness, my own capacity to know my own heart and choose my own path.

The amazing thing to me now is realizing that I didn't even question my parents' presumed right to dictate my choice of a mate. I didn't question their bizarre behavior at all. I didn't wonder why I couldn't choose to marry, when at the very same time my friend, Judy, was exercising her prerogative to do the same thing. And my parents were there for her wedding, happy for her. She was my age. It was OK for her to marry. It was not OK for me. I was beyond even asking why.

Twenty-two years later I was less than a hundred miles from home, wearing a very similar engagement ring, and beginning to discover just why my wanting to marry the man I loved had been so incredibly threatening to my father. He had been jealous. He was in a murderous rage because he was so jealous. He knew how much I cared about Kenny. He would not lose me to someone who might be more powerful in my life than he always had been.

Suddenly I understood what had happened the year before my aborted engagement to Kenny. I became terribly ill and lost my voice completely when Daddy came to Wellesley for a weekend in November of my freshman year. Kenny and I had become lovers less than a month before. I was torn between overwhelming guilt and the deep passion our sexual relationship awakened in me. I said to myself that my parents would die if they knew I had dared to be such a sinner. All the times my father had called me a whore flooded my mind. I didn't have any notion why sex was such an emotionally loaded experience for me. My friends seemed to handle it as a normal part of their lives. I was hysterical with fear that Kenny would hurt me, leave me, turn on me. He never did any of those things, but I had no peace of mind. Sex and fear were deeply connected in me. I didn't even wonder why.

When my father arrived on Friday afternoon, I was so ill I had no voice. I showed him around the campus anyway. We had dinner at a favorite restaurant in Boston with Kenny. The tension was thick between my father and Kenny. I couldn't speak or taste what I ate.

By Sunday, my eyes were swollen closed. My father left me in the infirmary where I spent the next three weeks recovering from this encounter between my first lover, whom I didn't choose and didn't remember, and my second, whom I thought was my first.

I had laryngitis and conjunctivitis. My throat and my eyes were swollen shut. I couldn't see and I couldn't talk. My physical symptoms were a perfect metaphor. I couldn't see what had happened to me with my father, and I had long ago been enjoined not to talk. "If you ever tell anyone, I'll have to kill us both." My body produced the perfect solution to my unconscious dilemma. And since sickness always got me nurturing from my father, getting sick was a brilliant solution. I managed to delay facing the conflict between my lovers for another year.

When that confrontation finally did come the following Christmas, I faced a pivotal decision point in my life. Had I found the courage to let go of my parents and opt for my own wants and needs, my life probably would have followed a very different direction. It was twenty-two years before I faced such a clear decision point again. By that time I had discovered and paid the price for not honoring my responsibility to myself for the quality of my own life. Even so, it wasn't easy then either.

But back in 1960 I simply kept going. I took the train back to Boston. I wrote papers and studied for finals. Just before exam break, Kenny called to tell me he wasn't coming to see me after all. He made an excuse that I knew wasn't real. I wasn't surprised. I had known we were finished on Christmas day in Alabama. The prospect of his coming to Boston had simply dulled the pain of that final goodbye for both of us. By this time I was so numb I almost didn't care.

That same weekend, on a blind date, I met the man I married a year and a half later. Before we had finished the trip from Wellesley to Boston, I knew there was nothing about him my parents could dare question. He was a super achiever, valedictorian of his high school and college graduating classes. He was from the right kind of family. He had the right ambitions. He was safe. I knew I would never again let myself be hurt as I was hurting then. I would never give my parents another chance to reject a man I had chosen.

Before that first evening's date ended, I knew we shared many common experiences. He, too, was living through the pain of losing a love. She had died in a plane crash that killed her entire family the summer before. She had been a Wellesley student. They had planned to be together in Cambridge that year since he had just begun Harvard Law School.

Both he and I had coped with pain since childhood by achieving academically and working very hard. We liked each other. We were so absorbed in talking with each other that we missed the turnoff to Wellesley on the way back to my dorm. When I said goodnight to him, I told myself that whether or not I ever saw him again, I felt better to know there was such a decent, bright, sensitive person around in the world.

He did call the next night. Soon we were together steadily, building a warm, good relationship. We found comfort and ease with each other and relief from our separate grieving. He introduced me to Modigliani at a retrospective in the Boston Museum of Fine Art. We catered a dinner party for one of his law professors. We studied together, and he marveled at how I could write papers with more ease than he allowed himself. We watched Winston Churchill on his funny round screen TV. We cooked duck and invited friends over for dinner. We spent weekends in New York. We loved each other. By October of my junior year we decided to marry the following summer.

I knew my parents could not object this time as they had before. There was nothing about this man they could fault. He embodied all the values they held. And most importantly, though we loved each other, there was not the intensity of attraction between us that had existed in my earlier relationship. There was not a strong sexual energy to arouse their fears and jealousies.

This time his parents wanted us to wait another year. They even flew to Alabama to persuade my parents to join them in resisting our plans. But my parents held firmly to their position. This was our decision. They could not stop us from living our own lives. It was one year since they had made their stand against Kenny. It was incredible.

Looking back on that time now, I am amazed that such a reversal of response could have happened so quickly. In the light of what I remembered in 1982, I now understand more clearly how this was possible. At the time I only knew I had found a way out of their grip on my life, a way that they had to accept and that I felt good about.

I loved this man and I admired and respected him. There wasn't the same excitement and strong attraction I had felt for Kenny, but that was part of what I liked about this relationship. I felt safe and I had my parents' blessings. Marrying him was the perfect solution to many dilemmas I faced at the time. I knew the script for my life was to graduate from college, get married, have children, and live "happily ever after." Somehow I also was supposed to have a career to make up to Daddy for my being a girl and for his missing out on the education and career he had wanted for himself. I was about to reach the first rung on that ladder. I would graduate from college the following year. What was I to do next?

My advisors at Wellesley spoke of graduate school and a career. Part of me yearned to continue my education, to explore the world of business, to live in New York or Boston and have a challenging job that would allow me to learn more about Economics, which was my major.

Another part of me was frightened of breaking out of the mold that had been cast for me by my family and our culture. It seemed so much easier to marry a brilliant man and support him in his career than to take those career and business risks myself. Bringing home the perfect son-in-law also solved my career dilemma with Daddy. My decision to marry allowed me to proceed to the next step in my script without having to struggle with what to do if I broke free from my parents' expectations for me.

We were married the following August, just before my senior year in college. We had a wonderful wedding, almost what I had dreamed of all my life. But I was still not free to assert myself about the details that were important to me. In the end, the dress and veil I wore were not what I wanted, not what I liked, not what I felt pretty wearing. But they were what my mother and one of her friends wanted me to wear.

A family friend who had been generous and good to me in many ways offered Mother the heirloom lace veil worn by brides in her family. The veil was lovely, creamy ivory and elegant. But the veil was not a part of the picture I had for myself as a bride. I wanted a soft beautiful veil that covered my face as I walked down the aisle. I wanted a lacy dress that was made just for me.

Once again I did not claim the courage to insist on considering my own feelings. Mother wanted me to wear the heirloom veil. Then a dress was offered that went with the veil. I went along with Mother, who didn't want to offend her friend by not accepting her offer. I didn't dare offend anyone.

The week before our wedding, I became dizzy and felt dizzy for much of the next two years. My body was signaling me that something was wrong. Since I was paying no attention to my own needs and feelings, my body was left to express those feelings that I didn't dare allow to come into my conscious awareness. I felt dizzy, lost, and vulnerable. I was abdicating responsibility for my life. I was committing myself to live through my husband to satisfy my parents' dreams for me to avoid hurting or disappointing them and to avoid growing up and claiming charge of me. I almost deceived myself completely, but my physical body gave me no peace for the next seven years until I began to find and claim my own course for my own life again.

Many times during the ten years of our marriage, I could have heeded my body's signals and searched beyond what was offered me by the medical doctors I visited. But, again, rather than thinking for myself and searching for my own truth, I followed what the authorities I had accepted in my life said I should do. At that time, those authorities didn't suggest psychotherapy though I was manifesting all the symptoms of a human being in great emotional turmoil and distress. I was in my 20's, nervous, developing an ulcer, unable to eat without indigestion, and I weighed 101 pounds on a 5'6" frame.

Finally, valium was prescribed. I accepted the relief it gave me, but I did ask lots of questions about its safety. My doctor assured me it was only a muscle relaxant, not a tranquilizer. And he told me it wasn't addicting.

Had he sent me to a good therapist at that point, I might have avoided a lot of difficulty later. Speculating about that is of little value now. What I experienced is what I experienced, and I believe those experiences were all part of the path I needed to follow to learn what I had to learn.

The valium allowed me enough relief to begin to take hold of myself and to find some direction for myself. Eventually, I had to release it and go through the painful experience of withdrawing from it. Discovering on my own that valium, in fact, was addicting was another step toward realizing I couldn't trust blindly what an authority figure told me. By this time, which was after the birth of my second daughter, I was beginning to emerge from the worst of my helpless nightmare and finding a glimmer of my own strength rising in me.

As I took my first tentative steps toward finding my own center, I gradually realized I was going to have to face the feelings I had been avoiding for most of my life. But, it was the loss of my marriage that brought me to my knees. I was devastated when my husband left me, and I realized he was in love with another woman. In desperation, I finally sought help from a therapist and found one of the best. In the fall of 1972, I began therapy at the same time that my divorce was granted. The fourteen years since have been exciting, painful, scary, and exhilarating as I have discovered myself and carved the real me out from the tangle of emotions and experiences I had hidden from myself through repression, disassociation, and amnesia.

I was devastated by the divorce. At times I felt as if I simply couldn't keep going. I was so caught up in my own pain, feeling rejected and desperate, that I had little energy for helping my children through the crisis of their loss. I did my best, but my best was far from meeting their needs at the time. I felt like a victim, and I acted like a victim. My therapist insisted that I get in touch with my anger, which was conspicuously absent from my awareness. I followed her direction and tried to express my feelings to my ex-husband as if he were present in the room with us. I could say the words, but there was no feeling to enliven them. The only feeling I knew was an overwhelming emptiness. I felt abandoned. I felt like I was about five years old. I felt no strength. I was terrified, afraid to be alone, and at the same time, wanting to isolate myself.

At one point, I called my parents and asked them to come be with me and help me with the children. My father called me back the next day to tell me that my mother was too upset by the divorce to make the trip. I would have to manage on my own. I think that moment was the first clear realization I had that there was something incredibly wrong in my relationship with my parents. When my mother's feelings were escalated over mine while I was going through the worst experience of my life, I began to notice that perhaps I might just be angry after all.

Always before, they had come when I needed them. When my children were born, they were there to help. When I spent three months in bed during my first pregnancy, my mother took care of me. But those were happy times, relative to what was happening now. I couldn't understand why my parents were more devastated by my divorce than I was. Looking back now, I realize that this was the first time they had to face that my life was not the story-book picture of perfection I previously had managed to maintain. My divorce meant my life was not perfect. That meant they had to face the fact that the abuse I had suffered as a child just might be taking a toll on my life. As long as I was able to maintain the facade of perfection, we could all pretend that what had happened hadn't really happened. Now the lid was off that illusion. Though I still didn't have a clue about why I felt so much like a devastated five year old, abused and abandoned, unconsciously, I think we all knew the jig was up.

For all of us the dark-sided nightmare remained hidden for another twelve years. But the process of self-punishing, painful, life-wasting destruction was unleashed. My mother became ill again, almost immediately after my divorce. That was the beginning of her trip down the awful path of encroaching senility to the helpless existence of an infant in a seventy-year-old body. My father took early retirement, supposedly hoping to travel and enjoy his remaining years. Instead, he devoted himself to caring for my mother as she became more and more disoriented, confused, and helpless.

I embarked upon a difficult fourteen years of troubled relationships with men, trying to discover how to put my life back together again, while unconsciously punishing myself for my very existence. Through all of that I also took over responsibility for my parents' care. The nightmare played on. It was three years after my father's death before I began to wake up to the hidden source of the terror the three of us shared, hidden deep within each of us, while we lived out the tragic script that we had created to distract us from what we had, each in our own separate ways, put out of our minds. Mother went out of her mind in the process. Daddy lost his capacity to function as strokes devastated his brain. I managed to fight my way out, taking advantage of every therapeutic process I could discover that might assist me in waking up and claiming my right to my own life at last.

CHAPTER VI

SEEING THE WHOLE PICTURE

I was thirty-one when I experienced my first divorce. I felt devastated and overwhelmed by the painful feelings and new responsibilities I faced. My daughters were eight and three. I was barely functioning. As I began my long journey through every kind of psychotherapy I could find, I was determined to heal myself. It wasn't an easy task.

My first husband remarried six months after our divorce. Three weeks later, I met and fell in love with Dean. He and I shared my long delayed adolescence. I was addicted to our relationship and clung to it well past the point where it was clear that he was not interested in the same kind of commitment that I knew I needed. Nevertheless, I persisted in trying to make him into the person I wished he was. I ignored my own needs and feelings in the process. I also refused to accept him as he was and honor the differences that existed between us. Finally, I was able to let go of this relationship when, after the workshop with Brugh Joy, I faced that I could not fulfill my own potential and live with the kind of open marriage he desired.

Just when I was healing from this second divorce and overcoming my feelings of sadness, failure, and loss, I met Jason. He loved me in a way I thought I had never experienced before; yet it was curiously familiar. He was capable of great compassion, gentleness and understanding. He was generous, and he encouraged me to take risks that I had never dared to consider. He was fun, witty, and delightful. Life was a joy and a celebration with him. He was wonderful to my daughters and taught us all a lot about loving each other and being nurturing in our home.

As our relationship developed, I discovered the dark side of him that was terrifying to me. When he disagreed with me or took issue with something I said or did, he sometimes became abusively angry, raving at me about my faults and blaming me for his problems. At these times, I had no way to break through his incredibly tough defenses. When this first happened, we were traveling in the Orient. I was half-way around the world with a man who seemed to be a total stranger and a terrifying one at that.

I marvel now at how well I handled traveling in a totally strange world on an emotional roller coaster with this man I loved, who loved me unstintingly one minute, and hated me with equal intensity the next. I was determined to enjoy my first trip abroad despite the ups and downs we were experiencing. But, by the time we reached Paris, I knew I would end our relationship as soon as we got home and return the ring he had given me for Christmas. I gave up all hope of salvaging what I had so treasured in our time together. While we were in Paris, he became quite ill and was unable to leave his bed. I set out to see the city on my own. I resigned myself to what lay ahead of me after the trip.

When we reached the airport to fly from Paris to London and then home, I, too, was ill with a fever and an upper respiratory virus. In the car on the way to the plane, he verbally attacked me yet another time. I told him I was defeated and prayed that he would let me get home in peace. "Please just leave me alone."

I managed the baggage while he returned our rented car. When he approached me in the middle of the airport after getting our boarding passes, he turned abruptly and his old familiar pleasant personality was back. I was dumbfounded and overwhelmed with relief. Now nothing was too much trouble for him to do to help me and nurse me back to health. I was his precious little girl once more. I chose to ignore the horrors of the past three weeks so I could cling to him once more, thanking God for the miracle of healing I told myself he had experienced.

The ordeal and ecstasy of the trip, the rapid change in his personality, and the terror I felt when the loving man abandoned me and the frightening one took over, stirred forgotten corners in my mind. This was incredibly familiar.

Gradually it dawned on me that I was recreating my relationship with my father. I could no longer avoid facing the sickness and pain I had absorbed as a child. With Jason, I recreated my experience with my parents so vividly that I could no longer fool myself about my childhood.

Throughout my adult life, I had attracted people and situations that stirred my buried child's rage, hurt, sorrow, and isolation. These old painful feelings repeated themselves in what seemed like an endless cycle. Work as I did through all kinds of therapy, I still had not been able to rid myself of this plague. What was wrong with me? Why did I continue to have hurtful relationships with men when what I thought I wanted most of all was a happy family and happy home life?

Now, in this relationship, I knew I had done it again. I was in love with a man whose erratic behavior stirred all my old, painful demons. More memories began to flood back to me, probably, because despite his moods and unpredictability, he did love me. Assured of his devotion, I felt safe enough to remember more and more.

My remembering process, which had begun in Atlanta four months earlier, took about two years. Ultimately, I faced that, separately and without the other's knowledge, both my mother and my father used me for their perverted sexual pleasure. My mother chose bath time and naptime until I was four years old and her brother was killed. When that tragedy occurred, she must have imagined that she was being punished for her sexual activities with me. She stopped. We read Bible stories instead. She turned herself to teaching me, playing school, telling me stories, trying to redeem herself and me from the sin we had known.

Daddy chose the closet when I was being punished, or his workshop, as I grew older. And when I was 9 or so, he left me alone. There was no explanation. Mother knew about him and me. She had exploded in rage when she discovered us together. She blamed me for ruining her life. She flailed at me, beat me, broke my nose. But it was two years before Daddy stopped. There were whispers that he almost had a "nervous breakdown" when he went away on a trip. He stopped for Mother; it hurt her too much. No one even told me what had happened.

All those previous years, he "comforted" me with sexual fondling when I was upset. He was my security, sick as it was. Suddenly there was nothing. I had been alienated from Mother after she found us together; now he was gone, too. I cried alone in my room for hours, feeling guilty, bad, awful, and not even knowing why.

The little girl that cried didn't know the bad little girl that had done those terrible things. She blocked the knowledge and memory of her secret sexual experiences, transforming herself from the bad girl to the good girl as fast as she could blink her eyes, crossing the backyard from the workshop to the house.

For the next 32 years, I kept repeating the pain and isolation, creating situations and experiences that hurt me in similar ways. From the time I rediscovered sex as a young adult, I thought I was crazy. Why was I terrified that my lover would abandon me? Why did I lose my sense of myself and become like a slave to him? Why was I suddenly suicidal? I could do most everything else successfully. Why were my relationships with men so incredibly painful and difficult?

I worked hard. I did everything I could to make my life worthwhile, to overcome the guilt I felt, but had no explanation for. I worked hard to try to earn love and respect. I loved my parents. I believed they loved me. I lived my life trying to please them and heal the deep unhappiness I felt in them and in me. I cared for them through their invalid years when each of them was helpless, unable to speak, walk, or let go and die. And still I couldn't seem to have what I craved with every fiber of my being: love, genuine love; the kind I could feel easy and peaceful and safe with; the kind I saw others have. Why did it elude me; why, when I worked so hard to earn it?

I didn't understand then that my first task was to learn to love myself and to stop the patterns of internal self-rejection I had practiced unconsciously all my life. By not remembering and facing my childhood pain and despair, I was, in effect, rejecting the damaged little girl within me. The rejection I experienced in relationships with men simply was a mirror for me of this internal rejection process I had not recognized yet.

In Atlanta in 1982, when I began to remember sexual experiences with my father, I had only quick glimpses of memory pictures. Seeing these pictures and feeling that I had had sex with Daddy was followed by an immediate denial that anything so awful could possibly have happened. But the memory pictures persisted and the feeling grew more certain.

Two years before meeting Jason, I dated another older man whose first name was the same as my father's. I realized then how much my attraction to him was focused on his name. At that time, I began to acknowledge to myself that I had had strong sexual feelings for my father. This pleased my Freudian therapist. He assumed and assured me that sexual fantasies about Daddy are a part of every female child's normal development. I was relieved to accept his interpretation and push back the memories that were threatening to break through into my consciousness.

Now, as I faced the unthinkable possibility that my father had used me for sex, I longed to protect my illusions about him, the image I had of him, the deep love I knew he had for me. I wanted to protect myself from even consider-ing that his love for me might have included sick, perverted experiences. I needed my father to be good. I needed my father to be the father I wanted. I needed my childlike perception of him even though he had been dead for more than three years. I didn't want to grow up, let go of him, and see what really had been there and had been so awful for me as a child.

So I said to myself, "You're crazy." I reminded myself of my therapist's words that all little girls fantasize and want sex with their fathers. It's just fantasy, not real. This must be my imagination.

But the memories persisted. Things began to make sense. Connections kept popping into my mind. I had found the missing piece in a puzzle I had never before been able to complete. I wasn't crazy. It was no wonder I had had the problems and pain I had struggled with for so long. It was no wonder my relationships with men had been so ecstatic, so painful, so confusing, and so devastating.

I knew that my father had carried a deep, unfathomable pain inside him that nothing would relieve. I had done everything I could to help him through his dreadful last years, but nothing shook his unhappiness. He would look at me with such pain and such love in his eyes. It was as if he couldn't bear to leave me and die. When I told him I loved him, he hung his head and shook it "no". That frustrated me enormously, and I considered it a triumph when I finally convinced him that he couldn't tell me how I felt about him. I taught him to shake his head "yes" and outwardly accept my love without protest.

Now I realized why he had been so convinced that I couldn't possibly love him. He and I had desperately needed to talk about what had happened so many years before. But I did not yet remember, and he couldn't talk. Probably he would not have wanted to face the issue if he had been able to speak (or perhaps his loss of speech was an unconscious means of insuring that this secret would be buried with him).

Gradually, as I sorted through these memories and connections, I began to feel what had been buried deep inside me and locked behind a door whose key I had lost along with my lost memory. There were so many feelings: shock, disgust, guilt, terrible guilt and shame, sadness, helplessness, hopelessness, and rage. For what seemed like a long, long time, my rage overshadowed every other emotion.

How could he have done this to me? How dare he violate me, a child, his child, and at the same time pretend to be such a wonderful, self-sacrificing father. What dishonesty, what massive deception, what sickness! Disgust. He was disgusting. He was dirty, nasty, horrible. He would abuse me sexually, then turn on me in his own guilty rage and chastise me for being a bad, nasty little girl. Why did I not tell on him? Why didn't I run away? Why didn't I fight him off? What was my responsibility in this ugliness? What could I, the child, be accountable for?

When I think of him now that my rage is spent, I know most of all how much I loved him. Despite what he did to me sexually when I was a child, he also gave me much that was valuable and loving. He was the source of what emotional warmth and connection I experienced after my grandmother died and my mother withdrew from me. Daddy was the center of my life. I was "Daddy's little girl" and my life was focused on making him happy.

"Daddy's little girl" was not the same child that experienced the strange sexual rituals with him in his workshop. "Daddy's little girl" loved to go out there and "help" him with his woodworking projects after dinner every night. She would slip across the backyard and knock on the door of the garage where he kept his tools and created wonderful wooden churches and crosses and liturgical plaques for our church Sunday school.

Once inside, she changed. He locked the door. He always kept that door locked. Then her world, her reality changed. She was in the hidden secret world now; the hidden secret world they shared.

It had started in the closet when she was only two. When she got very angry and had a tantrum, Mother would lock her in the closet in the bedroom she shared with her parents. The door was behind her bed. She would cry and wail, frightened and isolated, hot and enraged, stuck in that dark, hidden place. He would come to comfort her, cautioning her to be quiet. "Don't make anymore noise." If she'd be quiet and do what he told her, he'd let her out soon. "Don't make any noise; that's a good girl — that's Daddy's girl; Oh — Oh — o —."

Later he'd leave, making sure the coast was clear. Soon he'd return to free her; she'd been quiet long enough now. The punishment-comforting was over. "You can come out now. You've learned your lesson. Be a good girl now, be a good girl for Daddy."

The good girl didn't have anything to do with that bad, guilty, hidden-closet girl. The good girl worked really hard not to get into trouble. She didn't know why getting into trouble was such a terrifying possibility. She didn't know why she was compelled to be quiet, to be nice, not to bother anyone, not to upset anyone. She didn't know why she felt so different from other children. She didn't know why she didn't belong. Later, she didn't know why she was drawn irresistibly to that workshop to help Daddy.

When the lock clicked shut and he approached her to do those strange things, she knew she had no choice. It was scary and it hurt, and she didn't understand why this had to happen and why it had to happen so much. But she'd learned to get out of her body while he did those doctor things to her. She could watch the whole thing from the corner, up by the ceiling and that way she didn't feel anything. The one on the workshop bench was just a shell. She was the real one and this didn't happen to her. She just watched it all.

And when it was all over, and she took her hurting body back across the yard to the house, she left the bad-girl, workshop-girl behind. That wasn't her anymore. She was "Daddy's little girl" again and she was innocent. "Daddy's little girl" and the workshop-girl didn't even know each other at all.

"Daddy's Little Girl" learned to read; she escaped into books, every book she could find. She loved novels. There was another world in her novels; a world she held onto for sustenance; a world she would belong to someday. And when she read, she wasn't bothering anyone. She couldn't get into trouble reading. She was safe with her books.

She escaped into school, too. That was a world she could master, at least, the study, tests, and grades parts. She was awkward and shy with the other children. She was locked up inside herself; she didn't know how to play. She did know how to make good grades. And so she survived on grades and the respect she earned for herself in that way. She would make her parents proud and keep the secret, too.

The "workshop girl" and "Daddy's little girl" didn't meet for years and years. Not until I was 41 and began to remember, did "Daddy's little girl" even have a thought about the "workshop girl." And when she did, she couldn't believe what she was remembering.

"This couldn't have happened to me. My father was a wonderful man. He wouldn't have done anything to hurt me," I said to myself. "You're just making this up. He was the pillar of the church. What's wrong with you to even think such a thing?"

A battle raged inside me for months as I realized I couldn't ignore the vivid images that were coming to me. I could no longer pretend that my growing-up years had been normal and natural. But still I saw only still pictures, different and separate images that kept repeating themselves in my mind. There was no continuity to my memories, only flashes of scenes that had no beginning and no end.

I wrote in my journal. I talked with a close friend who believed me more than I believed myself. I had no therapist at the time. I had no desire to re-enter therapy with my former therapist to deal with an issue he had discounted and dismissed.

In my own therapy practice, I experienced an influx of women clients who were facing similar issues in their lives. Could I dare try to help them when I was dealing with my own childhood sexual experiences? I knew what the traditional therapeutic answer would be to that question. Don't dare attempt to help others when you may be blind to the damage in your own life and your own thinking.

Yet I knew first hand what they were facing, and I knew that through their sharing with me, they were gaining ground in their struggles just as I was finding healing in the process, too. I told them I was facing the same issue, and I let them know that I was not finished dealing with it either. We understood that we were working together in the fullest sense, seeking common goals. We were looking for healing in our lives and we were determined to find it.

I read about incest, and I attended conferences on the subject. Whenever I participated in a conference that focused on childhood sexual abuse, I came away confirmed in my understanding of what had happened to me. As a child I experienced many of the symptoms that go with sexual abuse. I was terrified of the dark and sometimes refused to sleep alone. I had repetitive nightmares about our house burning down. I worried obsessively about my father dying. I was an isolated child with few friends. I developed a phobia about fish. I washed my hands compulsively. I was sick a lot, especially with headaches, stomach aches, and sore throats. At one point, I was afraid to leave home to go to school. I blocked my capacity to visualize. I felt guilty, bad, different. I was severely depressed and I kept a protective wall around myself.

At these conferences, I heard about the devastating effects of incest on a child's life. I heard clinical discussions of the nightmarish aftermath of such experiences. I felt like a monster, some kind of freakish form of life that couldn't be expected to ever find peace, happiness, and health. There was little talk of successful treatment, and no one said, "I survived and I'm OK."

After one such conference, I cried for twenty-four hours. For the first time, I embraced the seriousness of the trauma I had lived with all my life. My buried hurt, pain, rage, and isolation broke through, and finally I allowed the child in me to express herself without judgment and criticism. The little workshop-girl was no longer alone and isolated. I welcomed her back into my life and did my best to comfort her and believe what she finally was trusting me enough to share with me.

I realized that not believing that hurt part of myself, while opting to hold onto my idealized view of my parents, was the worst form of self-rejection. I had been protecting my image of my father and mother at an enormous cost to my own life. I had kept the guilty secret for years so none of us would have to face the reality of what had happened. In the meantime, it had destroyed my parents' lives (at this time my mother was still alive but completely helpless and senile) and was taking an enormous toll in my own.

In my studying incest and treating its victims, I learned that breaking the vow of secrecy is crucial to ending the pathology. The victim must end her victim stance by speaking up and confronting her parents with what happened. Or if her parents are no longer alive, she can talk with other surviving family members so she no longer carries the entire burden of what happened. But how could one ever find the courage to upset everyone else in the family with such devastating information? Would she be believed even if she did speak up?

I read that no matter how the rest of the family responds, the incest survivor herself is freed through the act of telling. The key factor is releasing the burden of the secret from her own life. I was relieved to know that I couldn't possibly confront my parents since my father was dead and my mother senile. My daughters already knew. All I would have to do was tell my two first cousins and one aunt who were all of the surviving members of my family.

I was in for a surprise. I had invited Carolyn Conger to Oklahoma to present a workshop. In October, we gathered at my lake home for an intensive four day session. Strange dream images came into my mind as we listened to music at the beginning of the conference. I saw a witch on a broom, riding across the full harvest moon. I saw my mother's bed in her nursing home room. I saw a child. Carolyn suggested that I draw these images and see what might come from that experience.

Late that night I began my drawing. As the images took form on my paper, words began to come. I wrote. Page after page appeared before me, describing yet another incident I had blocked from my memory for thirty-four years.

My mother was enraged, understandably so. She had just come upon my father and me. She looked in the workshop window and saw what every mother would most dread to see between her daughter and her husband. Sex. Sex. Pure and simple. They, we, were having sex.

She was overwhelmed with her hurt, her rage. She was betrayed by the most important people in her life. She had no place to turn, no one to tell. For this was the unspeakable, the shame that couldn't be shared.

She feared my father, feared his rage, feared losing him, especially now that all the family she had was her senile father. (She never counted me as her family.)

And so she turned her rage, outraged, on me. I was seven years old. I was the only outlet she had. And I was guilty; guilty of the worst of crimes. I had seduced my father. Yes, it was my fault, and she would beat the sin out of me. She drug me across the backyard by my left arm. She pulled my limp, terrified form into the dining room. She pounded my head against the floor, shaking my body, striking me across the face, breaking my nose. She would destroy what beauty there might be that could do such damage. "You made him do it. You should die for this. You've betrayed me for all time. This sin I will never forget, never forgive."

Thirty-three years later she sat, senile and lost, in her chair, shrouded in the smell only nursing homes can create. It was cold November now, and I was ready to confront her with what I had discovered that night six weeks earlier. By this time I had cried my tears and grieved the loss of another illusion, the illusion of my mother's innocence. (At this time, I had not yet remembered my sexual experiences with her.)

I told her what I did know. I told her the part I remembered then. In her eyes I saw the acknowledgment. I saw her experience the moment we had both avoided for all that time. As our eyes met, my anger faded. "Mother, forgive yourself. Forgive me. I forgive you. I forgive me;" me, talking for both of us since she had long since lost the gift of speech herself.

And she reached up her withered hand and touched my face as I leaned over her chair. She gave me the healing touch of my mother's hand, my mother's love. And I touched her face, that face I loved so much. In forgiveness and healing, she gave me back my life. In forgiveness and healing, I gave her the release she needed.

Six weeks later, I sat with her, shared with her, loved her, at peace with her then and with myself, through the day she died.

Six months after I buried her, new pieces of the puzzle that bore my mother's image emerged. Again I denied what was opening before my inner eyes. This couldn't be. Not my mother; not the one whose innocence I had embraced with all that was in me needing an innocent parent to survive.

The memory pictures continued and became clearer and clearer. I did age regressions, using methods I had learned through Silva Mind Control. I made myself look and feel and re-experience the secret that was buried deepest of all.

Here I found a very different reality. Here I found in myself sexual feelings more powerful than I'd ever before dared to allow. Here I found a skilled female lover completely abandoned in the pleasure of another female's body; her child's. Bath time and nap time before I was four years old brought memories even more difficult to face and accept as my own.

I had kept my mother sacred in my mind as helpless, passive, the victim of her life; the victim because she never allowed herself to face the reality of her responsibility for her choices. Now, I had to see her active and choosing. She chose to use me, her daughter, to fulfill sexual needs she wouldn't allow my father to meet. I had to look at her active part in creating the pain I'd lived with hidden inside me for all these years. I had to see her clearly for the first time.

I'd only recognized this powerful, active side of her in photographs of her adventures during the decade of her 20's. She had traveled, escorting tours of high school students, exploring the Western United States. Always she was the beautiful, smiling center of every group. Her warmth and energy lighted the pictures. In them, I saw a woman I liked, a woman I wanted to resemble, a woman I knew only through the wonderful stories she told me about those glorious days of adventure and fun.

Her unhappiness and her marriage seemed to coincide. She had told me how nervous and upset she'd been the first year she was married to my father. She could no longer stand teaching her sixth grade class and resigned after that year. She was miserable. She must have known she had made a big mistake. She wasn't happy. Sex must have been a problem for both of them.

What had happened to my parents? How did they develop the sexual difficulties each of them had? How were they both so wounded that each of them separately and without the other's knowledge could have abused the child that I know they loved and wanted and focused their lives

around. They loved me and gave me all the love and support they had to give. Yet there was also this dark, secret,
hidden, shameful side of my growing up with them. What
had so damaged them that they could have, in turn, damaged me as they did?

I could only call upon my intuition, my own sense of
what might have occurred, to answer these questions.
There were no surviving family members to consult except
my aunt, my father's sister. Eventually, I talked with her.
Through our conversation and through remembering what
my parents themselves told me about their growing-up
years and their families, I put together clues and pieces that
seem to fit together. I was searching for a way to understand how they could have been so damaged themselves
and, in turn, passed that damage on to me.

Born in 1905 and 1906, they were raised in the shadow
of the Victorian Age, with its emphasis on sexual repression. With sex considered bad and forbidden as it was,
these normal feelings and urges had to be driven underground, suppressed, forced out of awareness. Driven deep
within and held down with such force, these normal, natural urges become daemonic.

Hal Stone and Sidra Winkleman in their book, *Embracing Our Selves*, describe this process:

*Sexuality and sensuality are natural energy patterns. If, for a
variety of reasons, these energies are considered unacceptable,
then they become daemonic . . . It takes tremendous energy to
keep our instinctual life buried. The longer and the deeper it is
buried, the more daemonic it becomes, and the more energy is
required to maintain the burial . . . We use the word daemonic
to establish a clear discrimination between natural instinctual
life and repressed or disowned instinctual life that has become
distorted. (p. 240-241.)*

My intuition tells me that my father, who was a conscientious, respectable, responsible man, first had explored
his sexuality with his older sister in the kind of sex play
that children's natural curiosity stimulates. He adored this

sister. I know that he suffered a facial stroke on the day she was married and he was the one who gave the bride away. He was devastated by her sudden death a few years later. I was born six years after she died. As a child, the highest compliment I could be accorded was to be compared with her. I loved for Daddy to tell other people that I reminded him of her because of my looks or my intelligence. I also may have been a substitute for her in the infantile sexual liaisons he and I shared.

Probably my mother was sexually abused, also. Again, I can only imagine what might have happened. Her father also ended his life senile and helpless. Perhaps he was suffering from the guilt a sexually abusive parent must feel deep within, even though he may have completely repressed the memories of what generated the guilt in the first place. Mother feared her father and tolerated him, but she never loved him with the devotion she accorded her mother. After her mother's sudden death, she was left to care for her father as he became more and more deaf, senile, and ill. She dreaded and feared becoming like him in her old age. She was relieved when he died, yet she never expressed any anger with him. I remember that he was a difficult person to be around. I didn't like him and stayed away from him as much as I could. I was afraid of him and felt guilty about not liking him more than I did.

Whatever damaged my parents during their growing-up years remained hidden and repressed deep within them. Yet these buried experiences affected all our lives profoundly. Precisely because of the deep repression, these energies were expressed in hidden, secret, destructive ways that were completely incongruent with what my parents believed in and wanted to express in their raising of me.

Everything in our lives was distorted as a result. I was driven to make them proud of me, to show them that I was successful, to be a credit to them, so we could all deny the destructive impact of our hidden sexual experiences on my psyche. We all three managed to live out the myth of our innocence as long as I was able to maintain my facade of normalcy and success.

No one noticed the difficulty I had with pregnancy and childbirth, the threatened miscarriage, the need for a Caesarean section because I simply couldn't release by body enough to allow my first child a normal delivery. She almost died in the struggle before my doctor resorted to the surgical delivery. No one but my husband and I had to notice my lack of pleasure in sex during my first marriage. We did acknowledge my physical health problems, headaches, stomach trouble, and colitis, but those seemed unrelated to anything else. At that time in my life, I understood no connection between my mental and emotional state and my physical health.

However, the turning point came with my first divorce. My facade cracked. I could no longer pretend to be the perfect daughter, unscarred and unscathed. My parents could no longer pretend that the hidden, secret sex had not harmed me. Though they may have long since repressed any active memory of those encounters, at some level within us, we all three knew that something was wrong which we could no longer deny so thoroughly.

From this time on, my mother's health declined steadily. Within a year she was found to have arrhythmia, a fibrillating heart beat, that would not be corrected when she was hospitalized for treatment. She lived in fear of dying at any moment, and my father began to treat her as an invalid. Her retreat into senility began; and within two years, she was lost in a world of her own, isolated, angry, and desperate. Though she lived for more than ten years longer, she was only a shell of her former self.

My father devoted himself to caring for my mother until her condition so deteriorated that he could no longer manage her care at home. After she entered a nursing home, he could not allow himself to enjoy anything. I tried everything I could imagine to help him adjust to living alone, but he refused any comfort. My children and I gave him an adorable dog to be his pal. Though he loved dogs, Daddy convinced himself that he didn't want this one, and gave him away.

That summer I planned a trip to Disney World with my daughters and invited Daddy to join us. I thought that would be just what he needed and also would be fun for all of us. I was aware of being glad Mother could be left behind so we could enjoy normal activities without having to plan everything around her needs. I am sure my old Oedipal feelings were at work, too. Now that she was out of the picture, I could have Daddy to myself and even pretend to be a family with him as father and me as mother.

The plans didn't work out. The day before we were to leave for Florida, he picked an enormous fight with me and absolutely refused to consider going on the trip. At the time, I was mystified by his behavior. I even stayed in town an extra day, waiting for him to change his mind. But he wouldn't budge from his position. Looking back at the experience now, I can see that the whole idea was much too threatening to both of us. It could have blown the lid off what we both had repressed for so many years. Of course, he said he simply couldn't leave Mother. I think the reality was that we both felt too guilty to allow the trip to take place. After the children and I left for Florida, I called to check on him. That night for the first and only time I ever heard him say the words, he told me he was getting drunk.

We stopped to see him again on our way back to Oklahoma. Though we had a tentative reconciliation, I knew that at a deep level something had shifted in our relationship and that it would never be the same again. This was the last time I saw him standing, active, and whole. It was late June, 1976.

By November, he had had a massive stroke after prostate surgery, and never was able to speak or walk again.

In the fall of 1984, I was invited to present a workshop and a paper at Bob and Mary Goulding's International

Redecision Therapy Conference which was scheduled for May, 1985. I could pick my own topic. Without a moment's hesitation, I submitted my workshop title: "Beyond Victim: Redecision and Healing After Incest." I knew I would have to finish my own working through of these issues in order to write the paper and conduct the workshop. This meant telling my cousins and my aunt about what had happened in our family and about the paper I was writing. I set these tasks for myself and committed myself to accomplishing them.

I first revealed my secret to my cousin who is ten years younger than I. She is my father's niece. For months I hesitated to talk with her about what I had remembered. I knew how much she loved and admired my father. I didn't want to upset her, to cause her pain, to intrude upon her life with this unpleasant, unthinkable revelation. When I finally mustered my courage to call her one morning, I was nervous and agitated as I waited for the operator to complete my call. After chatting casually for a few minutes, I told her I had something to tell her that was very difficult for me to share. I asked her if she had time to listen. She assured me that she did. And so I told her what I remembered and how these experiences had affected me. She knew about the difficulties I had had in my relationships with men, because for the past few years we had talked frequently and I had told her about my divorce from Dean. She wasn't surprised by what I shared with her now. She was supportive and wonderfully warm with her response to my pain and my difficulty in finally breaking the secret by sharing with her. Her acceptance strengthened me greatly. I was relieved and empowered by talking with her.

Still I was reluctant to tell her mother, who is my father's sister. I couldn't bear to think of spoiling her memories of her brother. And I secretly wondered if she would believe me or would defend my parents.

Again, I was in for a wonderful surprise. When I talked with her on the telephone, she was incredibly understanding. She said to me, "Honey, I always knew there was something terribly wrong in your family and terribly hard for you. This makes perfect sense."

Nothing could have helped me more. Not only had she believed me, but she also validated my perceptions. I couldn't believe how wonderful I felt to experience her love and understanding and acceptance. That day hastened my healing and brought a new feeling of peace and self-acceptance I never before had experienced. Her response was a blessing I had not expected, a gift I needed and had dared not hope to receive.

During this period, my relationship with Jason continued to deteriorate. There were times when we were delightfully happy and content with each other. There were other times filled with pain. I was in constant emotional turmoil and had developed a variety of physical symptoms which finally convinced me that I couldn't afford to ignore my unhappiness any longer. Ours were not healthy conflicts where feelings were expressed and released and problems solved. Instead, they were destructive, hurtful, abusive times which invariably ended with his leaving dramatically, declaring that our relationship was ended.

After one such exit, we both recognized that we had to stop the terrible toll these patterns were taking on both of us. Once I lived through the first few weeks of intense grief after Jason moved out, I was determined to get my life back on track and end our romantic involvement. It was January of 1985.

I wasn't able to begin writing my incest article until we had separated. Once I began to reclaim my life, the words flowed and I found new understandings coming to me as I wrote. I knew that ending my relationship with Jason was like stopping the incest with my father. I would no longer allow myself to be abused, no matter how much I grieved over the loss of the beautiful parts of our time together. For the first time in my life, I knew that I could take care of myself adequately in the world. I knew I no longer would be anyone's victim.

During this period, I started a therapy group for incest survivors. In the group, we dealt with tremendous anger as we struggled to trust other women. The deep rift between mother and daughter was reflected in the difficulty we had trusting each other. Because I had not completed my own healing process, I was not yet as strong and confident as I needed to be in handling the powerful emotions the group faced. When we disbanded for the summer, we were all grateful for the relief. The emotional intensity of the group was a challenge to each of us. Several women had left the group, unwilling to face the feelings they were encountering.

I was writing my incest article as the group was developing. I submitted it for publication in February, but I still hadn't talked with my other cousin. Telling him about the sexual abuse was the most difficult confrontation of all. I knew how much he loved my parents, and how special he was to them. I treasured my memories of him when I was a child and he called me "Muffin." Writing to him was the closest thing to confronting my parents themselves. I thought he couldn't believe me. Yet, he, too, was loving and accepting when he answered my letter. With his response and my article completed, I was ready for the Goulding's conference in May.

I arrived at the Asilomar Conference Center on the California coast, just north of Pebble Beach, feeling healed, excited, hopeful, and very much alone. When I presented my workshop, the responses I received were excellent. I realized once more how very much I enjoy leading groups and being a teacher.

I was determined to have completed my healing before this conference. But while participating in the various workshops and talking with others, I felt deep feelings stirring inside me again.

At lunch one day, a woman named Maggie Creighton sat down beside me. Chatting with her, I discovered that she is founder and director of the Cancer Support and Education Center in Palo Alto, California. She had just arrived at the conference and was to present a workshop that afternoon on her work with cancer patients. Because I liked Maggie and was interested in her work, I decided to select her workshop to attend that afternoon despite the fact that I had a ticket to Muriel James' workshop and had been looking forward to meeting her for the first time. I knew as soon as I began talking with Maggie that it was no accident that she had crossed my path that day.

During her workshop, Maggie led us through a guided meditation to uncover early decisions. After the meditation she asked us to write down the decisions we had discovered. Though I had no conscious awareness or memory of what I experienced during the meditation, I immediately wrote out three decisions; "I've got to do this alone." "I'll survive somehow." "I'll find a better way."

When I shared what I had discovered with the workshop group, my voice broke as I said, "I've got to do this alone." Maggie immediately invited me to move into my feelings and work with her. I responded by regaining my composure and assuring her that I was fine. She moved on to another person. Soon we took a break.

During that break, I saw clearly that I was continuing to follow that old decision to do it all alone rather than risk letting a group of relative strangers see my pain. I knew that I didn't want to continue in that old position so I told Maggie I wanted to change that pattern. Soon after I began to talk, I was sobbing. Maggie responded in a most loving and accepting way, encouraging me to breathe, to keep my mouth open, to let my long-buried, wordless rage, helplessness, sorrow, and shame emerge through whatever other sounds I made. The group gathered around me, silently supporting me as I released my pain, touching me gently, sharing this experience with me.

I realized that I had expected that they would leave. I thought they would be frightened by this ugly mess inside me, frightened as I had been frightened for so many years, frightened as my parents were of what I felt. But no one left. Instead they were with me, caring about me while respecting the boundaries between us.

My relief afterwards was enormous. Yet I knew I had not finished with this deep unveiling. The next day, I decided to work in my conference therapy group. I waited until the last possible time to speak. When I finally let myself share with the group, I told John McNeil, who was therapist that day, that I wanted to be free to flirt and feel confident and normal in relationships with men. As I talked, I again felt my old anguish arise. Would I ever, I thought, be free of this ancient pain I've encountered so often, faced, experienced, released, only to discover later that I still had not reached to the bottom of the place it filled inside of me?

Again I was aware of my fear that people would leave rather than accept this monster in me. All I could do was weep. Again, to my amazement, no one left the room or seemed terrified. I had lived my life imagining that no one would accept me if they knew how I felt inside. Despite the fact that I encouraged people to share their painful feelings with me, I felt that I should not dare claim the same privilege with others.

I was overwhelmed with the warmth and understanding I received from everyone in my group that day. I released my shame and my fear of other people knowing the real me. I accepted myself and the severity of the wound I had been so long in healing. The acceptance I felt from these two groups, from Maggie, my cousins, and my aunt combined to allow me to finally express what I had fought so long to eliminate within me. I felt a shaky peace emerging.

We were out of time for the group and the conference. And I knew I still wasn't finished. One of my friends from the group asked me if I planned to attend the workshop at Bob and Mary Goulding's home the week following the conference. She was going and suggested this might be just the opportunity I needed to complete my journey.

I protested that I couldn't possibly go. I had therapy appointments scheduled for the next week. I had a radio program to do on Sunday night. I had to make money, etc., etc. She suggested that I could, in fact, change all that. I told her and myself how impossible that would be.

That night I pondered. Could I dare put my personal needs for healing ahead of the responsibilities I imposed on myself for being available to other people, for being responsible to the radio station, and for being home for my daughter? I knew she would be happy visiting her father for another week. But I noticed that I was afraid of some kind of terrible punishment or loss if I dared to put my needs ahead of my self-imposed responsibilities.

The next morning as I walked to breakfast with my roommate, I told her how torn I felt. She encouraged me to stay for the workshop and to put myself in first place for a change. As I continued my internal debate, I saw my old friend, Gene Kerfoot, who gave me a few of his delightful comments about how I might be more valuable to other people if I were not so easily available.

I headed for the phone. My secretary was not happy with the task she faced of changing my full schedule. Instead of feeling sorry for her, I simply gave her the job, knowing that I was paying her to work for me, not for me to take care of her.

Feeling great, I said my goodbyes to my newly found conference friends. I was heading into a new time in my life, a time when I would be able to function freely, unburdened from my painful past. As I drove north toward Watsonville from Pacific Grove, I knew I was putting myself in the right place at the right time to complete the healing I wanted so desperately to have.

It was like coming full-circle to return to Mt. Madonna. Fourteen years earlier I attended my first therapy workshop there when I was just beginning my quest. I had not been back in the intervening years. Joining Bob and Mary and twenty-two others, many of them also therapists, I knew I was in the best possible situation to complete my work. The Gouldings are among the finest therapists practicing in the world today. Their model, called Redecision Therapy, is a combination of Transactional Analysis and Gestalt Therapy, with their own focus on finding and changing early, self-defeating decisions made by the child within us.

During the workshop, we worked with the Gouldings and with each other, with either Bob or Mary supervising our work. I started off working as therapist and feeling very good about what I facilitated for the man who worked with me. I was biding my time and deciding who I would trust to work with me when my turn came to be client.

When I finally took my place in the client's chair, I knew who I would request to be my therapists. I asked a couple from New York who seemed clear, sensitive, and strong enough to assist me through the territory I had to explore. Bob Goulding was supervising that afternoon and videotaping our work. I was sure I was in good hands.

I started off describing the empty place I had always felt inside myself. This empty, frightening feeling haunted me. All my life, I had worked hard, played hard, kept moving just to keep it at bay. Whenever I had enough leisure time, it surfaced to spoil my pleasure. And here in the quiet of Mt. Madonna, it was back again.

My therapists had me be that empty place and give it expression. Suddenly I realized that my empty place belonged to the little girl, nicknamed Muffin, who used to be me before she got split into "Daddy's little girl" and the workshop-girl. Muffin was invited to tell her parents how she felt about the sexual, physical, and emotional abuse she had endured.

As Muffin, I turned to the empty side of the sofa next to me, and visualized my parents sitting there. Though I had addressed them in Gestalt work like this many times before, never had my free child, Muffin, been present to speak with the full force of her feelings and her energy. My words came tumbling out, and they came with force and strength and absolute conviction.

"How dare you intrude on my body as you did? How dare you put your perversions and your crazy, sick sexual needs ahead of my need for love and safety and nurturing! How dare you blame me for your sickness and snare me in the guilt of your shameful activities! Why didn't you have sex with each other and leave me alone to be a child like other children, free to play and enjoy life and be innocent? Why did you torment me as you did and leave me feeling guilty, bad, dirty, different from other children, shy, afraid of being found out, and afraid to be myself? How dare you pretend to be so virtuous, so much better than other people! What hypocrisy! I hated hearing you confess your sins in church, only to leave and go right back home to another week of whatever you chose to do to me when you were angry or lonely or filled with desire. How could the people I loved and needed and had to depend upon, who said they loved me, hurt me so much? How were human beings capable of such destructiveness?"

I raged and wept until there was nothing more to be said, no more tears to shed. And when I was done, Bob Goulding came across the room from behind his camera, and sat in my parents' place on the sofa beside me. He reached over and pulled me close to him, his arm around me, giving me the best hug I've ever felt. With his eyes twinkling, he looked me in the eye and said, "F--'em and feed 'em beans!" Whatever that comment meant, it was just what I needed!

Delighted, I felt warmth and relief spread through me. It was as if, in that moment, I had a new father, a healthy, permission-giving, loving man who wanted me to be free to be exactly who I am. I felt myself incorporating him into my mind, replacing the old, sick, ashamed, guilty masculine energy I had always experienced before. In that moment, I knew I could do anything, accomplish anything

I set out to do. I now had the strength, the wholeness I had always sought. I was starting a new chapter in my life. I knew I was healed, free, normal, sane. I knew I could take care of myself. I knew I could now get the divorce I needed and free myself from the last vestiges of having been a "victim of incest".

That night I dreamed this dream.

I return home and I have a baby that I am going to take care of. It seems to be Jason's baby and mine. Someone wants me to give her a bottle of orange juice which is very bubbly. I decide not to. I think it will give her colic. The baby was in some kind of container, like an instrument case. I open the case and take her out. She has spit up on herself. I hold her up and take her into the ladies room to wash her feet and her legs. She smiles at me and I realize she has a mouth full of teeth. She has wonderful fat little legs. I am washing her feet and thinking how much I love her and how much I am going to enjoy this baby and taking care of her. She smiles again. I realize that it is unusual for a baby to have a full set of teeth. At one moment, her teeth go crooked, then seem to straighten out again.

My baby is my newly reclaimed child within myself. She has been restored to me through the memories I have regained and worked through as a result of my relationship with Jason. I demonstrate that I can take care of her properly and follow my own judgment about what will be good for her and agreeable to her. I refuse to give her the orange juice that someone else wants her to have.

Taking her out of the instrument case seems to represent my reclaiming her through the work I had done the previous day. The instrument case is significant because it indicates that she will enable me to express my creativity.

The child has vomited on herself while she was locked up in the case. She has rid herself of the toxic experience of the incest and now I take her into the ladies room to clean her up. This seems important as an affirmation of my femininity and a statement that I can care for myself now without feeling that I have to have a man's involvement in my life.

The feelings of love I experience for the child reflect the profound healing that is taking place within me. I am really pleased with my child and she with me. She smiles at me, and I see her full set of teeth. Teeth sometimes mean wisdom in dreams. Her set of teeth shows me that she is wiser than an ordinary infant since she has in fact been around for as long as I have, even though she has been locked away in her case. Her teeth becoming crooked are a clue to me that she is really me. My teeth used to be quite crooked before I had them straightened. Straightening my teeth was an important event in my life. It was one of the first things I did for myself to separate my life from my parents'. They had always insisted that my teeth were straight when in fact they were not. Taking care of this problem was an early step I took in beginning to extricate my life from their emotional control.

I loved this dream and still do. It reflects the new beginning I knew I had made and shows me capable of handling myself and my new life wisely and carefully. After years of being overly vulnerable to others and unable to keep adequate boundaries for myself, this reassurance was very important to me.

I returned home from California, ready to implement the changes I knew I was now ready to make in my outer life. The summer was filled with planning for a major change in my professional life. I had two books to write. I also was working through the ending of my relationship with Jason.

The therapy group for sexually abused women reconvened in the fall with a number of new members. After the work I completed in California with the Gouldings, I was much more effective as therapist for the group. I knew then that healing is possible, because I had experienced it myself. And, I knew that if I could heal my life, others could heal theirs, too, if they committed themselves to the process and stayed with their commitment until they completed their work. I told the group about my experiences in California, emphasizing how important it had been for me to let other people see the depth of my pain and comfort me.

The level of sharing in the group deepened. We thrived on direct, healthy communication, loving confrontation, honesty with our feelings, and lots of support and encouragement for each other. Over the summer, one group member had talked with her parents about the incestuous relationships she and her sister had with their father. When she returned to group, she was visibly different, relaxed and thinking clearly as she began to structure new kinds of relationships in her life. Everyone else was eager to congratulate her and hear about her experience. A new feeling of hope was kindled in everyone through our sharing.

CHAPTER VII

BEYOND VICTIM

Jason and I continued to see each other occasionally after our separation. Before the workshop with Bob and Mary Goulding, I clung to the hope that somehow, someday, we might be able to repair the damage to our relationship and be together again. After the healing I experienced there, I released him. When I returned from California, my decision to end our relationship was firm.

One morning in September, I got a desperate call from Jason. He had decided there was nothing left in life for him. He was going to California where he said he had made funeral arrangements for himself. He planned to commit suicide.

Knowing his pain was very real and realizing his capacity for destructive behavior, I was frightened. I tried to convince him he should get help; see a therapist or go into a hospital. He was adamant. His mind was made up. There was no further reason for him to live.

When I hung up the phone, I was stunned. This was painfully old and familiar. I had allowed Jason to push all my old emotional buttons. Once more, I struggled with feeling responsible for someone else's life.

Much of that day is a blur in my memory now. I do know that I went to talk with Jason in the hotel room where he was living. He was calm and deliberate. This was his solution to the problems he faced. He was of no value to anyone now, if he and I could not be reconciled.

I sat on the edge of the bed while he paced back and forth. In my mind, I was reliving the time my father threatened to kill himself if I dared to marry Kenny. As I watched this scene unfold before my eyes in the present, I faced the same dilemma once more: my life or his. Which would I choose? Would I sacrifice myself once more to a man trying to manipulate me emotionally? Or would I take responsibility for doing what I needed to do for myself and let him be responsible for himself, even if he chose death?

"It's my life or his;" the words kept repeating in my mind. "My life or his; my life or his." "Are you going to make the same mistake again?" I asked myself. "Can you risk choosing for yourself and then live with the consequences if he does kill himself? Can you live with yourself if you ignore your needs and feelings?"

I wavered. My old belief clicked into my mind. "I must do whatever it takes to save others, no matter what the cost to me." I felt the despair that followed that old thought. I remembered my more recently adopted beliefs. "I am responsible for me. He is responsible for himself. I do not control his life. He does not control mine."

I knew my answer had to be "no." I had created a second opportunity to play this suicide scene. I intended to do it differently now. My mistake the first time around had cost me dearly. I would not make the same mistake twice. I would not abdicate responsibility for myself to try to save someone else who was pretending I held the key to his life.

I told him our romantic relationship was over, difficult as it was to end it. He could not come back. But I also told him I would talk with him and help him in any way I could, short of hurting myself in the process. When I made my "no" clear and irrevocable, he was surprised but he seemed to relax. I told him I loved him and needed him alive. I wanted to know he was in the world and that we cared for each other even if we didn't do well living together. And I told him I was angry that he would consider abandoning me and leaving me alone to face the financial problems left after our involvement.

This confrontation with Jason was another enormous

step for me in moving beyond victim and into full responsibility for my life. By standing up to him and not allowing myself to be manipulated by his suicide threat, I conveyed to Jason my confidence that he could deal with his problems without our relationship. In effect, I told him I was not afraid of him and not afraid of his anger. I didn't think he was a murderer who would kill himself if he didn't get his way. I chose the way of love, not fear. I said "no" to the Saboteur in him that he was totally identified with at the moment. By letting him know I recognized that his strengths still existed despite his current identification with his Saboteur, I showed him that he too could refuse to be manipulated by this self-destructive part of himself.

At the same time, I symbolically stopped the incest with my father by refusing to play our old game. Unconsciously, Jason gave me the opportunity I needed to release myself from my father's hold on my life. It was a powerful experience for both Jason and me. From that point on, he started his journey back to financial and emotional recovery. And I knew beyond the shadow of a doubt that I had moved out of my old "victim" posture. I did not see Jason again for a year and a half, though we talked on the phone periodically about business matters.

Moving beyond victim meant that I was determined to enforce the terms of our financial agreements. It took about six months for Jason to re-establish himself financially. During this time, I made it clear to him that I would take whatever legal steps were necessary to make sure he paid me what he owed me. As soon as he could, he began making regular payments to me against the loans I had made to him during our relationship. These limits that I finally set with Jason around financial issues were crucially important for both of us in recovering from the damage we had done to each other during our romantic involvement.

Trying to rescue him financially was one of the most serious mistakes I made in our relationship. Despite my better judgment that told me to keep money issues out of our romance, I did not say "no" to his requests. I convinced myself that he would be successful with the ventures he was creating even though I had serious doubts about some of the choices he was making. He said I would be a full partner, but, in fact, he did not include me in many crucial decisions he made. His owing me money created great stress for both of us and was a major factor in destroying our relationship.

Once again I learned that sacrificing my best interests and my judgment in an effort to take care of someone else and secure his love was a disservice to both of us. It was loving too much, not loving responsibly. I ignored my own limits and boundaries and allowed myself to be violated in a way that caused serious damage to our relationship and to my financial security. Only when I restored those boundaries and kept them intact did we both begin to heal the damage we created. Now, two years later, we are able to be friends, having released and forgiven each other for the hurt we experienced in the past.

Jason has grown and changed in beautiful ways since our confrontation that day. He has found his life purpose and is dedicated to the Foundation he has created to help children experiencing the kinds of problems he faced as a child. He has kept his financial commitments to me. He maintains his emotional balance and composure now and so do I. Recently, we talked about what our relationship meant to both of us.

The impact we had on each other was powerful. The deep love we shared brought up all the painful emotional issues we both had to face. Through loving each other as we did and then releasing each other as we ultimately had to do, we both changed our lives dramatically. Our relationship helped us both face the best and the worst in us. Having seen and embraced the darkness and the light we encountered together, each of us separately has claimed the powerful resources we possess for living well and living creatively. We value each other and encourage each other, savoring a new appreciation of the mysteries of life and relationship. We couldn't possess each other. We couldn't merge our lives. But, as separate beings, we can affirm each other and the love we will always share.

In November of 1985, I made my second trip to the desert at Sky Hi Ranch to consolidate my healing process. This time the workshop was a two-week dream conference with Carolyn Conger. I battled with myself about going. The practical, conscientious part of me said I couldn't afford to take the time away from work and give up the income I would lose. The nurturing part of me told me I absolutely must go. I needed a rest. I needed to get away from my usual world. I needed a fresh perspective on my life. I needed a deep encounter with my higher self.

Intuitively, I sensed that I would meet a man who would be important in my life if I went to this workshop with Carolyn Conger. I wasn't sure I wanted to meet anyone new. My wounds from my recently ended relationship were deep and still painful. I wanted to be safe and solitary, yet I also longed to connect with someone with whom I could have a healthy, comfortable relationship. I had been alone since January. Maybe I was ready for this encounter I knew was coming if I went to the desert.

Several close friends not only encouraged me to go; they insisted. They could see more clearly than I how important this retreat was for me at this particular time.

I arrived at the Ontario Airport to discover that there was a snow storm in the desert. The usual transportation service to the ranch was not operating. I investigated renting a car but concluded that was too expensive for the two weeks I would have to keep it. A cab seemed to be my only choice.

I got in the taxi line, hoping I would find a driver willing to head out to the desert mountains in this weather. I didn't know exactly how to find Sky Hi since my plan had been to take the regular van service to the ranch from the airport. I didn't have any directions for getting there on my

own. I told the driver I drew that I knew the ranch was near
Apple Valley and that it was snowing there. He said he was
willing to risk the trip, so we set out on our adventure.

When we arrived in Apple Valley, we stopped at a con-
venience store to get directions. I called the ranch. There
was no answer. The phones were out of order because of
the storm. My driver made an announcement to the cus-
tomers in the store, asking if anyone knew how to find Sky
Hi Ranch. One man told us there was a sign down the road
where we were to turn. Encouraged, we set out once more.
By now, the snow was heavy and signs along the road were
hard to see. We missed the one we were seeking and had to
double back after realizing we had gone past it to the next
town. Finally we spotted the Sky Hi sign, and breathing a
sign of relief, headed up the mountain to the ranch. That
was exciting, too, with the roads as slick as they were. By
the time we arrived at our destination, I was deeply grateful
for the man I had been lucky enough to draw in the taxi
line at the airport. A former missionary, he was interested
in what I was doing and was a gentle, patient man as well.
Once more, I knew that I was protected by the energy of
love. My need for safe transportation had been met, and I
was at Sky Hi Ranch once more, five-and-a-half years after
my first experience there with Brugh Joy.

The difficulties I encountered getting there mirrored
the ambivalence I had felt about coming at all. At a deep
level, I knew I again would change my life profoundly
through this two-week retreat. I had been scheduled to
return to Sky Hi for a second workshop with Brugh the
summer I met Jason. I canceled that trip and took the path
through that relationship instead. Now that it was over, I
knew it was time to return to this place where my life had
shifted so deeply during my first visit.

Lunch was just beginning when I arrived, so I left my
bags outside the dining hall and went inside after bidding
my driver goodbye. Carolyn greeted me warmly and I
began meeting the other participants who had arrived the

day before. I had come on Monday rather than Sunday so I could do my radio program on Sunday night before leaving. As I sat down to lunch, I scanned the room to see if I recognized the man I thought I would meet. I checked out all the men I could see and drew a sigh of relief. There was no one there who was a likely candidate. I had been mistaken. It had just been my romantic imagination at work.

When lunch was over, I inquired about the location of my room. As I was getting my bags together, a man whose back had been turned to me during the meal asked if he could help. Surprised, I looked up at him and into the biggest, bluest eyes I could imagine. I knew I knew him and he knew he knew me. Our recognition of each other was immediate. His name was Bill. He helped me carry my bags to my room and invited me to hike with him and another woman that afternoon.

When the door closed behind him, I knew I hadn't been mistaken after all. This was the man I had known I would encounter. As I changed into my hiking clothes, I kept my excitement in check by chastising myself for not bringing my boots. They were heavy, and I hadn't wanted to carry them, thinking tennis shoes would be adequate. But I hadn't anticipated the snow. There was nothing to do but put on an extra pair of socks and dress as warmly as I could. I certainly wasn't going to decline Bill's invitation to hike.

That afternoon we began to get acquainted. I felt a pleasant connection with him and enjoyed talking as we climbed the mountain above the ranch. There was no urgency about anything here in the extraordinary beauty of the desert blanketed in snow. Two weeks of being in this wondrous place stretched before us. I felt as if time were standing still.

Carolyn's workshop was focused on dreams and dreaming. Following the same format Brugh had used, we had group meetings each morning and evening. Afternoons were free for us to explore on our own. For the first few days, I had lots of opportunities for dreaming. I was exhausted. I had had no idea how much I needed rest. Here in the quiet of the desert, my body insisted that I tend to its needs at last. I took long naps and went to bed soon after our sessions were over in the evening. I was recuperating from the stress of the past year, letting go, releasing myself and the fears and burdens I had been carrying.

The two weeks were a period of integration and deep healing for me. The work I did at this workshop was much more subtle than what I had experienced with Brugh five years before. I realized how far I had come in my own growth process since my first visit to the ranch. A new sense of health and well-being had emerged in me.

During this conference, I explored the Voice Dialogue process for the first time. Carolyn gave each workshop participant a copy of *Embracing Our Selves*, a new book by Hal Stone and Sidra Winkleman, which describes the Voice Dialogue process. There were several people at the workshop who were skilled with Voice Dialogue and had trained with Hal and Sidra. During the afternoons, we were free to have dialogue sessions with them as our facilitators.

I discovered parts of myself I had never considered before. I had been caught in a powerful struggle between the Pusher and Pleaser parts in me and my Rebel self, who was determined to see that I had some fun and some time to relax. The more the Pusher and Pleaser tried to control my life, the more the Rebel insisted on having its way. When the Rebel got its way, I enjoyed myself for a while, then my Critic punished me unmercifully for having been bad.

I had been dancing in this vicious circle for months, hooked on the guilt my Critic heaped upon me and paralyzed by the process. Now I could see how these parts had developed in me when I was a child, trying diligently to push myself to please my parents and keep all of us from having to face the dark sides of ourselves. The child in me had to sneak to have any fun, and usually managed to come out only when I was away from home at someone else's house. Yet I felt bad and guilty when I came home, sad that my life felt so different than my friends' seemed to feel. I convinced myself that there was something wrong with me. Subconsciously I held the deeply embedded belief that I was bad because of the hidden sexual abuse. This pattern of Pushing, then Punishing myself was an addiction I had held onto since childhood.

I also discovered the Bitch in me. It was great fun realizing I could use her for good purposes. For years I had tried to pretend she didn't exist. That denial worked until the Bitch erupted when I let myself be pushed way too far, usually by someone I loved a lot. Now, for the first time, I felt she could be my ally, not just an enemy I had to hide because I believed she, too, was bad.

The hurt, wounded Child in me, damaged by sexual abuse and hidden away for so many years, was also a central focus of my work. Since my session with the Goudlings a few months before, she had been healing steadily. Now I saw that a major concern was remembering to take her into account in my life. I realized I must accept her and her sometimes frightened reactions, especially with men. Rather than pushing myself to get rid of her fears and "be a normal person," I knew I had to accept this damaged child in me with love, compassion, and understanding. I don't have to let her fears control me, but I can acknowledge the reality of her feelings and the reality of the abuse she experienced. She is a part of me and she is trusting me and the world more all the time. But I don't have to expect her to be perfectly rid of the past that was so hurtful for her.

My Voice Dialogue sessions, my hikes on the mountain, my visits to my desert teacher (the wonderful cactus tree I had found five years before), and the times I shared with Bill, all allowed me more and more release. The highlight of my letting go came on Saturday when there was an energy balancing session for our entire group. Two people were appointed by Carolyn to stand at the head and foot of the balancing table during the entire session. Their responsibility was to hold the energy and help to keep it focused as each workshop participant took his turn lying on the table. Each person received energy channeled to him by these two and by the other group members who were invited to approach the table and channel energy, also.

I sat, comfortably propped up with pillows, meditating quietly as the balancing session began. Along with the other group members, I approached the table to share energy with each person as he took his turn. My inner sense told me I would be the sixth person on the table.

When my turn came, I lay down, grateful and ready for this opportunity to receive. As I relaxed and centered myself, I felt powerful stirrings throughout my body. I sensed energy shifting and moving inside me. It was as if I were being gently and carefully realigned, brought back to balance and out of the distortions I had created, as I had misdirected the pure, perfect energy of my life. Most of all, I felt deep peace and contentment as I lay there, filled with brilliant white light, connected with all of myself, with everyone else in the room, and with the love of God. When this experience seemed complete for me, after what was probably only three or four minutes, I quietly returned to my pillows on the floor and rested.

Just as the time after my balancing session with Brugh was a a life-changing experience, so were the moments that followed this healing ritual. I leaned against my pillows and experienced a profound knowing as it emerged within me. *I didn't have to take care of anyone else. It was enough to be me and take care of my own life. I could just be here. I didn't have to get up and go to the table. I didn't have to do anything.* There were plenty of others to share energy and help. I was deeply grateful for what I had received and I didn't have to reciprocate immediately. I knew I would return these gifts in many ways as I lived my life. There was no rush, no urgency. I was here and that was enough. This was the healing for me; *not having to do for someone else.*

Though I had voiced these same beliefs and even been able to act on them previously, I had never before known their validity with every fiber of my being. When I said "no" to Jason, I had acted on these principles. But it had been a struggle to do what my head knew was correct and my insides still questioned. Now there was no struggle. Now I simply knew. I was healing in the very core of my being.

For the rest of the balancing ritual, I relaxed and gave thanks. Gratitude for every experience of my life flooded my consciousness. I was released. I was free. It was finally my turn for my own life. I was grateful.

I am convinced that energy work is the highest form of healing. I had confronted these same issues many times. I had made tremendous progress, but still I hadn't really possessed the issues I understood intellectually. I could make them work, but effort was still involved. Now I knew my struggling was over. There was a deep integration within me. Now this knowing was truly mine and would always be mine. I was at peace with myself.

The next day there was a similar healing ritual for a cancer patient who joined our group for the morning session. I was intensely interested in her sharing and the work Carolyn did with her. At the time I had two clients at home who had cancer. I wanted to learn all I could about working with them.

Again I felt released as I listened to the woman who was sharing her story. This was her life, her creation. She was asking for help and the group was there, ready and available to share energy with her. What she did with that energy was her choice. It was not mine. In a similar manner, I would work with my clients when I returned home. The outcome would be theirs to choose. I knew a new balance would emerge in all my work with my clients, and I knew I would be a much more effective therapist as a result.

That Sunday afternoon, we began a period of fasting
and silence that lasted until Wednesday morning. My first
period of fasting and silence during the workshop with
Brugh had been tense. I was worried about being without
food for three days. The more my mind focused on hunger,
the more anxious I became. By the last night of the fast, I
devoured a novel in an effort to distract myself from my
thoughts of food.

This time the period of fasting and silence was completely different. I enjoyed the time, being in touch with
myself without any of the usual distractions. I liked hiking
with Bill without talking. I worked on the manuscript for
my first book. I was relaxed and confident and in charge of
my mind. I thought very little about food, but I did enjoy
the three times a day I had either juice or herbal tea. I was
peaceful and calm. By the last night of the fast, I experienced a high that was extraordinary. I was acutely attuned
to myself and to the Universe. The joy I felt was beyond
anything I had known before. I knew I could have continued the fast for several more days.

From my journal that night:

> Joy fills my heart,
> A deep, still, peaceful joy
> Unlike any feeling I've known before;
> I know now who I am.
> I am love — able to give and receive
> In peace, safety, and calm.
> I am full. I am whole.
> I am me - at last. I am free.
> For two days, I have not eaten,
> And still I am not hungry.
> I am full with a different food
> That fills my spirit mouth
> And satisfies my soul's hunger.

During the entire workshop I was dreaming and
working with my dreams in small groups of workshop

participants. My dreams were clearer and more focused than usual. And they affirmed the growth and integration I was experiencing.

When I attended my first dream workshop with Carolyn Conger at Lake Tahoe in 1981, I was able to remember only one or two dreams during the entire two weeks. That was before I remembered my experiences of sexual abuse. The 1981 workshop helped to shake loose some of my deeply buried pain so I could face it later; but, at the time, I was enormously frustrated because I could not remember my dreams as other people seemed to do so easily. As long as my incest memories were blocked, my capacity to remember dreams was impaired, too. Now my dreams were clear and I was able to remember them easily. This was another affirmation of the healing I had experienced in the intervening years.

Carolyn asked each of us to write a myth to share with the group during our final evening's dinner celebration on Friday night. The Pusher and Pleaser in me were busy, urging me to get started on my myth and write a really good one. But I was also aware of the Child in me that didn't want to be pushed. My Rebel informed me that perhaps the most growing thing for me to do would be not to write a myth at all. That suggestion was appealing. I had never before dared not fulfill an assignment. I decided to explore that possibility.

For the next few days I enjoyed not thinking about a myth while other people were busy working on theirs. This was a delightful new freedom. If I didn't feel like doing it, I didn't have to do it. I liked this new choice I had finally decided to allow myself.

On Friday afternoon, Bill sat at the desk in my room, laboring over his myth while I relaxed with a book. When he left to go to his private session with Carolyn, I had a sudden desire to write. Taking my pad and pen in hand, I found words flowing rapidly onto my paper. Within fifteen minutes, I had written a myth that I really liked and wanted to share that night. The best part was that it had come to me freely, without any conscious effort on my part and without any stress or strain. I was delighted with this effortless experience of creation.

During dinner that night, Bill proposed a toast which everyone enjoyed. To my amazement, I rose to my feet and responded with my own toast, a poem that paralleled the one he had presented, but gave it a woman's perspective. My playful, creative self appreciated having the Pusher and Pleaser back off so it had room to function freely and spontaneously.

When we shared our myths, I again felt great ease and freedom. I found myself moving forward to read mine without any nervousness or anxious anticipation of what sort of response I would receive. This was what I had to share. It was mine and it was OK. Here is my creation:

The Goddess, Conscientious Perfection, harnessed her golden steeds and journeyed into the desert, seeking even greater perfection and enlightenment. But when she arrived, the desert was blanketed in snow. Her golden steeds had never encountered such sticky, slippery terrain, and she was forced to proceed without them when they refused her every command.

However, Conscientious Perfection was not to be daunted. She proceeded despite this loss and soon discovered herself in the midst of a large group of fellow seekers, dreaming their journey and moving about without concern about propriety, perfection, and pride. Conscientious Perfection was drawn into this powerful energy, finding herself more weary than she had realized; weary of trying to maintain her position of perfection, conscientious direction, and dedicated productivity.

Toward the end of her desert sojourn, the great Goddess, Dream Mother, appeared with a task for all the Dream Travelers. "Write a myth," she said. "Tell a tale, teach a lesson, integrate your learnings, reach into the depths of your creative nature and draw forth wonders beyond what you've ever dared explore. Beat a beat, tap your drum, play your instrument; let your telepathic, intuitive genius be your guide. Release yourself.

Flow — flow, flow . . ."

Conscientious Perfection was soon hard at work, composing a perfect myth, weaving the tale of her past, the tale of her woeful journey from childhood to the full-bloom of her Perfected, if not frenetic, present life.

When, lo, to her amazement, her steeds deserted her again. She found herself bored with this old tale, tired of performing; indeed refusing to perform at all. Yet still she toiled, trying as best she could to create what the great Dream Mother desired.

Finally, while tapping her toes, and beating her knee, she knew a truth like none she'd known before. In that moment, Conscientious Perfection saw, with a clarity that could come only in the almost smog-free desert air, a vision, appearing before her eyes. The great God of Mirth and Play stood before her, laughing, joking, silly-moving to her toe-tapping, knee-drumming, rhythmic beat. "I bring you a gift," he said. "But first, I must know, are you willing to pay the price?"

She loved gifts, so Conscientious Perfection was thrilled as she quickly agreed to do whatever was necessary to claim this gift God Mirth and Play had brought for her. "Forget the myth," he said. "Let Dream Mother be entertained by those who relish their task." "For you," he roared, "there's a new name in store. Give me your yellow pages, give me your efforts, give me your tale of antiquated, outworn, no-longer-relevant woe."

Gladly, Conscientious Perfection gathered her pages, her notes, her books, and her tapes. God Mirth and Play took them all, and with a deliciously juicy laugh, roaring and dancing, beating his feet, he invited Conscientious Perfection to join his dance. Shaking off her reticent, conscientious, stuffy self, she slipped into his grip. Laughing and giggling, and silly-making, she lost her senses, she lost her mind, she lost herself. Spinning her around and around, God Mirth and Play proclaimed her Transformed, for that was the word, the energy all the seekers sought. When her spinning stopped, she heard him say, "A new name is in order for you now. I greet you and dub you: Princess Peaceful, Playful Possibility."

As I read these words, I felt a new power within me.

People were laughing. I could be funny. In those moments, for one of the first times in my life, I felt like my mother must have felt when she told her funny stories and had a roomful of people enjoying her antics. I had that same capacity for fun, lightheartedness, and humor in me. I knew this also reflected my healing, release, and forgiveness of my mother. Now I could claim exciting parts of me that are like her without feeling as though I might lose myself and be swallowed up by her helpless, negative dimensions.

The following morning, during the last group session before we said goodbye to each other and headed home, Carolyn played Sans Saens' Symphony #3. Lying on the floor, we centered ourselves and opened our hearts to the vibration and energy of this powerful music.

As I listened, I saw myself stepping out of my head through my crown. A butterfly emerged from a cocoon. I became the butterfly and flew about. I lighted on a twisted, beautiful stick, resting there, before I flew into my heart.

Next I was in a cathedral filled with organ music. A magnificent wedding was taking place. I was being joined in an inner marriage with myself.

Then my parents were present, healthy and whole. I felt tremendous love, healing, and forgiveness. I assured them that I am well now, beyond the hurt and pain from our incest experiences. I soared with the music, tears of love and release flowing from my eyes.

I returned to Oklahoma later that day. The next night on my radio program, I talked about the conference I had attended and invited listeners to share their dreams. I was confident and relaxed in a way I had never been before. It was easy to help callers explore and find meaning in their dreams. I knew I had discovered new dimensions of awareness and creativity in myself and that I was able to tune into higher sources of understanding that literally seemed to speak through me now. Since that time, dream work has been a regular and important part of our Sunday night radio therapy group.

That was two years ago. My life has changed dramatically since that time. Though I have experienced some difficult challenges, I know deep within me that no matter what I encounter, I am OK. I have faced and resolved the financial crisis left after my separation from Jason. I have moved past my old fears of money to a new ease and confidence that my financial and emotional needs are always met when I do my part to fulfill my life purpose.

I completed my first book the following January. After sending it out to lots of publishers, I put it aside. Almost a year later, when I finally got the response I wanted from a good publishing company, I took my manuscript out again and did yet another rewrite. In the meantime, I began writing a biweekly newspaper column. The discipline of writing on a regular basis, and within a specified amount of space, improved my writing significantly. As I rewrote my manuscript, I was grateful that I had developed my skills by following the inner guidance I had received to write a newspaper column. My Higher Self was helping me to accomplish my goals and satisfy the intention I set six years earlier to fulfill my potential for service.

The final version of my book was a vast improvement over what I had written less than a year before. The day *Nurture Yourself To Success* arrived at my office in its final form was one of the most exciting times I've ever experienced. Since then, I've been even more inspired to complete this book and enjoy every step of the process. Now I know I really can write and produce a book. One of my lifetime dreams and goals has become a reality.

My relationship with Bill continued for the next eighteen months. He was a marvelous, loving presence in my life. We attended a number of workshops together and enjoyed wonderful weekends. He was growing and so was I. We shared a delightful period of supporting and appreciating each other. I received much that I needed to complete my healing. I experienced a stable relationship with a kind, loving man. He was much like the positive side of my father. Being with him helped me integrate that dimension of my relationship with my dad.

But our growing led us in different directions. And the difficulties of maintaining a long-distance relationship took their toll. Ultimately we decided to release each other from our romantic commitment and continue our friendship. I will always love him and value the time we shared.

Currently, I am facing many transitions. My older daughter was married recently; my younger daughter graduated from high school two weeks later. My house was robbed, and I was forced to part with treasured possessions I had always valued: jewelry and other items that connected me with my parents, grandparents, and great-grandparents. My book came out. My younger daughter left home for college this fall.

For the first time in my life, I am truly on my own. Part of me is frightened and most of me really is excited. I feel whole and healthy, ready for new adventures and ready for the loving relationship with a man that I know I am able now to accept, allow, enjoy, and commit myself to nurturing. I won't settle for less than exactly what I want and know is possible for me. No more compromises to please anyone else or placate the frightened child in me who used to think she couldn't survive without a man, no matter how he treated her.

I am free from the pain of my past. I am grateful for all I have experienced and all I have learned through those experiences. I love being me and being alive and being filled with love. I am excited about what the future will bring. I enjoy the present. My work is improving every day. Life is good.

No matter what the difficulty there is to overcome, healing is possible. The crucial factor is commitment to learning to nurture yourself, moment by moment, and day by day, for the rest of your life.

Having shared my own story, I want to turn now to

exploring with you the stages and steps in the healing process as I have experienced it and as I have shared it with others in therapy over the past eleven years. I have changed names and created composites in the stories of the women you will encounter in the rest of this book. Join me now and become a part of a weekly therapy group for women who were sexually abused as infants, children, and teenagers. I am therapist for the group and I share my own process and experiences as I explore with these women and assist them in healing their lives.

CHAPTER VIII

STAGES AND STEPS IN THE HEALING PROCESS

The healing process after incest/sexual abuse involves a progression of five major stages:
1) Recognition: Owning and Remembering Incest/Sexual Abuse
2) Beyond Denial: Releasing Rage and Sorrow
3) Mastering the Fundamentals
4) Forgiveness and Confrontation
5) Transformation

These are not distinct linear stages that move in an orderly progression from start to finish. Each is a process that coincides and overlaps other steps in the healing experience. But all of the elements of this process are essential to healing the pain and damage that result from sexual abuse experienced during childhood or adolescence.

I work with sexual abuse issues in the context of the fundamental model I have developed for healing, no matter what the underlying pain or problem happens to be. Let's look first at that model which serves as the foundation upon which the healing process specific to the experience of incest/sexual abuse rests.

FUNDAMENTAL MODEL FOR HEALING

GOALS:
1) To expand your conscious awareness so you notice without judging your mental, emotional, physical, and spiritual processes.
2) To shift your life out of the painful, Self-Sabotaging

energy of fear and into the powerful, healing, enabling energy of love.

OBJECTIVES:
1) To heal your Inner Child of the emotional pain and psychological wounds you experienced growing up in your family and your community culture.
2) To heal your Adult Self and its thinking patterns so you learn to use the power of your mind to create a positive, loving reality in your present life and the future you are designing.
3) To heal your Parent Self so it becomes an Enabling Force in your life rather than an instrument for Self-Sabotage.
4) To open to your Higher Self and deepen and enhance the essence and quality of your spiritual life.

STEPS ESSENTIAL TO REALIZING THESE OBJECTIVES:

1) Learning to center, ground, and shield yourself in the energy of unconditional love and developing your Aware Consciousness, which flows from this centered position.
2) Taking responsibility for all aspects of the reality you create for yourself in your life.
3) Learning to recognize your Internal Saboteur and how it operates in your parent, adult, and child ego states.
4) Recognizing the abusive relationship that exists between your Internal Saboteur in all its forms and your Child-Self, which is the essence of who you are.
5) Developing your Nurturing-Enabling Self which will:
    A) Set limits with your Internal Saboteur and stop its abusive activities.
    B) Encourage and accept your Child-Self; listen to what it shares with you; recognize its needs and feelings; allow it to express its needs and feelings in healthy, appropriate ways.

6) Clearing your thinking processes so your thoughts are grounded in the energy of love rather than fear.

7) Learning about the boundaries that separate one person's life from another's; learning to respect these boundaries and set limits for yourself and with other people.

8) Reparenting your Child-Self through meditation: creating a new past for yourself; an ideal, loving reality for your damaged Inner Child to inhabit while you go about the daily business of your present, adult world. Transforming the destructive unconscious programs your damaged Child-Self created; integrating your transformed Child-Self into your daily life.

9) Finding and fulfilling your life purpose with guidance from your Higher Self.

10) Moving through self-love into love and service that affect your community and the larger world.

11) Deepening and developing your spiritual life; the quality of your relationship with your Higher Self and with God/Goddess/All That Is.

12) Practicing forgiveness in a moment-by-moment, day-by-day discipline of opening to love while acknowledging and releasing guilt, anger, sadness and fear.

Within the context of this Fundamental Healing Process, let's look now at the stages that are specific to healing your life after incest/sexual abuse.

ESSENTIAL STAGES IN THE PROCESS OF HEALING YOUR LIFE AFTER INCEST /SEXUAL ABUSE

STAGE I: RECOGNITION: OWNING AND REMEMBERING

STEP ONE: Recognizing that a significant number (ten or more) of the patterns that are common in the lives of sexually abused women exist in your life.

STEP TWO: Beginning to remember; recognizing and

acknowledging that you were sexually abused; dealing with the denial and self-doubt that accompany remembering previously forgotten sexual abuse.

STAGE II: BEYOND DENIAL: RELEASING RAGE AND SORROW

STEP ONE: Releasing the denial and self-doubt that served to help you avoid your rage and sorrow.

STEP TWO: Owning your rage and sadness; experiencing your anger at having been a victim; feeling the vulnerability, helplessness, and overwhelming sadness you felt as a child and feel again now in the face of the memories that have emerged; taking responsibility for the temptation to nurse these old wounds and to cling to them.

STEP THREE: A) Deciding to do whatever is necessary to get well; B) Taking responsibility for beginning and completing the healing process; C) Using the energy of your anger to move out of the victim's posture.

STEP FOUR: Uncovering and changing any conscious or unconscious guilty beliefs that you are doomed to be a victim forever. Affirming, "I am healing my life and growing stronger moment by moment, day by day. I am committed to completing my healing process."

STEP FIVE: Recognizing, accepting, expressing, and releasing the feelings of rage, humiliation, shame, guilt, sadness, fear, isolation, and differentness that accompany the experience of incest/sexual abuse.

STEP SIX: Uncovering the guilty belief, "Incest/Sexual abuse is bad. I experienced incest/sexual abuse; therefore, I am bad." Changing that belief and affirming, "I am innocent and I deserve love."

STAGE III: MASTERING THE FUNDAMENTALS

A) Creating a healthy reality for yourself in the present.
    STEP ONE: Learning to recognize and say "no" to

your Internal Saboteur, consistently and effectively, moment by moment, so you stop compulsively repeating abusive, self-sabotaging patterns of thought, feeling, and behavior in your daily life.

STEP TWO: Accepting and feeling compassion for the damaged, wounded child within you; noticing without judgment when your Saboteur attacks your Inner Child; protecting your child and stopping your Saboteur.

STEP THREE: Nurturing your Inner Child with words of love, encouragement, and appreciation; strengthening your Nurturing-Enabling Self so it fills the space your Saboteur previously occupied; committing yourself to transforming your Saboteur by continuing to set limits with it so it learns to respect your authority over your own life.

STEP FOUR: A) Recognizing how your boundaries were violated when you were sexually abused and how you continue to allow similar violations of your boundaries in the present; learning to respect your boundaries and set limits for yourself and with other people.

B) Creating a healthy past reality for your Child-Self; a new past for her to occupy in a new home with new parents or in a transformed version of her old family. Allowing her to live there while you are involved in your current adult reality and the future you are desiging.

C) Healing your damaged Child-Self and integrating her into your present life. Being her therapist and having regular sessions with her after she moves into her new home.

　　1) Assessing her difficulties through research and observation.

　　2) Understanding her needs, her feelings, and her impact on your life.

　　3) Embracing her in love.

4) Transforming her destructive unconscious programs.

5) Integrating your transformed Child-Self into your daily life.

STAGE IV: FORGIVENESS AND CONFRONTATION

STEP ONE: Understanding the why and the how of forgiveness; beginning the process of forgiving and releasing your abuser and yourself.

STEP TWO: Recognizing and taking responsibility for the burden you have carried by keeping the incest/abuse secret and thus protecting yourself, your abuser, and your family from facing what happened.

STEP THREE: Preparing for the confrontation; continuing to face your rage, express your feelings, write in your journal, and work with your dreams. Working through your fears of confronting and facing conflict by practicing simulated confrontations with your therapist and in your therapy group.

STEP FOUR: Beginning the process of forgiving and releasing your abuser and yourself.

STEP FIVE: Accepting that parts of the incest/abuse experience may have been pleasurable; forgiving yourself for any pleasure you felt when you were abused and releasing your guilt for feeling pleasure in the present. Affirming, "I now allow myself to experience pleasure without guilt."

STEP SIX: Confronting your abuser and your family.

STEP SEVEN: Completing the forgiveness process.

STAGE V: TRANSFORMATION

STEP ONE: Changing your image of yourself so you tune out victim consciousness promoted by your Internal Saboteur and tune into active creator consciousness supported by your Nurturing-Enabling Self.

STEP TWO: Taking responsibility for your experience of sexual abuse and for how you deal with it as an adult.

STEP THREE: Accepting the place of your sexual abuse experiences in the context of your whole life; appreciating the value of living through and working through these experiences for your spiritual growth and evolution; taking responsibility for having chosen your family and chosen these experiences for your soul's growth in this particular lifetime (if this perspective fits you).

STEP FOUR: Transforming these painful experiences into creative purposes and goals for your life.

STEP FIVE: Letting go; accepting the moment-by-moment discipline of forgiving and releasing the past completely and living successfully in the present.

STEP SIX: Trusting yourself and your capacity to nurture yourself successfully; celebrating the joyous future you are creating with every loving choice you make in the present.

CHAPTER IX

THE WOMEN'S GROUP

You are invited now to join the Tuesday women's group and see how the stages of the healing process unfold in the lives of eight women who are members of the group. This is an on-going group; the group continues as new members join and as old members leave. When a new person comes into the group, each member introduces herself, sharing something about herself and where she is in the healing process. Since this is your first session with the group, we will begin with introductions. You will be invited to share something about yourself after you have met the others.

MARTHA: Let's begin with our energy circle. (*Group members join hands, close their eyes, and center themselves in the energy of unconditional love. Focusing their attention on the heart chakra, each member is invited to feel into the energy of love and visualize that energy moving from her heart up to her shoulders, then down her arms and into the palms of her hands. Through her hands, she feels her energy connecting with the energy of the women on either side of her as she attunes herself to the others and feels into the energy of the group as a whole. After a minute or so of this silent sharing, I squeeze the hands of the women next to me and they pass this signal on around the group, indicating that our energy circle is complete.*)

Today we have a new member present so let's introduce ourselves and share with her whatever you feel will help her to know you better. As you speak, you may want to reflect upon where you are now in the healing process. I'll begin.

You and I have already met, but I would like to tell you a little about where I am in relationship to this group. This group is very important to me. I, too, was sexually abused as a child by both my parents. As I have worked through my healing process, I have learned through my own experiences what this path is like. As I work with group members, my own healing deepens and expands. So, I gain as much as I give. Though each one of us has our own unique story, we also have lots in common. We are all in different places in the healing process and that helps, too. We can see in other members both where we have been and where we are headed. We are like mirrors for each other. We see parts of ourselves in everyone else. When one person works through an important issue, everyone here shares in that process and benefits from the experience. The group energy is much more powerful than the energy of any one person. By joining together in this way, we multiply the impact of the work we do.

Katherine, will you share now in whatever way you choose?

KATHERINE: My name is Katherine, and I've been in this group since it first began. About six months ago, I finally realized that I really was sexually abused by my father when I was a child. Before then I never was quite sure, though many of the sexual abuse patterns fit my life. For the past three years I have gone through periods of believing I was abused, followed by long periods of doubting myself. When I believed myself, I felt better and was much more productive. When I doubted myself, I was anxious and depressed. This whole experience has been quite a struggle for me, but now I am beginning to believe I really will get well. Before I started therapy here with Martha, I had seen four different therapists over a period of about fifteen years. Although I worked hard in therapy, the sexual abuse issue never came up. Before I got into emotional difficulty, I had a very successful career as a college professor. Now I feel like I've lost ten years of my life in the nightmare I've been through. I'm forty-two years old and I've never been married.

(Katherine is an attractive woman, tall and slender. She is wearing a comfortable outfit, slacks and a cotton sweater in a shade of peach that is lovely with her auburn hair and green eyes. Her keen intelligence is obvious as is her sensitivity and still somewhat fragile sense of herself. Despite her early career success, she has lost confidence in herself as a result of the serious emotional problems she has experienced. Rebuilding her self-confidence, overcoming her fears and anxieties, and channeling her strong creative abilities are major goals for her now.)

MELISSA: Hi! I'm Melissa and I've been in the group almost a year now. I'm twenty-six and I'm single. My boy friend and I have been going together for about three years. I'm not sure about our relationship. Sometimes I think we get along great, and sometimes I just know he's not the one I want to spend the rest of my life with. But it's a comfortable relationship in lots of ways. He's done some growing recently. He always responds when I put my foot down, but I get tired of being the one who has to do that to get even a little of what I want in a relationship. I like my job. I work for a landscape architect. I'm his assistant. I enjoy being out of doors which I get to do on this job. But I don't think this is what I want to do for the rest of my life either. I'm thinking about maybe going back to school, but I'm not quite sure yet just what direction I want to take. I was sexually abused by my father. I remember parts of it distinctly and parts of it have come back to me in dreams. I've talked to my younger brother about what happened, but he's the only one in my family I've told. I want to talk to my mother and my father both, but it's really hard. I'm used to taking care of everyone in my family and trying to make them happy. Talking about sexual abuse sure isn't going to make them feel very good. So I haven't done that yet. But I'm getting close. I'm getting a lot better at confronting other people. I've been able to talk to my boss about several important issues recently and with good results. So I'm getting there. I have two brothers, and my parents have been divorced since I was ten years old. My father remarried soon after the divorce and is still married to my step-mother. She's bossy and I can't stand her. My mother has been married and divorced a couple of times. She always seems to need me to take care of her, and I get tired of that. None of my family lives here now. That was scary when they all moved away to different places, but it is good for me to be on my own and where I can't be doing things for my mother all the time.

(Melissa is a down to earth, beautiful young woman. She is dressed in her usual casual style, jeans and a t-shirt, but she is immaculately groomed and looks radiantly healthy. Her presence in the group is immediately apparent. She is soft spoken and a bit shy, but when she shares, her honesty and perceptiveness are apparent. This is her first experience in therapy. She is dedicated to the process and is progressing rapidly. Her dreams, which she records faithfully, are elaborate, rich, and complex.)

JEANETTE: Well, I've been in this group almost a year, too. But I'm never sure I'm really getting any better. *(At this point, several group members interrupt Jeanette and point out to her that her Saboteur is speaking. She relaxes, smiles, and continues.)* Actually, I am getting back into my drawing. I've been to two classes this week and what I did is pretty good. At least, the teacher seemed to like it. And I did clean up my apartment. I came into therapy because I'm phobic, have been for years really, but now I've started to get tired of it. I moved out of my home and into an apartment because I got so phobic about the house. Then I found I was getting the same way about my apartment. I can't keep just running from place to place trying to get away from my fears. So I realized I have to do something. I've been in therapy before. I fight it a lot. But I've got to get better. Recently my grown daughter told me she just can't have a relationship with me if I don't straighten myself out. That really got my attention. And I've done some real positive things since. I have discovered I can say "no" to all those crazy fears my Saboteur cooks up. I don't have to get involved in all that foolishness. And I feel great when I don't.

(*Jeanette is in her mid-fifties. She is an attractive woman with startling blue eyes that seem to mirror the pain she has experienced. Divorced about ten years, she has three adult children. She is an extraordinarily gifted artist with a unusual capacity for portraits that catch the essence of her subjects. She has lived in fear for years, doubting herself and her talent. Yet she is a wonderfully determined woman, an active athlete despite arthritis that is becoming more troublesome. She has many friends and is good at sales. When she was a child, she was repeatedly abused sexually by a man who ran a neighborhood filling station. She remembers these abuse experiences, but discounts the impact they had on her. Her Internal Saboteur is powerful and abuses her unmercifully. When she allows her Saboteur to be in charge, she becomes depressed and suicidal. Yet she has learned that when she takes responsibility for herself and says "no" to the fearful creations her Saboteur generates, she feels powerful and in charge of her life.*)

ELAINE: I'm Elaine. I've been coming to group since January. It's still hard for me to talk. I haven't seen my family for two years. I just had to cut myself off from them. Sometimes I feel really bad about leaving my sister and my younger brother — he never did anything to hurt me. But I'm afraid if I try to see them, my mother will find out and turn up, too. And I don't want anything to do with her. Or my father. When I was six, he was hospitalized and diagnosed a paranoid schizophrenic. After that, we just never knew when he would explode. And I usually was the one who got blamed for what happened. I'm the oldest; I had to take care of my brothers and sister most of the time. My mother always tried to confide in me about all her problems. She acted like she was so perfect and such a martyr because she was married to Daddy. Now I'm realizing she had as big a part in the problems as he did. I'm really glad I finally got away. Since I finished college, I've been completely on my own and I feel good about that.

(Elaine is a petite young woman; she is dressed casually and attractively. Her eyes are large, curious, and intelligent. They also seem to plead for understanding. She is remarkably perceptive and is strongly committed to her therapy process. Currently, she is living an isolated life; she enjoys her work as a research assistant, but she lives alone and doesn't allow herself much social activity. She had a more active social life prior to beginning therapy two years ago. When she started seeing her first therapist and looking at the issues in her life and the pain she had suppressed, she moved into her own apartment so she would have time and the privacy she felt she needed to deal with the feelings she was uncovering. Gradually, she became more and more afraid of other people and isolated herself further. She writes a lot, recording her dreams and keeping a journal. Her short stories and poems are exceptional and she hopes to begin publishing her work soon. During our first therapy session, she asked that I not ever touch her or give her a hug. I agreed, with the understanding that when she felt ready to change that agreement she would tell me. Recently, after working through an especially important dream, she asked me to give her a hug. She now wants to begin to break out of her self-imposed isolation and enjoy life more. She has had many dreams which are strongly suggestive of sexual abuse, but she is not yet sure of all she experienced as a child. She is afraid of men and terrified of sex.)

GAYLE: I'm Gayle. I've been here in group for two years now. When I first remembered the sexual abuse in my life, I was dumbfounded. But the little girl in me knew what she had experienced, and I finally started to listen to her and take her into account. She was furious and hurt and neglected. For years I had been "Daddy's girl". Everyone in our family knew I was his favorite. I'm the youngest by quite a few years, and he and I always were extremely close. We talked about everything and really understood each other. He always told me I was wonderful and could do anything. He's just so special. But Mother was another

matter. She played helpless in lots of ways, and I was supposed to look after her. In many respects, our roles were
reversed. I was like Daddy's mate and she was like the little
girl. Now I see how powerful she really is with that role she
played. Since I confronted my father about the sexual
abuse, things have been different in our family. At the time
we had the confrontation session, he denied everything.
But he did it in such an amazing way. He said he would
accept whatever I needed to believe if it would help me. I
always was such an imaginative child, as he put it.
Obviously, I was making all this up now; and, if it helped
me to do that, then he would let me imagine whatever I
needed to. He showed no emotion. I was so furious to be
told I was just making it all up. I didn't even talk to Mother
about the sexual things she did with me. Somehow that
seems so much harder to face. Since that day and that
session with my parents, it hasn't been mentioned again. I
was so afraid they would reject me completely. That didn't
happen, but things are different. I'm more independent
now. I don't go on vacations with them anymore. I don't
play the old helpless games with Mother. But there is still
more work to do. I've been letting myself sort of drift for a
while. Yet I know I need to dig in again and finish dealing
with what I've only partially completed.

(*Gayle is a lively, intelligent, and very expressive woman in
her early thirties. She is single and enjoys men, but doesn't let
herself get really close to anyone. She is very creative and
talented, but she is not yet allowing herself the full expression of
her power. Her Saboteur, disguised as her "little girl" has been
telling her how nice it is just to "drift" with her therapy for a
while. "It's just too scary to step into the unknown any further."
Because she has learned to listen to her little girl and honor her
feelings, it is hard for her to see how her Saboteur now is using
the "little girl" to undermine her progress. And the helpless
voice of the "little girl" is a lot like the helpless position her
mother played so well. It is very seductive for her.*)

LINDSEY: I'm Lindsey and I think you're going to be

glad you've decided to join our group. My life is very different now. I first confronted my father with his sexual abuse of me two years ago. It was a terrible scene. I had flown home to Oregon because I knew I had to face him with what I had remembered. When I told him, he screamed at me and denied it all. And I got no support from my mother, either. Even my sister, whom I'm sure was abused too, backed down and refused to support me. For over a year I was estranged from my family.

Then I had a very important dream about my home in Oregon and my parents. I felt that somehow the dream was telling me that emotions were shifting within my family. Two days later I got a phone call from my father. I told him that the only way I would re-establish our relationship was if they were willing to come here for family therapy sessions with me. They drove down, but only my mother would go with me to talk with Martha.

During that session, I told her how I felt about her not protecting me from my father when I was a child and not acknowledging now what I experienced then. I was really angry, and I let her know just how I felt. She seemed to understand that day and even to accept the reality of the abuse. She kept urging me just to put it out of my mind and not cause anymore trouble or upset my dad again. I told her it was time she started acting like a mother instead of a helpless child. I told her I needed her help and her support, and I wanted Daddy and her both to come for a session with Martha and me. She vacillated and hedged; it was obvious she was afraid to take a stand with Daddy on my behalf. But I let her know that if she wanted my respect and any kind of relationship with me, she was going to have to grow up herself and face the reality we had all been hiding from for years. When we finished, she told me she would talk to Daddy and try to get him to come back with her for another therapy session.

She didn't succeed that day. They left town later that afternoon, but eventually I got a letter from my dad. About six months later, he agreed to come to therapy with me, and he and Mother came back here for a week. Dad and I had two therapy sessions with Martha; then Mother joined us for the third session. We had planned for four, but she got into her old sickness pattern and was having blood pressure problems and threatening to have a stroke. So they left after our third encounter.

During the sessions with Dad, I managed to stay centered pretty well, and I just didn't buy into his excuses and his denial. He got up and tried to leave the room once, but Martha acknowledged how frightened he was feeling and assured him that our purpose was not to place blame or attack him; it was to face something that had to be faced if we were going to be able to have any kind of family relationship in the future. He settled down, returned to his place on the sofa, and we continued. I talked with him about lots of issues, not just the incest. We talked about his relationships with his family and with Mother's; about how there never had been healthy boundaries in those relationships either. I told him I always had felt like the disposable child in our family; the focus was always on someone else, except when he was using me for sex. Even when Mother introduced herself to Martha, she said she was Ellie's (my sister) mother, not mine. I confronted her with that, too! I kept pressing the point that they were the parents and I was their child, and it was time they began acting like grown-ups. I'd had to be one for a long time.

Dad never actually acknowledged the incest, but he did stop denying it. I think he realized that I knew what had happened and that I wasn't going to back down. The closest he came was, "Let's say maybe it did happen — then what?" I really wasn't after making him confess. I know it happened and at some level, maybe buried deep in his unconscious, he knows, too. What really mattered to me was letting go of the burden of keeping the incest a secret and putting them on notice that I wouldn't play the old denial games with them any longer.

When Mother joined us for the third session, she was heavy into getting both of them off the hook by being sick herself. She played that one to the hilt, but I also confronted her on her role in the incest drama, even though she was pretending to be too fragile to deal with me. Again, what really mattered to me was not buying into my old sick ways of relating to them. I was able to stay clear with them through the whole time. I wish they had stayed for the last session, but they left a day early.

Since then we've gotten along much better. I set limits very effectively with them now, and they treat me with respect I never had from them before. My father is more active in his community and does some volunteer work now. Even Mother's health has improved and she's dealing with her mother and her sister in more effective ways.

My life is enormously better. I had ended a destructive relationship with a man several months before these meetings with my parents. I spent four months alone, facing myself and my part in the destructiveness of that relationship. The following spring, soon after my encounter with my parents, I met a really wonderful man. With him, I've had the first healthy relationship I've experienced. We were married eight months ago, and we're communicating well and appreciating each other more all the time.

(Lindsey is thirty-one; an attractive woman whose keen intelligence is immediately apparent. She owns her own business and is quite successful with her professional life. Throughout her therapy, she has been thoroughly committed to the process. The healing she has accomplished is an inspiration to other group members. She is well liked and highly respected by them. Her having faced her family, gone through the estrangement, and emerged in a healthy place demonstrate to others in the group that healing is possible. She is honest with her feelings and her current dilemmas. Lindsey knows she must take the damaged child within her into account in the present day challenges she encounters, so she doesn't let herself get caught in her old, self-punishing patterns of behavior. She talks about the dailiness of

*her work with herself; how she must renew her commitment to
herself moment-by-moment and day-by-day, to continually
strengthen herself and complete her healing. Lindsey has been in
therapy for four years.)*

EMILY: I'm Emily. I've been in group four months and
I've been working with Martha for about a year now. I'm
finishing up my undergraduate degree; then I have one
more year of training before I'll be certified as a teacher for
handicapped children. I wasn't actually abused sexually,
but my father was real seductive and inappropriate in the
ways he related to me. And he always made me feel real
uncomfortable. My parents were divorced when I was five.
Before that I was really close to my dad, but I can't
remember much after that. I do know my mother was terribly upset by the divorce, and she was pretty much
unavailable emotionally after that. I felt really sorry for her
and tried to protect her — especially when my dad was
critical of her. But it was like there was nobody there for
me after the divorce — except my little brother. I tried to
take care of him, too. At least we had each other.

When I was ten or so, Mother filed a court case to end
Daddy's parental rights. She refused to let us see our dad
because of her fears that he might abuse me sexually. I
sometimes wonder if she wasn't sexually abused herself
and doesn't remember it consciously. Dad really was inappropriate with me; he made all kinds of comments about
my body that embarrassed me; he gave me a very explicit
book about sex and read it to me. I always felt so tense
around him, like I had to be sure I would keep the limits
with him, since I sensed that he might not. But still Mother's trying to cut me off from him completely was really
hard on me. Eventually the courts sent my brother to live
with my dad in California and left me with Mother. That
was really awful. I didn't have my brother or my father.
Despite the weird stuff with my dad, I still loved him and
wanted to see him. He was at least strong enough so I could
be angry with him. I couldn't even feel angry with my mom

because she seemed so weak.

I got into drugs and drinking in my early teens. It was my way of trying to escape. I went through chemical dependency treatment when I was 17, and I've been sober now for seven years. But I've really had problems in my relationship with Bryan. We just broke up six months ago after being together for six years. I'm just now getting where I can talk about him without crying. I was so in love with him. I thought everything was just perfect, except we didn't really have a sexual relationship. He said we shouldn't do that until we were married. In the end, he told me he was having affairs with lots of other women all during our relationship. He said he was addicted to sex. I was devastated.

Since I've been seeing Martha, I've been working on my relationship with my dad and learning how to set limits, especially with him. He was very concerned about me when Bryan and I broke up. I think he knew my problems with Bryan had a lot to do with the problems in my relationship with him. So he called and told me he was coming here to see me and wanted us both to meet with Martha for four sessions.

I was happy about that but afraid to trust that he really would do it. He's always made lots of promises he hasn't kept. This time he came through, though, and I think he has changed a lot. He acknowledged all the sexual stuff and all the ways he used to make promises and then not keep them. He also admitted his confusion about limits. He's been in therapy, too, for the past year. He even told me he has a monogamous relationship with his wife now. It was hard to talk to him about all the things I confronted him with, but I really feel good now that I did it. He made three commitments to me: that he won't be sexual with me or ever cross sexual lines with me; that he will not abandon me; and that he'll keep his deals with me about helping to pay for my education. And I believe him. He's grown and I've grown. I used to have such a barrier up to protect myself from him. I felt like I had to be responsible for keeping anything sexual from happening between us. Now I feel more like I can relax around him. I really hated to see him leave to go home. Since I talked to Dad about all this, Bryan hasn't seemed like such a big deal. And that's a big relief too.

(Emily is an attractive twenty-five-year-old woman. She, too, is committed to her therapy and has made substantial progress in the past year, culminating in her recent confrontation with her father. She wants to feel more comfortable with her sexuality and her beauty so she can enjoy men without being afraid of how they will respond to her. Though she did not have direct sexual experiences with her father, his seductiveness produced similar guilty, self-punishing behavior patterns and distorted relationships with men. Her most devastating feelings relate to abandonment, issues around her parents' divorce, and their subsequent fighting over her and her brother. She has a stronger sense of herself and less self-doubt than most victims of direct sexual abuse.)

JANICE: I'm Jan. I'm really shy about talking in here. It's just too embarrassing to tell anyone what happened to me. My mother was really crazy. She's dead now; died of cancer about two years ago. I hated her. She used to do all sorts of weird, sick stuff to me; sexual things. And she would cut me and put strange things inside me. It was so awful. I feel so dirty and so bad because of it. My dad was involved in it, too, though it was just sexual abuse with him. He didn't cut me or anything. I still live with him, and I'm just beginning to be able to stand up to him a little. It's like I was brainwashed by all the torture and all the things they told me. I've tried to kill myself several times; that got me in the hospital where they gave me lots of drugs. I took every kind of pill they had. But since I've been seeing Martha I've gotten off the pills and I've stopped being suicidal. At least I can say "no" to my Saboteur when it gets real wild and tells me to do away with myself. I don't cut myself anymore, and I'm gradually losing weight, too. But I've still got a long way to go to get over all this stuff. It's almost impossible for me to cry. I didn't dare show any emotion when I was a child, or they would do worse stuff to me. Now that makes my therapy hard, because I tend to just disconnect when my feelings start to come up. That's what I did to survive as a child. Recently I've been having Rolfing sessions, and that's helping me loosen up and get more in touch with my feelings. I know I have to get them out so I can get well. But it sure isn't easy. I am making some new friends though, and I do real well with my job. I still don't make enough money to move out, and I'm afraid of what he'd do if I did. He hasn't tried anything sexual with me since my last suicide attempt. I think he knows not to since I did that the last time he tried. But I'm still real afraid of him. Recently I did talk to my brother, though. That was a big breakthrough, because he told me Mother abused him, too. I was so surprised. I felt very close to him for a week or so, then he got real defensive and won't talk about it anymore. I told him he ought to get help, too, but he's afraid to do that. So now I feel cut off from him again. He used to be real awful to me when we were little.

(Jan is thirty years old. She is very bright and very dedicated to her therapy. She writes copiously in her journal and has told me more through writing than through talking. She is hungry for love and affection and is terrified that I will abandon her in some way. Whenever I go out of town, she becomes quite anxious though gradually she is becoming more secure. I am very firm with her. After gaining adequate trust with her, early in her therapy with me, I told her I would not take anymore phone calls telling me she was suicidal. I told her I would be glad to talk with her about what she was doing that was constructive and creative. She was furious, but she got her suicidal impulses under control. Previously, no one had dared to relate to her strength in this way. She still tends to use her helplessness and her victim position to manipulate. Given the severity of the abuse she experienced, it is difficult not to allow her helplessness to control our relationship. But that would only delay her recovery. My effort is

to let her know I care about her and that I know she has the strength she needs to heal her life. It will be a long road, but she is well on the way.)

Now that you have met our group, perhaps you will share something about yourself as if you, too, are a group member. You might take time out now and write an introduction for yourself, paying particular attention to the abuse patterns you notice in your life and where you are in the healing process.

I also suggest that you read my first book, *Nurture Yourself To Success*. It will introduce you to the therapy model we use in the group and help you learn to recognize your Internal Saboteur. The book also teaches you about centering and limit setting, central elements in nurturing yourself successfully. There is an important section on anger and its relationship to your Internal Saboteur. And there are questions and exercises that will assist you in uncovering destructive messages and patterns in the ways you relate to yourself and to other people.

In addition, you will want to purchase a beautiful blank book for keeping your own personal journal and recording your dreams. There are a number of excellent books which will assist you in working with your dreams. I recommend *Creative Dreaming* by Patricia Garfield, published by Ballentine Books, New York, in 1974; and *Dreams: Discovering Your Inner Teacher* by Clyde H. Reid, published by Winston Press, Inc., Minneapolis, Minnesota, in 1983.

Subliminal tapes are another wonderful resource to help you in your healing process. I have used them with great success for the past two years. Because they require little effort to use and because they communicate directly with the unconscious mind, they are an important tool for creating healing change. Obviously it is crucial that these tapes be well prepared and carefully selected. I recommend the wide selection of tapes published by Midwest Research, Inc., 3275 Martin Road, Unit S-129, Walled Lake, Michigan 48088. As you begin your work, you will find these particular tapes especially helpful:

    Tape #63 Personal Power Dynamics

    Tape #7   Overcoming Fear and Worry

    Tape #65 Relieving Anxiety

    Tape #14 Getting It Done! Stop Procrastination!

    Tape #47 Developing a Winner's Attitude

    Tape #6   Loving Relationships

    Tape #19 Mutual Sexual Satisfaction

If you are willing to commit yourself to your own healing process, you will be amply rewarded for your efforts. The key is sticking to the process and getting help for yourself along the way. I urge you to find an excellent therapist and enter a therapy program that includes both individual and group work. Eventually you may also choose to have family sessions as you reach the point of confrontation.

Shop around for a therapist who has experience dealing with sexual abuse. Not all therapists are prepared to handle these issues, so make inquiries. Look for people you know who have grown through their therapy and can recommend a therapist who is effective with sexual abuse issues. Arrange for a first appointment to determine if you think you will work well with this particular therapist. If not, continue your search until you find a good fit for you. But please don't let "therapist looking" or "therapist hopping" become a way to avoid getting down to the work you must begin.

CHAPTER X

OWNING AND REMEMBERING
INCEST/SEXUAL ABUSE

STAGE I: RECOGNITION:
OWNING AND REMEMBERING

Now that you have joined our group, we will review the stages in the healing process and explore these stages more deeply. When you read *Nurture Yourself To Success*, you will find an in-depth explanation of the twelve elements of the Fundamental Model for Healing. In the chapters that follow in this book, I will expand on the Essential Stages in the Process of Healing Your Life After Incest/Sexual Abuse. Let's begin with Stages One and Two.

STAGE ONE: Recognizing that a significant number (ten or more) of the patterns that are common in the lives of sexually abused women exist in your life.

STAGE TWO: Beginning to remember: recognizing and acknowledging that you were sexually abused; dealing with the denial and self-doubt that accompany remembering previously forgotten sexual abuse.

The capacity to center, ground, and shield yourself in the energy of unconditional love is essential to any healing process. Read through the description of the centering process that follows and then close your eyes and allow yourself to go through the experience. If you have trouble remembering the whole process, you can tape record the directions and then listen to your tape to guide yourself. Be sure to read slowly as you make your tape so you will give yourself enough time to fully experience each step.

Feel for the center of your physical body. Straighten your spine and move your torso, seeking a centered position, so you are not leaning off to one side or forward or backward. If you are standing, make sure your knees are relaxed, hips tucked in slightly, and body weight balanced on both feet. Then notice your breath, making sure it is flowing openly, so you are exhaling completely and inhaling fully. Your eyes can be closed or open with your concentration focused in the area of your heart.

Visualize a beam of pure white light streaming down from above your head, entering your head through the crown. Experience feeling this white light-love energy flowing from the top of your head, down through the center of your body, and out through the soles of your feet, pouring down into the earth, cleansing your body and nourishing our planet.

Now focus your awareness in the area of your heart, at the center of your chest. Feel into your heart and open yourself to the flow of unconditional love. You may feel a tingling, vibrating sensation. You may feel great warmth, or even a cool energy. Discover how you experience the energy of unconditional love and mentally affirm to yourself, "I center myself in unconditional love."

Imagine the white light in the earth beneath you becoming a system of roots. These roots extend down from your feet and reach to the core of the earth. They bring you nurturing and stability. See your root system clearly and feel how it supports you. Mentally affirm, "I am centered and grounded in unconditional love."

Spin the white light around your waist and down to your feet, forming a cocoon enclosing the lower half of your body. Spin the light up to enclose the upper half of your body as well. Visualize yourself surrounded in light and mentally affirm, "I am centered, grounded, and shielded in the energy of love."

Now open your awareness to the space around your physical body and attune yourself to your energy field. Feel into the vibration of love and white light surrounding your body. Experience this white light flowing all around you and through you, filling you with the energy of love and protecting you from any approaching negativity. See yourself beaming this love *energy to others, through your eyes, your hands, your heart, and your thoughts.*

Again, visualize the cocoon of white light that encompasses your energy field. Mentally, change that brilliant white light into pure, clear quartz crystal. Look out from your place within the crystal and visualize a black arrow coming toward you. Watch as it comes closer and closer and notice that it stops as it touches the outer edge of your crystal shield. Change the arrow from black to gray, and from gray to white. As the arrow becomes white, it enters your crystal shield and becomes crystal, too. Your shield expands.

Now visualize a flight of black arrows coming toward you from a great distance. Watch them coming closer and closer to your crystal shield. Again, they stop as they come to the edge of your shield. Transmute the arrows from black to gray to white. See them entering your shield and becoming crystal, too. Your crystal shield expands and enlarges, just as you grow and enlarge your being through your every encounter with the challenges life brings.

Once you center yourself in love, you can access your Aware Consciousness. It flows from this centered, loving position within you. Your Aware Consciousness notices what you think, what you feel, and how you interact with others while you are in the midst of these experiences. It views your inner mental and emotional processes and your outer behavior without judging you, criticizing you, or comparing you with anyone else. It is an unconditionally loving state of awareness that is beyond ordinary consciousness. While ordinary consciousness operates without noticing the moment-by-moment choices you make about your thoughts, feelings, words, actions, and moods, your Aware Consciousness registers these choices.

Your Aware Consciousness also enables you to notice patterns in the choices you make. When you see the patterns that emerge in your thinking, feeling, and behavior, you have options that are not available without this awareness. The moment you can see a pattern operating in your life, your new perspective robs the pattern of its previously unchallenged power over you. When you see a pattern, the conscious part of you that recognizes it is separate from the parts of you that are caught up in it. By separating yourself from the pattern, you can choose to lift yourself out of its hold on you.

This is like the difference between watching a movie and being a character appearing on the screen. The character on screen is part of the action and the drama. He can't see what is coming. He can't tell how the plot will unfold. But the audience has a different perspective. It sees the larger picture, and is aware of more than any individual character on the screen can perceive. The audience can sense approaching danger, see how the drama is unfolding, and know how a tragic outcome might be avoided; but it has no power to influence the conclusion of the drama.

In your own life, you are both audience and actor. Your Aware Consciousness is like the audience, able to see your life unfolding, and able to recognize your patterns of thinking, feeling, and acting. It can alert you to how a pattern is operating, even as you are in the midst of the pattern's unfolding. By alerting you, your Audience-Aware Self creates choices for you. Once you see a pattern emerging, you can choose to continue in that pattern and play it out to its usual conclusion. Or, when you see the pattern, you can interrupt it and think, feel, or behave in a different way.

The key to this new level of choice is love. If you notice your patterns from a loving perspective, you will be able to change them if you decide to do so. If you notice your patterns from a judgmental, critical, or angry perspective, change will be next to impossible until you shift your consciousness from a fearful to a loving point of view.

Criticism and self-abuse do not facilitate growth and change. Rather they are the activities of your Internal Saboteur, unconsciously designed to keep you stuck in your accustomed self-defeating habits and patterns. Loving awareness and evaluation of your internal process and your external behavior allow you to change and grow in an atmosphere of encouragement and self-acceptance.

Self-love and self-acceptance are essential to healing your life after sexual abuse. When you read about the patterns that are common in the lives of women who were sexually abused as children, notice how you respond. Are you critical of women who manifest these patterns? Are you critical of yourself if you find these patterns in your life? Do you use awareness of these patterns to abuse yourself more or do you take a different route?

It is possible to see these patterns for what they are: reflections of rage, sadness, and guilt that were pushed deep into the unconscious mind during childhood. When you were a child, there was no other obvious way to handle such overwhelming feelings. The fact that these patterns are prevalent in the lives of many women means that you are not alone and isolated with your pain. You can recognize these patterns and claim the healing choices that are yours when you bring them into conscious awareness.

It is remarkably easy to turn anything into a weapon for self-abuse. Sometimes a client will tell me that she cannot bear to read a particular book. "It hits too close to home. I can see myself on every page. I can't bear to think I am like that."

I suggest to her that she can look at these patterns from a loving, rather than a fearful, self-sabotaging point of view. From a loving perspective, she can see that she is not alone with her pain; others have similar problems; there is hope for her; she can heal her life if others can. She is not crazy and isolated with her difficulties.

When Katherine first heard me talk about the patterns I was identifying in the lives of sexually abused women, she approached me at a weekend retreat. "Do you think it is possible that I was sexually abused?" she asked. She knew she recognized many of these patterns in her life, and she knew she had been puzzled by them for years. Why couldn't she say "no" to men who wanted to have sex with her? Why was she filled with so many fears? Why had a relationship with an older man thrown her into such mental and emotional turmoil?

I asked her what she thought. Did she think this was a possibility? She replied that she knew it must be. She was excited. She felt good to see this opening that had previously eluded her. Perhaps now she would be able to heal her life after so many years in therapy.

After that first discussion, Katherine and I did several hypnotic regression sessions. When she had entered a relaxed state of consciousness, I invited her unconscious mind and her Higher Self to carry her back in time and space to whatever earlier time in her life she needed to see clearly in order to help heal herself in the present. Consistently she went back to the same scene. It took place in her bedroom with her father when she was three years old. Her mother was away. Her father was caring for her. He was doing "sexual things" with her, but she couldn't see exactly what was happening. She could see his penis and she could feel how terrified she was.

Immediately after these regressions, she was relieved and much less anxious. She felt more powerful and in charge of her life, having faced and acknowledged what had happened to her as a child. But later when her rage emerged, or threatened to emerge, she was too frightened to face her feelings. Instead of risking these feelings, she denied them and chose to doubt herself and what she had remembered. She told herself she must be making it all up. Her father couldn't have done such things. Thus she kept her anger at bay while creating more anxiety and depression.

Katherine stayed in Stages One and Two of the healing process for over three years, alternating between denying and acknowledging what she had experienced as a child. But during this period, she gained strength in many areas of her life. She moved out of her parents' home and into her own apartment again, and she continued to develop her skills as an artist. Her paintings were exceptional and she began showing and selling them at art fairs and festivals. She learned to take responsibility for the ways she created anxiety for herself. As she saw how she scared herself, she no longer felt helpless in the face of fears she had previously assumed attacked her from some terrifying source outside herself.

As Katherine gained confidence in her capacity to be in charge of her feelings, she more readily acknowledged her angry feelings about current experiences. She became less afraid of her anger and learned to express it in appropriate ways, setting limits with others and getting over her fears of their being angry with her. She and I had many strong confrontations during this period. I refused to buy into her helpless-victim stance and treat her as if she were hopelessly sick. As she expressed her anger with me and with the group when she was confronted there, she realized that anger does not destroy relationships. Throughout this period of her growing, I related to her strength, insisting that she could be well and deal with life as effectively as anyone else.

This period of growth and integration was set in motion by what she remembered in the hypnotic regressions. The childhood experiences she remembered gave her new hope that she could overcome the pain that had plagued her for so long. Though she subsequently doubted what she had remembered, she never dismissed it as a possibility. During this period, she would tell group members that she might have been sexually abused. She had remembered such incidents in hypnosis, but she wasn't sure she could trust that process. Just admitting sexual abuse as a possibility strengthened her. It was as if the child within her was relieved even to be believed partially. As Katherine gained more control over her life, her Child-Self was able to settle down a bit. Katherine had to know, through experience, that she had adequate control over herself before she could allow her rage and sorrow about her sexual abuse to emerge.

She had experienced a confusing combination of being both over-protected by her parents and sexually abused by her father when he had been drinking. The over-protection robbed her of developing self-confidence and seduced her into believing she could not survive without her parents' support. This belief kept her from fighting with them, asserting herself, expressing her anger, and extricating her life from theirs. She remained emotionally, and sometimes financially, dependent upon her parents and unwilling to face her anger with them. The unspoken understanding between Katherine and her parents was that as long as they protected her, she was to protect them in return by ignoring what had happened. This unconscious collusion between her and her family kept her stuck for years in a child-like attitude of helplessness about her emotional life and her emotional needs. She had to discover her emotional strength and power before she was ready to break the symbiosis with her parents, let go of them, and face into her rage and sadness.

Other members of the group have moved through Stages One and Two much more quickly. Gayle worked rapidly once she recognized the self-destructive patterns in her life. Through voice dialogue, she got to know parts of herself she had not been aware of previously. The "little girl" in her was relieved to be noticed and invited to speak. Her angry self was slow to emerge because her Protector-Controller had kept that part silent for so many years. Anger was a monster when it erupted in her father. Gayle's Protector-Controller decided early in her life that her survival depended on not upsetting him by letting her anger show. Her Saboteur fed on her repressed rage and turned on her with cruel comments and critical, self-destructive suggestions. Though she was good at nurturing others, and felt a special obligation to take care her mother, Gayle rarely used her nurturing self to take care of her own needs and feelings. As she began to see how starved and rejected her "little girl" felt, she focused on tuning into her Child-Self and listening to what she had to say. It wasn't long before her "little girl" reminded Gayle of sexual abuse experiences she had buried inside herself and tried to forget.

Gayle called me one afternoon in great emotional turmoil. At work that morning she had begun to write the words, "bad girl, bad girl, bad girl," over and over. Soon more words came pouring out of her onto her paper. Her "little girl" was telling her what had happened with her father and how frightened and devastated she felt. Gayle took the rest of the day off to take care of herself and come to grips with what she had to face. We arranged time for a second therapy session that week and met soon after.

Through voice dialogue and hypnotic regression, she remembered more and more of what she had experienced with both her father and her mother. Her rage was powerful. So were the parts of her that wanted to protect her parents and herself from what she had uncovered. Her Saboteur was both blatant and subtle in the ways it attempted to turn her anger into denial, self-doubt, and attacks on herself.

Gayle's greatest fear was losing her parents' love. She was especially concerned about her father. Though he had abused her sexually, he also had given her lots of nurturing, encouragement, and permission to be herself and express herself. He continued to help her financially. She felt dependent upon him. She knew she was not supposed to grow up and leave him. She certainly was not to tell their secret. The bond between them was strong. At the same time, the confidence she developed because of his support and affirmation of her enabled Gayle to stay with her healing process. She wanted to come out on the other side of her pain, and she wanted to do that quickly. Within six months, she decided she was ready to confront both her parents.

Elaine is just beginning to move beyond the first two stages of the healing process. In recent weeks, she has admitted aloud in the group that she suspects she may have been sexually abused. She has discussed this possibility with me in individual sessions for the past eight months. Her dreams frequently suggest sexual pain and confusion. (See page 188) She tells me and the group she has remembered some things that are too embarrassing to tell yet.

Early in our work together, Elaine was very abusive of herself. She criticized herself unmercifully and allowed her Internal Saboteur to dominate her thinking. Her basic belief was that she was bad, guilty, and dirty. Whatever she did, she evaluated from that point of view.

I taught her to recognize her Internal Saboteur, who operates out of this negative, fearful belief system. Next she learned to set limits with her Saboteur whenever she recognized that it was becoming active in her mind. By saying "no" to her Saboteur, Elaine was able to separate her identity from its negative pronouncements. She realized that there is much more to her than she had previously realized. And the formerly unrecognized parts of herself that she now allowed into her awareness are parts that badly need her love, acceptance, and compassion.

She had a dream that painted a vivid picture of what was happening within her. In this dream, she saw herself as a five-year-old child. She was leaving a place that felt like a hospital where her father was being held against his will. As she walked down the hallway with her mother and an older sister who seemed to be about eleven, she was very frightened and sad. The older girl was angry and blamed her for her father's illness.

When she worked with this dream, she saw clearly how she had been identified with the angry older sister. For the first time, she was deeply aware of the feelings of the young child within her who felt so frightened, sad, rejected, and responsible for her father's problems. She realized that her angry stance against herself was both a way to avoid those painful, scary feelings and a way to punish herself at the same time.

She still doesn't remember the exact circumstances of her father's first hospitalization when she was about five or six. But she has always felt responsible for what happened to him. Prior to his going into the hospital, she was close to him and enjoyed him. Afterwards there was a tremendous rift between them. She concluded that she was a bad, evil person who was different from others. She deserved her father's anger and her own constant self-punishment.

Feeling responsible for her father's illness was a defense against her vulnerability and the pain of losing their close relationship. When a child experiences deep pain, loss, and lack of support during an early traumatic experience, she will find a way to believe she caused the disaster. Thinking she caused it gives her a feeling of control over what happens around her. This illusion of control keeps her from the overwhelming realization that life is such that she is enormously vulnerable to the people who are most important to her. Even though great guilt accompanies the blame she places on herself, the illusion of control keeps her from feeling her vulnerability; she opts to pay the price of guilt and self-punishment in exchange for this false sense of power and control.

Now Elaine is in touch with the five-year-old child she abused and avoided in this way. As she drops her angry stance against her Inner Child, she can approach her with love and compassion. Gradually her five-year-old self is beginning to trust her and open up to her. She is revealing some of her secrets, letting Elaine know how much she has forgotten.

Soon after her dream, Elaine began having flashbacks. Memories came back to her of all kinds of events she had not remembered. After several weeks, she noticed that all these flashbacks were of pleasant events. All of them took place outside the home where she lived as a child. She accepted that, as they learned to trust each other, her

Child-Self was sharing memories that were pleasant and not frightening. After this realization, she began having flashbacks of painful experiences inside her home. As she tells me more about her life with her family, she also is more open in group and participates much more actively than she did at first.

Melissa remembered sexual experiences with her father when she was doing Gestalt two-chair work. She was concerned about frequently having sweaty hands and feet and feeling embarrassed whenever she feels threatened by close physical contact with another person. In her Gestalt work, her first memory to return was of her father giving her a back rub and letting his hands wander "where they shouldn't have been." Later she had dreams of more direct sexual experiences between them. Dreams alternated with memories returning until she pieced together more and more of what she had experienced. She realized that her sweaty palms and feet were like memory markers. They reminded her repeatedly of her anxiety and dread of being touched as she had almost forgotten that her father had touched and abused her.

Jan had a dream experience soon after she began therapy with me. During the night, she had the same dream five times, waking up between segments, then going back to sleep and going further with the dream. In the first segment, she saw her mother entering her room, going to her desk, and getting a candle. At that point, she awoke feeling very frightened. In the next segment, the first scene was repeated and now her mother approached her bed with the candle. Again she awoke terrified. Step by step, the process continued, waking and dreaming, until the whole experience unfolded. Horrified, she watched as she saw her mother putting the candle in her vagina.

As Jan told me this dream, she remembered more about the severe abuse she had experienced from her mother. She remembered her mother cutting her with knives; molesting her sexually in the bathroom just before a dance recital; using a variety of objects to invade her body. She remembered hours spent in a closet being punished for her mother's actions. I believed her. She had much more difficulty believing herself. It was not until several months later, when she found the courage to mention what she had been remembering to her brother, that she got confirmation of her memories that she couldn't refute. Her brother told her he, too, had been abused by their now dead mother.

She didn't remember and acknowledge her father's role in abusing her sexually until later in our work. Facing the issues between them is much more frightening and difficult because they affect her daily life. Her father is still alive, and Jan lives with him. During one session, I commented that he had a role in her abuse because he didn't stop her mother's crazy behavior which had to have been obvious to him. That statement seemed to switch on a light deep inside her. She saw her mother putting her in her parents' bed where both of them would have sex with her. Though he never used knives and strange objects to hurt her, he was an active participant in her sexual abuse.

Once Jan remembered the abuse she experienced, she faced another problem. As a child, she learned to disassociate herself from her feelings when she was abused and afterwards. She simply didn't feel. Her mother trained her not to feel by cutting and punishing her whenever she cried or made any kind of protest. Now, when she approached her feelings in working with me, she would "disconnect" and go numb. This defense was an effective way to help her survive the overwhelming pain she endured as a child. But, in the present, it blocked her recovery process. Jan had great difficulty expressing herself verbally, but she was able to write about her experiences. The letters she gave me told me much more about her than she was willing to speak aloud. When I read what she wrote, her words flowed so naturally that it was hard for me to imagine why she had such trouble expressing herself verbally. Finally, she explained to me that it sometimes took her hours to write a paragraph.

During this period in our work, Jan was learning to recognize and disidentify from her Internal Saboteur. Her Saboteur was terribly destructive, modeled as it was after both her parents, who abused her so severely. She had obsessive thoughts about suicide and frequently cut herself with razor blades, compulsively repeating what her mother had done to her when she was small. She was hospitalized several times for suicide attempts before she started therapy with me.

I consistently identified the voice of her Saboteur whenever that part of her spoke during our sessions. Whenever she called me between sessions threatening suicide, I pointed out how she was allowing her Saboteur to control her. I told her firmly to get in charge again and say "no" to its destructive suggestions. At those times, I also asked her to write about the anger she was trying to suppress. I knew her repressed feelings were fueling her Saboteur's attacks. Gradually, she gained confidence in her capacity to withstand her Saboteur's assaults.

When I felt she was ready, I took the risk of telling her I would no longer take calls from her about feeling suicidal. I would, however, talk to her whenever she had something positive and constructive to share with me. I wanted to stop stroking her for her destructive episodes and start stroking her for taking control of her life. I also wanted to communicate to her my confidence that she can be as well and normal as anyone else, if she chooses to be.

Though she was quite angry about this confrontation, she called me later that same day to tell me she had acknowledged her anger with her father over an incident involving her car and had confronted him openly for the first time. She continued to use the times she checked in with me by phone to report progress rather than despair. In the months that followed, she gained increasing control over her Saboteur. It certainly did not go away, but Jan learned to see it for what it is: the voice of fear that feeds on repressed feelings, especially anger.

At the same time, she was learning to nurture herself with enabling, encouraging messages from her newly evolving Nurturing-Enabling Self. I did my best to model for her how loving consciousness works by setting limits with her Saboteur, and stepping into its place with positive words of affirmation and encouragement. Though her strength began to emerge, she still was blocked in expressing and releasing her rage in ways that would give her lasting relief from her inner torment.

I began working to desensitize her to touch so she could take another step toward healing herself. I knew she needed to be Rolfed to loosen her body and loosen the emotions she had buried within it. But she was terrified of letting our male Rolfer touch her.

During one of her sessions with me, Jan complained of severe pain in her neck and shoulders. I invited her to sit on the floor in front of me so I could rub her neck. She agreed, and for the next few weeks, she was able to talk more freely. As I massaged her neck and shoulders, she could speak without having to look at me. I told her how much pain and tension I felt in her body and urged her to schedule a session with Erik Dalton, a Certified Rolfer who is a wonderfully gifted healer. Eventually, she took that step. Though her first sessions with Erik were extremely painful for her, she was excited with what she felt and what she knew she was accomplishing. She stuck with the process and began to tell others in group how much her Rolfing sessions were helping her. Best of all, her energy was beginning to flow much more freely and she was actually expressing her feelings without disconnecting. A new life and light radiated from her face. We both knew she had taken a giant leap forward in her healing process.

From these experiences of different group members, you can see that there are many ways of remembering and facing incest/sexual abuse. Specific techniques for facilitating recall include hypnotic regression, voice dialogue, dream work, Gestalt work, psychodrama, and Rolfing, as well as working with specific memory pictures and spontaneous memory flashbacks. In the next chapter I will describe these techniques and how they can be used in Stages One and Two of the Healing Process.

CHAPTER XI

TECHNIQUES FOR FACILITATING RECALL OF SEXUAL ABUSE

HYPNOTIC REGRESSION: When I do hypnotic regression work, I am careful to go slowly. First, I teach my client to relax and enter an altered state of consciousness. I want her to become skilled at meditating and entering a centered, balanced place in consciousness. She will be able to use this capacity to help herself through the painful experiences she will encounter later in the healing process. And it will be a resource that will help her relax, live more successfully, and use visualization and mental programming to attain her goals.

As she becomes familiar with working in this way, we may begin to do hypnotic regression work. The objective is to assist her in facing whatever it is that she needs to remember from her past in order to create healing for herself in the past, present, and future. I may talk and lead her into a relaxed state of mind, or I may suggest that she relax herself in the ways she has found most pleasant and effective for her. I point out to her that she is always in complete control of what she chooses to do. She can follow my suggestions or not. She can go at her own pace. We honor her own inner wisdom about what she is ready to uncover and what must wait until she is more fully prepared to face it.

As she relaxes, I talk with her Protector-Controller part, appreciating how its dedicated work on her behalf has assured her survival to this point in her life. I point out that she is no longer living in the situation she encountered as a child. She is an adult now, and she has many more choices open to her for caring for herself and insuring her happiness and success. I suggest that the Protector-Controller's work will become easier if it is willing to allow her to explore territory that it has previously kept hidden in order to protect her from emotions that would have been overwhelming to her as a child.

Even with this gentle coaxing, her Protector-Controller will not allow her to go further or faster than it deems to be safe for her. By acknowledging its presence and asking for its help, I establish my respect for its role and my appreciation of its power. I also make clear that our intention is not to change or do away with her Protector-Controller. Rather it is to make life more pleasant and successful for her.

Once she is in a relaxed state, I lead her to a place where as a child she felt comfortable and safe. This may be a real place or it may be an imagined place. As she approaches it, I suggest that she notice the smells, the sounds, the visual beauty, and the feel of being here. I want her to have a very rich sensory experience of being here and feeling safe. I suggest that she find a comfortable spot to sit down, relax, and learn. Then I invite her Higher Self and her unconscious mind to assist her in her work by taking her back in time and space to whatever earlier experience in her life she may need to see clearly and to take into account in order to bring healing to her life in the present. I ask her to make no conscious effort at all, but simply to stay open to whatever words, images, feelings, smells, or sounds may come quite spontaneously into her awareness. I then invite her to share with me whatever she notices, keeping her eyes closed, and becoming more relaxed with every word she speaks.

I watch closely to notice changes in her facial expressions, her coloring, and her breath while also paying attention to unconscious movements she may make with her body. If I see an interesting change in her countenance, I may ask her what she is experiencing at that moment. Otherwise, I wait to see what she reports when she is ready.

Sometimes, clients will go immediately to a powerful, highly charged experience that deals directly with sexual abuse. Others will revisit less intense experiences and work their way back gradually to their most painful encounters. This may take place over a number of weeks and a number of different regressions. I honor whatever pace the client sets as the appropriate pace for her.

If she becomes very frightened of what she is remembering and feeling, I invite her to step out of the body of her Child-Self and watch from the position of the adult she is today. I also suggest that she visualize her Adult-Self being held in the loving embrace of her Higher-Self as she watches the scene that is unfolding.

Once she has seen what she experienced as a child, I ask her to step into the scene as her Adult-Self and approach her Child-Self. I suggest that she approach her Child-Self gently, introducing herself and telling her Child that she is from her future, that she is now an adult who is powerful and wise, and that she has come to help. I ask her to visualize her Adult-Self and her Child-Self surrounded in white light and love as she begins this healing process. I invite her to hold her Child-Self, if that is agreeable with the child, and to listen quietly to whatever her child has to say; to be open to her child's feelings; to allow her to cry or rage, shake or scream; whatever her Child-Self needs to express she will allow and accept. And when her child seems satisfied and complete with this experience, I ask her to bring her child back inside herself where she can keep her close to her heart and safe in her care.

When I bring her back to the present reality, I give her suggestions for coming back slowly, integrating what she has learned, and feeling the healing she has experienced. I remind her that she can return to her special internal place for learning and growing whenever she takes the time to go inside herself, relax, and take herself there.

I ask clients to tape their sessions, and especially regression sessions, so they can review what they experience. I also suggest that as soon as possible after the session, they write about the experience and expand on anything they have remembered. Frequently, more memory and understanding come to them during the writing process.

DREAM WORK: I ask each of my clients to select a beautiful blank book that is to be a tribute to her dream life. She is to record her dreams in this book, dating them, giving each dream a title, and leaving space in the book for recording her work with the dream and her impressions about its message for her. I also suggest that she bring her dreams to her individual therapy sessions and to group.

There are many fascinating techniques for working with dreams. For me, working with a dream is like listening to music or studying a painting. Like art and music, dreams usually do not use direct verbal communication. The challenge is to sense into the message being communicated by the dreamer's unconscious mind and presented through images, symbols, and stories with casts of characters that all reflect dimensions of the dreamer herself.

The Gestalt dreamwork process is always fruitful. The dreamer becomes each of the objects and characters in her dream, giving each a voice and speaking for it as if the dream is occurring in the present. Different parts of the dream may dialogue with each other. Invariably, fascinating dimensions of the dream's unique meaning for the dreamer emerge as she releases herself to this process. The dreamer also can write for each object and character in her dream and work with the dream in her journal in this way.

Another interesting technique that can be used in individual work or in groups with participants working in diads, is to ask the dreamer to tell her dream in the present as if she is currently dreaming it. The listener writes out the dream narrative, leaving double spaces between the lines as she records it. She then selects the images, symbols, and characters that strike her as important to the dream and asks the dreamer to associate to each one. As the dreamer reports her associations to each item, the listener records what she says. When this process is completed, the listener then reads the dream narrative back to the dreamer, substituting the dreamer's associations for each image, symbol, and character as it appears in the dream story. The meaning that emerges is usually quite clear to the dreamer.

Carolyn Conger, who is a wonderful dream work therapist, often has her workshop participants use Tarot cards in dream work. The dreamer draws a Tarot card to represent the significant symbols and characters in her dream. She then associates to the symbolism of the Tarot card as a pathway to a deeper understanding of the symbolism of her dream.

Dream work defies logical, linear thinking and requires right brain, creative, intuitive processing. When I listen to dreams, I release myself into experiencing the dream as the dreamer describes it. If I find myself pushing to understand what the dream is about, I step back in consciousness and release my efforting because I know it will not work. Understanding of the dream comes in intuitive leaps and flashes of awareness and connections. It cannot be forced.

Here is a checklist of possibilities to consider when working with dreams. I have compiled these suggestions from notes I took during the two-week dreamwork conference with Carolyn Conger that I attended in November of 1985, and from my own experience working with dreams.

CHECKLIST OF SUGGESTIONS FOR DREAM WORK

1. Access your centered aware consciousness and your Higher Self as you listen to a dream or work with your own dream. Ask for guidance and help. Stay open to receive what comes to you without forcing or pushing the process.

2. Look at all the characters in the dream; notice what each is doing; notice whether or not the characters are people who are known to the dreamer: Are they unknown, unidentified people? Are they the same sex or the opposite sex from the dreamer? If they are unknown, same-sex characters, they may represent the shadow side of the dreamer. If they are opposite-sex, unknown characters, they may represent the dreamer's animus/anima. (See Clyde H. Reid's *Dreams*, published by Winston Press, Inc., 430 Oak Grove, Minneapolis, Minnesota 55403, pages 32-40.)

3. Is there a theme to the dream? What title does the dreamer give the dream?

4. Remember to work with the dream in the present tense, as if you are dreaming it now.

5. Notice the feelings in the dream. What feelings did the dreamer experience in the dream? How did the dreamer feel when she awoke from the dream?

6. What is the context within which the dream occurs? What is going on in the dreamer's current life?

7. What numbers appear in the dream? What is their numerological significance? With the numbers one through seven, consider which body energy chakra may be indicated. Chakra one is the root chakra; two is the sexual chakra; three is the solar plexus or emotional chakra; four is the heart chakra; five is the throat chakra; six is the third eye chakra; and seven is the crown chakra.

8. Ask the dreamer to associate to the words, symbols, objects and characters in the dream.

9. Check your body reactions as you tell and hear your dream.

10. Look for what is missing or incomplete in the dream. What is being denied? What symbols seem really out of place in the dream? What do you wish were in the dream that is missing?

11. Act out the dream with other dream group members taking the parts of different characters and objects in the dream.

12. Draw images from the dream and see what emerges in the process.

13. Be the various parts of your dream. Let each part speak or write.

14. What question is the dream posing? Why are you dreaming it now?

15. Look for collective, archtypical aspects of the dream. (See Reid, pp. 41-52.)

16. Is this a repetitive dream or part of a series of similar dreams?

17. What sensory modality is coming through in the dream?

18. What word games or puns are there in the dream?

19. What sort of movement is there in the dream?

20. What is the activity level in the dream? Is this an active, high-energy dream or is it a passive, quiet dream?

21. What is the point of view of the dreamer? Is the dreamer seeing herself in the dream or is she in the dream action herself?

22. How vivid is the dream? What colors appear in it? How is this dream unusual?

23. Characterize the major quality of each character in the dream. What is a one-liner that describes each person in the dream?

24. If it is an unpleasant, frightening dream, how would you re-enter the dream and change it? Repressed rage often is projected onto monsters, tornadoes, scary people, or other forms that chase and threaten the dreamer. In working with such a dream, it is useful to imagine facing the monster, whatever form it takes, and subduing it. Then the

dreamer can demand that the monster give her a gift and serve her. In so doing, she becomes master of this previously feared and disowned aspect of herself. Then, before she goes to sleep again, she can suggest to herself that if she has another frightening dream, she can take charge in her sleep, face her monster, subdue it, and demand that it give her a gift.

Sexual abuse frequently comes up in dreams, even when the dreamer has no conscious memory of these experiences. Jan's memory was jogged by her candle dream. Elaine has had many dreams that point to sexual abuse; yet, for many months, she questioned the validity of her dreams and denied what they were showing her. Here are selected entries from her dream journal which she shared with me especially for this book.

ELAINE'S DREAMS

6/2/86 Me, mom, dad, and a baby, my sister. We are discussing abuse, I guess. My father says that he put his finger inside her (the baby). I see him doing what he was describing to this baby — my sister. I am not mad at him. I rationalize it away, thinking he was probably just washing her real good or something. But I am outraged at my mother. I turn to her and yell, "So what has happened to me?"

Dad is sexually abusing me or wanting to and the police are after us.

6/20/86 I am with high school friends . . . We have a real pretty little girl with us. She is playing in the sandbox, and we are talking to the sandbox attendant about how this park is better than some in Houston. A black little girl comes up to us and says, "Someone messed on my body." She raises her dress and there is blood on her leg. I can't tell if she means someone raped her or just peed on her. I start to ask her questions like, "Who did this? A man or a woman?" At the same time, the sandbox attendant (a woman) stops the conversation and takes the little girl's torn dress and says, "It gives me the creeps just holding this." The black girl walks away naked but looks different now. Now she is swinging her hips and has a body like a little woman. A little black boy meets her, but he has big muscles and looks like a little man. They dance and prance away together. I wonder if he did it to her or if it was someone else. I think that she wasn't really an innocent little girl and she knew what was going on and she asked for it.

6/28/86 I have a penis. It is like a little boy's penis and it's in the middle of torn, jagged flesh.

8/4/86 There is a married woman and she is seducing me. I am a young boy at first — I think — but then I am me —a girl. She is always looking at me and something is wrong with my foot. She wants us to go where we are alone and she is rubbing some ointment on my foot very seductively. I did not resist at all although I feel funny about it — I do not resist. I know it is wrong. Her husband surely can see what is going on. I take her to the movies 'cause she wants to go, but I don't think that's the only place we're going. I think we're going somewhere to be alone. We meet a friend of mine on the way. I tell her we are going to the movies and she seems to know something is wrong. She looks at me like why are you doing this? But I go along anyway. I didn't resist. I was a boy when it first started, I think, but when I resigned to the situation I was me — a girl.

10/20/86 I'm in some war zone or slave place or prison. Some tough girl wants me to let her have sex with me — to be hers all the time. To show me she means business, she gets a large knife and stabs and slowly cuts another girl (who was with me) in the chest. Then she threatens me with the knife. I wimp out and cry, "Please don't hurt me — I'll do anything." We take the other girl to get medical attention, and I become "her girl". Then she beats me up almost to death and is sorry — it is for no reason — she just got mad at me or something. I give her what she wants, but after she beats me almost to death I could care less if she kills me. I want her to in fact — I don't care anymore. She has taken everything I have anyway — I have no dignity left.

These dreams began before Elaine started therapy with me. She was seeing another therapist, a male, in another city at the time of the June dreams. The August dreams came after she had begun to work with me. It was a year before she was ready to acknowledge what the dreams were showing her and begin to deal with her feelings about being abused by both her father and her mother.

Her feelings of guilt and responsibility because she didn't resist are a strong theme in the dreams.

6/20/86 *"I think that she wasn't really an innocent little girl and she knew what was going on and she asked for it."*

8/4/86 *"I did not resist at all although I feel funny about it — I do not resist. I know it is wrong . . . But I go along anyway. I didn't resist."*

10/20/86 *"I wimp out and cry, "Please don't hurt me — I'll do anything.""*

It was only after she had the 7/10/87 dream recorded below that she began to see herself with enough love and compassion to transform her guilty feelings into the unacknowledged rage they covered. Here is her journal account of that dream.

7/10/87 *It's my birthday and we're having a party. Three men I work with in my present waking life are there laughing and being noisy.*

Then there is a scene with a little girl with her hands behind her covering her bottom.

Then there is a 4 or 5-year-old little girl. She tells on her daddy, and they keep him in the hospital. Mom and smaller sister are walking away from the hospital and Mom won't explain what happened. She has a disgusted and angry, displeased look on her face. The little girl runs back to the door of the hospital and is looking in. It is dark outside and the light is on inside the hospital door. There is an older sister there who is angry at the little girl. I (as the dreamer and observer of all of this) step forward and comfort the little girl. She wants to see him and I hug her and feel her pain. I feel her missing him, his attention, and I feel the abandonment. She doesn't understand.

This dream was a turning point in Elaine's healing. Previously she had been totally identified with the angry older sister, blaming her "black" Child-Self for what had happened. When she was finally able to feel her Child-Self's pain and identify with her loss and her hurt, she could acknowledge the sexual abuse she had experienced. As she released her guilt and owned her rage, she was ready to move beyond denial and doubt into the next stages of the healing process.

VOICE DIALOGUE: Voice Dialogue is a communication process developed by Hal Stone, Ph.D., and Sidra Winkelman, Ph.D. Their excellent book, *Embracing Ourselves*, is an in-depth explanation and exploration of this exciting method of self-discovery.

Voice Dialogue uses Aware Consciousness and an Aware Ego to tune into the various subpersonalities that exist within us. In a Voice Dialogue, you are invited to move from the position you occupy as your whole integrated self into whatever different chair the subpersonality to be accessed within you chooses to occupy. Suppose we want to talk with your Protector-Controller part. I invite your Protector-Controller to select a place to sit. When you move to that position, we begin our dialogue. I address your Protector-Controller, acknowledge its presence, and invite it to speak. During our dialogue, we call you by your given name, talking about you, rather than identifying you with your Protector-Controller. This helps keep your Protector-Controller separate from the rest of you.

The purpose of Voice Dialogue is not to get rid of or change any of your subpersonalities. Rather, it is to help you get to know all of your parts, especially the ones you have been unaware of and have disowned. Different parts manifest different personalities, different thought patterns, feelings, beliefs, and purposes. When you are able to see and understand these different energy patterns within you, you have choices available to you that previously did not exist. Instead of allowing yourself to be completely identified with any one subpersonality, you can use your Aware Consciousness and your Aware Ego to notice that part, hear what it has to say, and take it into account. But, because you do not become identified with it, you have a choice about whether or not you let it determine how you choose to feel, think, or behave.

In Voice Dialogue work, it is especially helpful to listen to parts of yourself that your Protector-Controller has kept hidden and suppressed. It decided early in your life that your survival depended upon not letting these parts show. In Gayle's work with Voice Dialogue, she got to know her "little girl," which she had neglected and ignored for years. She also uncovered her Angry Self, which had been hidden because of her fear of upsetting her father and setting off his rage. Her Internal Saboteur emerged, threatening her, discounting her, and trying to con her into complacency. She also talked with her newly emerging Nurturing Self and vowed to strengthen that dimension of herself.

Tremendous amounts of energy can be tied up in battling among various subpersonalities. Gayle's Protector-Controller required lots of energy to keep her Angry Self under wraps. Her Internal Saboteur heaped abuse on her "little girl" and did battle with her Nurturing Self. As long as these conflicts took place outside of conscious awareness, she had no way of reclaiming her energy and lifting herself out of these powerful internal conflicts.

Through Voice Dialogue, Gayle became aware of these inner dynamics. With Aware Consciousness and her Aware Ego, she learned to recognize when these different energy patterns were operating. Through that recognition, she could take charge of herself, see what was happening within her, accept all her parts, and create inner harmony. Instead of constant competitive struggling inside herself, she could lift herself above the struggle, accept the differing parts of herself, and not allow any one part to dominate and control her life.

Voice Dialogue facilitated her remembering the sexual abuse she had experienced. It allowed the "little girl" within her space, acceptance, and an opportunity to speak. As her Child-Self felt honored and allowed, she finally trusted Gayle enough to tell her what she had kept hidden for so many years. Gayle was ready to listen and believe herself, despite objections from her Saboteur. However, her Protector-Controller still keeps a tight hold on her Anger, which continues to block Gayle from completely releasing her rage about her abuse.

GESTALT THERAPY: Gestalt Therapy is a powerful approach which is useful in dealing with many different kinds of issues. There are a number of excellent books which describe Gestalt work. If you are not yet familiar with Gestalt, you may enjoy two of my favorite books: *The Gestalt Approach and Eyewitness To Therapy* by Fritz Perls and *Gestalt Therapy Integrated* by Irving and Miriam Polster.

I have used the Gestalt approach in my work with clients and with myself for many years. Because of its emphasis on experiencing in the present rather than talking about problems, Gestalt Therapy asks the client to speak directly, as if they were physically present, to the people in her life with whom she is experiencing challenges or conflicts. The client visualizes the person in question and, in her mind, sees that person in an empty chair. She then speaks to him, telling him how she feels, what she wants, what she needs, what she fears, or what her awareness in the moment of experiencing is. At appropriate points in this process, the therapist directs her to switch chairs and become the other person with whom she has been speaking. She then responds as she imagines he might if he were present. As the dialogue evolves, she may or may not arrive at a resolution of the issues between them. Whether or not a resolution occurs, she benefits from expressing herself honestly and having the opportunity to put herself in the other person's shoes. Through this process, the effective Gestalt therapist creates opportunities for clients to deal directly with their own projections onto the significant people in their lives.

In a Gestalt encounter with her father, a woman (who was sexually abused but does not remember) may tap into her rage. Through expressing these potent feelings, she may uncover parts of her blocked memory. This was the case with Lindsey. She remembered her sexual abuse in the course of Gestalt encounters with her father.

Other Gestalt techniques can also be helpful in recovering blocked memory. Intensifying feelings, exploring and expanding body gestures, deep breathing, and working with various parts of the body all are effective means of tapping into repressed material.

REBIRTHING: Rebirthing is a breathing process developed by Leonard Orr and described extensively by Sondra Ray in her many books, as well as by Jim Leonard and Phil Laut. (See *Rebirthing In The New Age* by Orr and Ray; and *Rebirthing: The Science of Enjoying All Of Your Life* by Leonard and Laut.)

In a rebirthing session, the facilitator of the process helps the client breathe in a specific pattern. By breathing in this pattern for an extended period of time, the client unblocks memories, feelings, and issues that have been locked inside her. The altered state of consciousness, which is induced through the breathing process, carries the client directly back to emotional experiences that need to be released. Where there has been sexual abuse, rebirthing may take the client to the pain that is stored in her body and associated with the abuse. By staying with her breathing and breathing her way through the physical and emotional pain she encounters, she begins to clear these experiences from her body.

While I have found rebirthing sessions very helpful to me and useful for my clients, I do not subscribe to the claims some Rebirthers make that rebirthing is the ultimate cure for everything. I refer clients for rebirthing sessions as an adjunct to their therapy and have found it to be very effective in helping to bring up and clear painful emotional issues. However, there is still much work to be done to heal the damage that results from sexual abuse and to learn to live and nurture yourself successfully in the present and the future.

FLASHBACKS: Often as the remembering process gains momentum, clients report flashbacks that are very vivid and frightening. I suggest that they honor each flashback by writing down what they remember in a special notebook they keep for that purpose. In this way, they acknowledge the memory, own it, and honor it. Writing down the flashback helps to deal with the fear associated with painful memories. Sometimes flashbacks relate to terrifying experiences that were totally blocked from conscious memory for years. Putting the memory on paper is like facing it and taking charge of it. This helps the client to let go of her fears and to feel some mastery of what she is uncovering. It also helps to stop compulsive repetitions of the same flashback memory.

STILL PICTURES: Sometimes clients have a still-picture memory, like a snapshot, of one scene that in itself may seem innocuous or suggestive. Usually they report that this one picture has haunted them for years. During body work, regressions, meditation, journal writing, Gestalt work or psychodrama, they may recover the previously missing memories that precede and follow the snapshot scene. Often the whole experience is one that was particularly frightening and abusive. The snapshot is like a marker, noting that a forgotten experience is buried beneath the still-picture memory.

These still pictures can be the focus of a hypnotic regression. I take the client back into the remembered scene and then move her forward and backward in time to assist her in recovering the experiences that preceded and followed the snapshot.

JOURNAL WRITING: Keeping a journal of dreams, feelings, experiences, and insights and breakthroughs during therapy is essential to the healing process. Over the years, I have found that clients who value themselves enough to write about their growth process heal their lives more thoroughly and more quickly than those who choose not to write. A personal journal is a wonderful companion and teacher. It also makes fascinating reading in the months and years to come. Frequently, when I reread my personal journals, I am amazed to realize that a particular dream I had six months earlier was precognitive. My journals also help me recognize how much I have changed and grown since the time when I wrote a particular passage. Writing is enormously helpful to me in discovering and knowing more and more about who I am.

By writing when you are in a centered, meditative state of consciousness, you may find that words come to you without conscious effort or direction. What unfolds may be guidance from your Higher Self that will be very useful to you in your daily life. You also may open blocked memories while writing in this way.

All these techniques for remembering are useful in Stages One and Two of the Healing Process. The denial and self-doubt that accompany remembering incest/sexual abuse are the work of the Internal Saboteur who is intent on keeping the abuse hidden where it can continue to destroy the secret victim's life. Denial and self-doubt cover the powerful and terrifying rage the victim of sexual abuse is afraid to face. And this suppressed rage fuels the Saboteur's attacks on her honesty, her integrity, her sanity, and her life itself. It is essential that she overcome her fears of anger and move into recognizing, accepting, expressing, and releasing the rage and sorrow that lie just beneath her memories of the abuse she endured. Opening into those feelings moves her into Stages Three through Five in the healing process.

CHAPTER XII

BEYOND DENIAL:
RELEASING RAGE AND SORROW

STAGE II: BEYOND DENIAL:
RELEASING RAGE AND SORROW

STEP ONE: Releasing the denial and self-doubt that served to help you avoid your rage and sorrow.

STEP TWO: Owning your rage and sadness; experiencing your anger at having been a victim; feeling the vulnerability, helplessness, and overwhelming sadness you felt as a child and feel again now in the face of the memories that have emerged; taking responsibility for the temptation to nurse these old wounds and cling to them.

STEP THREE: Deciding to do whatever is necessary to get well; taking responsibility for beginning the healing process and using the energy of your anger to move out of the victim's posture.

STEP FOUR: Uncovering and changing any conscious or unconscious guilty beliefs that you are doomed to be a victim forever; affirming, "I give thanks that with God's love, I am healing my life and growing stronger, moment by moment, day by day. I am committed to completing my healing process."

STEP FIVE: Recognizing, accepting, expressing, and releasing the feelings of rage, humiliation, shame, guilt, sadness, fear, isolation, and differentness that accompany the experience of incest/sexual abuse.

STEP SIX: Uncovering the guilty belief, "Incest/sexual abuse is bad. I experienced incest/sexual abuse; therefore, I

am bad." Changing that belief and affirming, "I am innocent and I deserve love."

The first step in this second stage of the Healing Process
is letting go of the denial and self-doubt that have served to
help you avoid your rage and sorrow. The Protector-
Controller part of you may have decided early in your life
that hiding your feelings was the smartest way to survive in
your family. The problem now is that continuing to hide
your emotions keeps you stuck in the pain you are trying
to avoid. Denying your anger and sadness creates depression and physical illness. It blocks your creativity and
keeps you locked in a perpetual victim position.

When you deny your anger and sadness, you reject the
parts of yourself that have those feelings. This self-
rejection is painful for you and has destructive consequences. When you drive your grief underground into
your unconscious mind, it comes back to haunt you. You
fool yourself if you think you get away with denying it.

In fact, your feelings are expressed, whether or not you
do so with conscious awareness and conscious control.
When they are expressed outside your conscious awareness and control, your Saboteur is in charge. It feeds on
repressed anger and sadness and attacks you and the people
closest to you with critical, judgmental, fearful comments
certain to create pain, unhappiness, and depression. You
may notice yourself caught in behavioral patterns like
being late, losing things, forgetting, pouting, refusing to
communicate, closing down sexually, withdrawing from
relationships, whining, feeling depressed and overeating or
not eating at all. Physical health problems like headaches,
stomach aches, colitis, arthritis, and cancer also emerge
when you stuff your feelings.

Perhaps you think that you don't deny anger. Instead,
you feel that you are angry too much of the time. Little
things set you off. You use your anger to intimidate others.
You try to manipulate and control people with your rage.

You certainly don't believe you have trouble expressing your anger.

If this pattern fits your experience, take another look. Chances are that the intensity and frequency of your anger reflect rage and sorrow that are buried deep within you. Instead of getting to the root of what hurt you in the first place, you hide from your painful, vulnerable experiences and block them from consciousness. You don't allow yourself tears. You are afraid of feeling vulnerable and sad. Instead, you hide your sadness behind anger, creating an invulnerable facade that probably fools you more than it convinces anyone else. Your anger feels powerful to you, and that is preferable to feeling vulnerable. Therefore, you express lots of anger in the present, directed at yourself and at the people who are closest to you. You rage at your children and your mate. You are always angry, but you deny the real sources of your rage. And you don't get relief and release from this distorted form of self-expression.

Perhaps you rarely express anger, but you cry a lot. You feel as if you experience sorrow much of the time. You probably cry when you are sad and when you are angry. It is difficult for you to stay with angry feelings without collapsing into sadness, which is more familiar and lots less scary for you. You learned as a child that tears were OK but anger was not. You got strokes and attention when you cried. So you discovered you could use tears to manipulate other people. You cry when they are angry with you, hoping to guilt them into feeling sorry for you instead. But, your tears have no end. No matter how much you cry, your sadness is not relieved. You, too, are avoiding your deepest feelings, especially your rage, and hiding behind a facade of helplessness and overwhelming vulnerability. You wear the mask of the victim and come to believe it yourself.

Why do you hide from your genuine, deeply buried rage and sorrow and distort them as you do? Why are you so terrified of these emotions that are key to freeing yourself from the pain of the past?

As a child, you learned from your parents how you should handle your emotions. If your parents were at ease with feelings in themselves, they taught you to respect your emotions and express them in healthy, appropriate ways. But, if your parents were afraid of their feelings, they taught you to fear them, too. You either learned to stuff your feelings inside yourself and express them in indirect ways, or, to use your feelings to frighten, manipulate, and control other people.

If you were emotionally, physically, or sexually abused, you are especially terrified of anger. As a child, you lived in fear of your parents' rages. You knew that your physical survival depended upon not upsetting them. You developed powerful unconscious patterns for suppressing your feelings, sacrificing yourself, and trying to keep the peace with your parents at all costs. At the same time, you may have been abusively angry with your siblings, especially the younger ones. As an adult, you may sometimes abuse your spouse, your children, and anyone else you see as less powerful than you are. But, still, you deny your anger with your parents, even when it is obvious to anyone else that your parents were severely abusive, discounting, and destructive with you. If you were a youngest or only child, you didn't have younger siblings to abuse. You tend to direct your anger at yourself, specializing in self-destructive behavior, depression, and suicidal fantasies. You also hold onto your self-destructive patterns, sacrificing your life and blocking your feelings to protect yourself from the risk of enraging your parents.

Jan's parents made sure she kept her feelings to herself. If she dared to cry, her mother cut her with a knife and locked her in a closet. It was just as dangerous for her to express anger. The severe brainwashing she experienced taught her to bury her feelings deep inside. When she became a teenager, she turned to alcohol and drugs to escape her pain. Gradually, she became more and more overweight, using food to comfort herself and weight to hide her sexuality.

Wendy came into therapy after she attempted suicide. She denied that the incestuous relationship she experienced with her father had had any effect on her. Though she was terribly unhappy, she chose to continue her alcohol and drug abuse rather than face the rage and sorrow she had repressed. Death seemed to her the only solution to her misery. She left therapy after discovering that she had the AIDS virus.

Jeanette hides her sadness and vulnerability behind a facade of anger and toughness. Her phobias and anxieties force her to face her vulnerable side which she tries desperately to hide from herself and from other people. It has taken her a long time to trust the group and her place in it, and it has been very hard for her to share her real feelings. Recently, she has become more open in talking about her grief which she avoided for years. Her first husband was killed when she was 20 years old. They had been married only a few months. Her buried sorrow and rage over this loss speak to her constantly through the pain of her arthritis. Since she began expressing herself honestly and facing her buried feelings about her sexual abuse as a child, Jeanette is taking better care of herself. She has improved her diet, has regular massages, is seeing a doctor for medication to help control her arthritis, and has stopped drinking. She is also becoming much more powerful by setting limits with her Internal Saboteur with its fearful, phobic thinking patterns.

Veronica denied that she had been sexually abused when I first asked her. Six months later, during a session when she seemed restless and distracted, she told me about how she and her younger sister fight constantly when they are together. She described some of the patterns in her sister's life, and I asked if she thought her sister might have been sexually abused. Surprised by my question, she told me of her own abuse and acknowledged that she knew her sister had been abused, too. Instead of facing their rage with their father, they had taken these powerful feelings out on each other. By fighting constantly with each other, they made sure they would not form an alliance and face what their father had done to both of them. As long as they fought, the family secret and their guilt and shame remained hidden. They protected their father by jealously fighting with each other like two women trying to share the same man.

Elaine's buried feelings manifested themselves in severe self-abuse. Early in her teen years, she made a critical decision. She couldn't stop her parents' abusive treatment of her. But she could stop her reactions to them. She vowed that she would never let them see her cry or show any emotion again. She would deny them the pleasure of seeing that they had any impact on her. At the time she made this vow, it was a survival decision. It helped her feel her own power. As soon as she could, she exercised that power and left home. But though she left her parents behind, she did not escape from abuse. Now she tormented herself with suicidal, derogatory thoughts and was unable to eat much of the time. When she accepted the reality of the abuse she had experienced, she had to make a new decision about allowing her feelings to be seen by her or by anyone else. This was a tough step for Elaine. Her old decision had been useful for her. It had enabled her to escape. It was hard to release it. But she realized that though it was a brilliant move when she was trapped at home, it was costly to continue to abide by it now. When she finally allowed herself to express her rage, she reported to the group the following week that she was now hungry and enjoying eating for the first time in months.

If you are denying your rage and sorrow over sexual abuse, you will notice some of these patterns operating in your life.

1) You doubt the memories you have recovered and deny that sexual abuse could have occurred in your family.

2) You are depressed. You cry a lot but rarely feel relieved by your tears. You feel hopeless.

3) You experience lots of physical health problems. Headaches are especially common among victims of sexual abuse. Stomach problems, colitis, sexual dysfunction problems like vaginismus, eating disorders, arthritis, and cancer all reflect deeply buried emotions.

4) You are a perpetual victim. You feel helpless and bewildered by the difficulties you consistently attract into your life.

5) You are angry and explosive with the people closest to you. You deflect your buried rage and sorrow onto them while continuing to deny the true source of your pain. Your anger never seems to be relieved despite the frequency of your outbursts.

6) You refuse to allow anyone to see how you feel. This gives you a feeling of power by denying that other people have impact on you.

When you face the true sources of your deeply buried pain, you will experience enormous relief. If you release your self-doubt and denial and allow your true feelings to emerge, you will discover that you aren't overwhelmed by these emotions that have always seemed so terrifying. You really do have all the strength you need to face what you have to face.

Your Protector-Controller part will not desert you as you begin to claim these feelings that it has helped you hide. Your Protector-Controller has been on the job in your life since your early childhood. You can trust that it will keep you as safe now as it has in the past. It will make sure you encounter your feelings in manageable doses that are not overwhelming. It also will see that you are in a safe situation where you can handle the pain you encounter. You will feel relief and new freedom each time you face, express, and release a part of your old, painful emotional burden.

This is the second step of the Rage and Sorrow stage of the recovery process. Now you own your rage and sadness and allow yourself to feel your anger at having been a victim of sexual abuse. At this point, you still feel very much like a victim. You are outraged that this could have happened to you. You alternate between periods of blaming rage and times when you are totally identified with your vulnerable, helpless, devastated Child-Self. Your feelings are as strong as if you were experiencing the abuse in the present.

Your challenge is not to get stuck here. Be aware of any temptation you feel to nurse your old wounds and cling to them. Some people stop their growth at this point, becoming addicted to the highs of their rage and the lows of their sadness. They may go off on crusades to save the world, punish abusers, look for other victims, and stir up their feelings, too. But if you allow yourself to get caught here, you avoid moving ahead with your healing. And, until you heal yourself, you won't be genuinely helpful to others who face similar problems.

In the third step in this stage of recovery, you allow the power and energy of your anger to lift you out of your victim posture. You take full responsibility for doing whatever is necessary to complete your healing. This means making a commitment to stay with the healing process and not allow yourself to be sidetracked along the way. Your Internal Saboteur will be active here as it will be in all the stages of your healing. Watch for its fearful, negative comments and its cunning, conning suggestions that are designed to seduce you into stopping your work before you have completed it. Remember your Saboteur is devoted to your eventual self-destruction. It is not going to welcome and support your commitment to healing yourself and taking control of your life into your own hands. But, as you set limits with your Saboteur and refuse to allow it to defeat you, you will gain strength and your Saboteur will gain respect for you. Eventually, you will transform its power, creativity, and determination into positive forces in your life.

Steps Four and Five are uncovering your unconscious guilty beliefs that you are doomed to be a victim forever. Your Saboteur clings to these beliefs. It reminds you that "you'll never really be any better or any happier than you have ever been. How could you be? You're a bad, guilty girl and you don't really deserve happiness and pleasure. You are a victim, you always have been, and you always will be. There is no hope for you. You might as well give up now and save yourself a lot of trouble and expense chasing after what you can't ever have."

Listen for the voice within that tells you that you are doomed to be a victim forever. That belief is a logical conclusion for a sexually abused child to draw. When you were a child, you knew deep inside yourself that you did not deserve the abuse you were experiencing. You also felt that you had no real power to stop the adult who was abusing you. This feeling was especially strong if your abuser was one or both of your parents.

But, instead of seeing your parents as bad, you decided that you were the bad one. Somehow, someway, you must be different from other children. You must have deserved what was happening to you. Surely, your parents, whom you loved and needed for your survival, couldn't be the bad ones. What they did and said must be true. Probably they told you on numerous occasions that you were a bad girl who caused all their problems.

The beliefs, that you are doomed to be a victim and that you are bad and deserve the punishment you receive, have determined much of your behavior and experience. Look back at the patterns that are common in the lives of women who were sexually abused. Most of these patterns derive directly from one or both of these beliefs. In order to change your life and free yourself from compulsively re-enacting these destructive patterns, you must change these beliefs.

Meditation is a powerful way to transmute old beliefs that interfere with your happiness and success. The meditative process that follows is adapted from suggestions by Lazaris on his audio and video tapes titled, *The Secrets Of Manifesting What Your Want* (Published by Concept Synergy, P.O. Box 159(M), Fairfax, Ca. 94930.)

Relax yourself in whatever way works best for you. (If you are not familiar with meditation, see Nurture Yourself To Success, Chapter VIII, Centering Yourself, pp. 52-54). Once you have relaxed your body, quieted your mind, and deepened your breath, visualize yourself going down a stairway into a dusty basement. As you enter the basement, notice the cobwebs, smell the smells you encounter, and let yourself see any old toys or relics from your past that are stored down here. Walk through the basement, looking around and exploring. In the far corner, you will notice a doorway that you haven't seen before. Feeling curious about that door, you open it and find yourself looking into a very simple, brightly lighted room that has no windows. Directly across from you on the opposite side of this room, there is a beautiful bookstand holding a very large, leatherbound volume. Move across the room to examine the book. On its cover, in gold letters, the title is embossed: The Book Of My Beliefs. *The author's name is also inscribed in gold. To your surprise, your name is written there.*

See yourself opening this large book that you have created and turning to the page where you find this belief inscribed: "I Am Doomed To Be A Victim Forever." *Notice the elaborate lettering and the richness of the paper on which it is written. Now, with lots of energy and gusto, tear that page out of your book of beliefs. Be quite dramatic with your actions. Rip the page up into tiny bits. Hear the sounds of the paper tearing and ripping. Feel your hands making those movements. Let the experience be as vivid as possible.*

When you have torn the page to bits, you notice an old-fashioned potbellied stove located in the corner of this room, just to the right of the door through which you entered. Turning around, you throw these bits of your old belief into the fire and watch as the flames rapidly consume them. Satisfied that you have disposed of your old belief, return now to your book of beliefs. Beside it you will find a wonderful, large pen that writes in gold. Take this pen and carefully, with great attention to the detail of each letter, enter this new belief on a fresh page of your book. "I am fully responsible for every aspect of the reality I create. I am never a victim."

Look carefully at the new belief you have inscribed. Read the words and commit them to memory. When you are ready, close your book of beliefs and leave this special room, shutting the door behind you. Return through the basement, climb the stairs, and gently bring yourself back to the place where you are.

When you have completed your meditation, take the time to write your new belief on several cards or memo notes. Post your new belief in places where you will see it often. Your bathroom mirror is a good spot. Put another copy in your car, one on your refrigerator, and others wherever you will see them frequently. Affirm your new belief repeatedly. Remember that reprogramming your mind requires consistent effort and determination. Work intensively, asserting your new belief until you feel completely at home with it and absolutely convinced of its truth.

When you feel ready to do so, use this same meditative process to change the old belief, "Incest/Sexual Abuse is bad. I experienced incest/sexual abuse; therefore, I am bad." Tear it out of your book of beliefs, tear it up, and burn it. Replace it with a beautifully inscribed new belief, "I am innocent and I deserve love." After your meditation, post your new belief in your favorite places for reminding yourself. Affirm it frequently. Work with it until you have integrated it completely.

Writing your new belief as an affirmation is another important part of making it true for you. Take a pad of paper and divide it into two columns. In the left-hand column, write your new belief. Continue writing it over and over, listening to any objections to it that come up in your mind. When you hear an objection, write that objection in the right-hand column. Continue writing your affirmation and your objections until you can write your affirmation twenty times without any objections arising.

AFFIRMATION	OBJECTIONS
I am innocent and I deserve love.	
I am innocent and I deserve love.	
I am innocent and I deserve love.	Not me. I'm bad and dirty.
I am innocent and I deserve love.	I'm guilty. I hate myself.
I am innocent and I deserve love.	You're a bad girl.
	You caused it.
	You know you did.
I am innocent and I deserve love.	You're kidding.
I am innocent and I deserve love.	Don't make me laugh.
I am innocent and I deserve love.	
I am innocent and I deserve love.	
I am innocent and I deserve love.	Is it possible?
I am innocent and I deserve love.	Maybe.
I am innocent and I deserve love.	
I am innocent and I deserve love.	Yes!
I am innocent and I deserve love.	
I am innocent and I deserve love.	

You may fill pages before you reach a point of resolution. Keep writing and keep listening to your objections. However long it takes you to make this change, stay with the process until you know you believe the affirmation you are writing. The effort you make in going through this exercise will reap dividends for you for the rest of your life.

You may find that it works best for you to go through this belief changing process taking smaller steps than the ones described above. Elaine found that she couldn't embrace the affirmation, "I am innocent and I deserve love," until she first worked with the statement, "Maybe I'm not bad after all. Maybe I am innocent." She had to admit the possibility of her innocence before she could claim it and affirm it directly.

Changing these beliefs will enable you to take a giant step forward in your healing process. You are not a helpless, doomed victim. You are innocent. And you are free now to own and express your rage and sorrow about the abuse you experienced. Using the affirmations listed below will help you to take full responsibility for the pain you have suppressed.

"I create my own reality."

"In the past, I created my depression and physical symptoms by suppressing my emotions."

"In the past, I chose to be a victim to avoid my rage."

"In the past, I chose to see myself as bad rather than face my rage."

"I choose now to own my rage and sorrow and free myself from the past."

The key to the sixth step in this stage of the healing process is allowing yourself to EXpress rather than continuing to DEpress these powerful feelings you have avoided and denied. Now you will feel a range of emotions you never before have allowed yourself. You will feel joy, excitement, bliss, and pleasure, as well as rage, sorrow, fear, humiliation, shame, and isolation. Your pleasurable feelings will be much stronger and richer now as you stop suppressing your painful feelings. The truth is that to the extent that you suppress one feeling, you suppress all the others as well. Because you have held so many deep, hurtful emotions inside you, you have missed out on joys in life that you richly deserve to feel.

As you open into your feelings, you will find that they present themselves to you when you are in a safe situation to face them. This may occur when you have private time at home, or time with a trusted friend whose support and caring is an enabling force for you. You may encounter your pain during individual and group therapy sessions. You probably won't be overwhelmed with your emotions in the midst of a busy day or an important meeting. But you may find them spilling out in your closest relationships with mates, children, and associates at work. Certainly, you will want to share with the people who are closest to you that you are working through some deep issues and hope they will be aware that you may not be your usual self. Your mate can be a wonderful source of support, but he may need help in dealing with his feelings about the abuse you experienced and the ways your healing process is affecting your relationship. Therapy for him during this period can be invaluable.

When you feel your emotions rising, let yourself breathe. You will notice that your tendency is to hold your breath and shallow breathe as soon as you encounter your feelings. This is a fear response and serves to block your releasing what you need to release. If you hold your breath and shallow breathe, you won't experience much relief. You will feel worse rather than better when your feelings subside. When you allow yourself to breathe deeply and fully, you will breathe your way through your feelings and gain a great release in the process. You will feel a burden lifted. Your heart will be lighter, and you will have new energy available to you when you complete each emotional release experience in this way.

Gestalt Therapy, Psychodrama, and Voice Dialogue are all effective therapeutic tools for expressing and releasing feelings. In Gestalt work, you imagine the person you need to address sitting in an empty chair across from you. Tell him what you are feeling, making sure you express feelings rather than thoughts or blaming judgments about him. Then change chairs, take his part, and respond as you intuitively feel that he would. Continue this exchange until you feel complete with the process.

In Psychodrama, you select other people to play the various roles in the scene you are about to enact. This can be as simple as having your therapist role play the person you wish to address, then changing roles with her and hav-

ing her take your part while you take the part of the person
you are confronting. The exchange can continue as long as
is necessary for you to feel closure on this particular experience. More elaborate Psychodramas involve your select-
ing a number of group members to play different roles in
the scene (often with your family) that you wish to re-
enact. You may play yourself with another person functioning as your alter-ego, coaching you and making suggestions. Or you may ask someone else to take your part so
you can watch the scene unfold from the perspective of one
who is outside the drama. At different points in the experience, you may take different roles in the family to feel
what each person's position is like. The process continues
until there is a sense of completion.

In Voice Dialogue, you play all the parts of the various
energy patterns that are within you. Your Protector-
Controller may speak, followed by the angry part of you,
the hurt part of you, the damaged part of you, and the wise,
understanding part of you. The objective is not to achieve
any resolution among these parts. Rather, it is to listen to
what each has to say in order to understand and accept
more fully all of your experience and all of who you are.

Writing is an enormously important part of the express-
ing/releasing process. After an experience with Gestalt
work, Psychodrama, or Voice Dialogue, write about your
experience in your journal. As you write, you will learn
more about yourself and integrate what you are discovering. Your written account of your therapeutic experiences
will be invaluable to you as you move on into later stages
of your healing. By taking the time to honor what you learn
along the way, you will create a fascinating memoir for
yourself and deepen your understanding of the unique
human being that you are. Taking yourself seriously
enough to write about what you feel and what you discover
honors who you are. It also gets those long-buried feelings
out of you and onto paper. When you read back over what
you have written, you will have a new perspective on your-

self. Writing validates you and helps you to see yourself as
worthy of your own attention. With your feelings expressed in such a tangible way, you will find that you can release
them much more easily.

In therapy sessions, I use batacas (foam padded bats
made especially for therapy) to help my clients express
their rage in a way that goes beyond words and allows sheer
physical release. There are rules that govern the use of
batacas. In a bataca fight between two people, there are no
head shots, no blows to the breasts or genitals, and a time
limit that is agreed upon before the fight. There are no
winners or losers. The object is to fight fair and to learn
that anger can be expressed within a context that requires
self-control and self-discipline. When the batacas are used
to express rage with someone who isn't present, an empty
chair is an effective target. It is OK to hit the chair or to hit
a wall with the batacas, but it is not OK to hit yourself with
them or to use them in destructive ways.

Through using the batacas, my clients experience how
much better they feel when they acknowledge and release
their anger. Letting go of anger in this way is fun; no one
gets hurt, and people feel good about each other after a
bataca fight is over. Energy is strong and relief is immediate
and obvious. Everyone learns that love and anger co-exist
and that anger is nothing to fear. Instead, it is simply an
emotion to acknowledge, to express, and to release.

It is interesting to see how differently people react to
being handed a bataca. Children appreciate them instantly. Usually they spot the batacas and ask about them
before I introduce them. They love to have a bataca fight
with me or with each other or with their parents. Children
also enjoy imagining that they are hitting people they are
angry with when they pound on an empty chair. I explain
to them that hitting with batacas is OK because there are
rules and because no one gets hurt. This is different from
hitting other people to hurt them or to punish them.
The object of hitting the chair is for them to feel better;

it is not to hurt the other person. It is to acknowledge, to express, and to release their anger in order to take good care of themselves.

Adults' reactions to batacas are much more varied. Some people look as if I have given them a bomb or a disgusting object when I hand them a bataca. They are suspicious and don't want to touch it. I comment on their reaction, and we explore why the bataca is so threatening. It may take several sessions or several months for them to decide to risk taking a swat at an empty chair. These people are so afraid of their rage and have stuffed it inside themselves for so long that they are terrified of an object that is obviously designed for expressing the monster emotion.

Others will take much more readily to the bataca and enjoy the release they experience with it. Couples often break through long-standing barriers in their relationship when they have their first bataca fight. They discover that fair fighting is fun and relieves their tension with each other.

Batacas help people to move into the energy of their anger and to express rage that is deeper than words. This physical release of anger is just as important as expressing it verbally. When my clients are using the batacas, I remind them to keep breathing and to make as much noise as they want when they hit the chair.

Body therapies are also important in releasing buried feelings which are stuck in the body. Rolfing and Hatha Yoga are both helpful in letting go of old emotions. Sometimes in group when we are dealing with lots of anger, I lead the group in the "lion" yoga posture. The "lion" involves taking a deep breath and releasing that breath in a loud roar while bending forward from a kneeling position. The face and eyes are stretched into an exaggerated open position, the mouth is stretched into a large oval and the tongue sticks out as the roar sounds. To avoid self-consciousness, we agree not to sneak peeks at each other as we all roar together. The relief and the release are delight-

ful. Again we learn that anger is OK and that letting it
go in healthy ways feels great. On other occasions, we
may have a group scream, which is not quite so threatening
as the "lion."

After releasing anger, I suggest that my clients allow
themselves to create a revenge fantasy. Letting your Child-
Self imagine getting back at the person who has hurt you is
an important step in letting go of your anger. In fantasy,
you can be cruel and punishing, vividly picturing yourself
getting even with your abuser. Once you have created your
revenge fantasy and carried it out in your imagination, you
can release the fantasy and release your rage with your
abuser. Letting go is much easier when you give the Child
part of you this opportunity to retaliate. Remember that
fantasy is fantasy. It is not equivalent to taking action. But
it does take into account the part of you that wants to
strike back before it will let go.

You may wonder how long it will take you to move
through this stage of expressing and releasing your rage and
sorrow. My experience is that this process varies with each
person who faces it. You will go at your own pace and you
won't express all of your feelings at any one time. Chances
are this phase of your healing will require several months
or possibly several years, depending upon how diligently
you work and how willing you are to focus your energy on
fully expressing and releasing your feelings. Trust that your
Protector-Controller and your Higher Self will guide you
at the pace and rhythm that are ideal for you.

As you move into your feelings about the sexual abuse
you experienced, be aware of the resistance you will
encounter within yourself. The Angry-Child part of you
wants to be acknowledged, heard, and accepted at long last.
The Protector-Controller part of you is reluctant to allow
your Angry-Child to express herself. Your Saboteur is
opposed to the whole process. At times you may feel that
the battle inside you is overwhelming. Your fears may seem
stronger than your capacity to heal yourself. If this is your

experience, remember that love is always stronger than fear. Your task is to love and compassionately understand the Angry-Child within you. Listen to her and encourage her to speak. Congratulate yourself on every step you take in expressing your feelings. Appreciate your progress and encourage yourself along the way.

Elaine was able to address her mother with her rage much more readily than she was her father. She had always seen her mother as being strong. But, because her father had been ill for many years, she was accustomed to protecting him from any feelings of hers that might upset him. She also denied the power of her anger with him by holding onto the belief that she had been responsible for causing his illness and hospitalization when she was six years old.

Elaine had rejected the Vulnerable Child within herself for years. When she saw her father's vulnerability, she wanted to protect him from her anger because she could so identify with his pain. But, by protecting him, she was rejecting the vulnerable, Hurt Child in her who had suffered from his loss and from his abuse of her. The temptation for her was to hold onto her illusion of control by telling herself she was responsible for his illness. This gave her an excuse to punish herself endlessly for his plight while avoiding her own Vulnerable Child-Self that had loved her father deeply, been abused by him, and then abandoned when he became ill. She had to work through this dilemma before she could express her rage with him.

This issue came up in group when Elaine showed the other group members pictures of her baby niece and of her father holding the baby. As she struggled with her feelings of responsibility for her father's obvious unhappiness (the picture of him revealed a man who looked very tense and miserable), Jeanette became intensely involved in Elaine's work. She could see clearly that Elaine was not and could not be responsible for her father's life and his choices. She was enraged with this man who had not been an adequate father and had abused his daughter. And she was angry with Elaine's self-punishment in lieu of facing her rage with him.

Jeanette was deeply identified with Elaine, who represented her own younger self. Elaine is close to the age Jeanette was when her first husband was killed. Over the years since, Jeanette has felt responsible for his death and punished herself with phobias and anxieties rather than facing her vulnerability and grief over losing him. Her father was not a strong, adequate man either. Jeanette's rage, which finally emerged in Elaine's behalf, had been buried for years. She had not been willing to direct it at her father and her dead husband whom she felt she had to protect from the power of her feelings. When she saw young Elaine doing the same thing, her outrage finally broke through her defenses.

Jeanette's anger helped Elaine move past protecting her weak father from her rage. Before the end of the group session, Elaine expressed her anger with her father for the first time in Gestalt two-chair work. Each time she releases part of her long-buried anger in a therapy session, she feels much stronger and happier and reports at her next session that she is enjoying both life and food.

Be aware that you may block your own rage by thinking you must protect "weak" parents or other people from the power of your feelings. The truth is that you are also afraid of letting yourself experience the depth of what you feel. We all have much more strength than we sometimes want to admit. In our culture, we are taught to think it is a noble act to protect those who seem to be weaker than we are. Yet, by seeing ourselves as stronger, we discount them. We also discount ourselves because the corollary of this belief in weakness in others is that we also are too fragile to face all of what we will encounter in life. As long as we hold onto this myth, we block our own growth by telling ourselves lies like, "It's just more than I can handle." Then our hidden expectation emerges. The unacknowledged aspect of our belief in weakness is that we can expect others to protect us when we feel frightened, weak, and helpless. Certainly, there are many times in life when friends and family give us much needed love and support. Yet, no one else can handle for us the emotional challenges we must face, express, and release. Our feelings are our own, and only we can clear them.

Clearing your feelings includes both expressing them and releasing them. You may find that you have more difficulty letting go of your feelings than you do expressing them. Long-buried emotions are like old friends. Even though they keep you depressed and unhappy, at least they are familiar. Letting go of them is like taking the training wheels off your bicycle. You aren't quite sure you really know how to ride without them. But once you discover how much more fun your bike is and how much you enjoy riding with your new freedom and power, you certainly don't long to put them back on again.

Here are some tips to help you truly release your feelings, rather than going over and over them endlessly.

1) Be intentional about letting go of your feelings when you express them. Set your intention to let go in all the work you do with your rage and sorrow.

2) Breathe as you feel. Keep your breath moving as you experience your emotions. Deep breathing with your feelings is the most effective way of clearing them.

3) Visualize your pain, sorrow, and rage leaving your physical body as you express these emotions.

4) In addition to expressing your feelings verbally, put them on paper. Writing your feelings gets them out of you and onto paper where you can leave them and have a record of their impact on your life. Read what you have written from the position of your Observer-Aware Self. See these emotions as part of your past, which you can fully own now and release.

5) Create a revenge fantasy to satisfy the part of you that wants to get even before it will let go.

6) Other forms of creative expression are also very useful in releasing your emotions. Playing the piano, writing poetry, drawing, painting, and dancing are excellent ways for allowing emotional release. As you free yourself from your buried rage and sorrow, your creativity will be enormously enhanced. Your pleasure from creative activity will be much greater also.

During my healing process, I took ballroom dancing lessons for the first time since sixth grade. Learning to move my body gracefully and to dance freely were important in reclaiming my sexuality. I realized when I discovered Latin motion how deeply I had blocked myself from ever doing anything that might be sexually provocative. I was never to flirt with another man because I knew I had to protect my father and me from his jealous rages. When I finally was able to move my hips as my instructor taught me, I had a strong visual image of my father turning over in his grave. Now I love to dance and feel the freedom I reclaimed in this way.

7) Find a Certified Rolfer and arrange to have a series of Rolfing sessions. Rolfing is extremely helpful in loosening up emotions that have been locked inside the body for years. As the Rolfer helps you open your body, your emotions will move through you much more freely than before. If you were sexually abused, I think Rolfing is essential for full healing and recovery.

The regular practice of Hatha Yoga is an excellent way to maintain the benefits you receive from your Rolfing. Yoga helps you stay flexible and keeps your body free from emotional buildup. It is a discipline I intend to continue practicing for the rest of my life. Because of the stress my body endured over the years that I blocked my memory of sexual abuse, I know I must take especially good care of my physical health now and in the future. In addition to practicing Yoga regularly, I have periodic, tune-up Rolfing sessions. I also enjoy massage and foot reflexology and find them helpful in relieving tension, enhancing my health, and healing my body.

Be aware that releasing your feelings means giving up the unconscious payoffs you experience from holding onto them. When you let go of your buried rage and sorrow, you will no longer enjoy feeling like a victim, being a cry-baby, or staying sick, depressed, and helpless. You won't stay stuck in confusion and you won't act like an abuser yourself, playing the bitch with the people you love the most. You will be free of your addiction to these old behaviors and well on your way to new experiences of joy and pleasure you've never known before.

CHAPTER XIII

MASTERING THE FUNDAMENTALS

STAGE III: MASTERING THE FUNDAMENTALS

A) Creating a healthy reality for yourself in the present

1) Learning to recognize and say "no" to your Internal Saboteur, consistently and effectively, moment by moment, so you stop compulsively repeating abusive, self-sabotaging patterns of thought, feeling, and behavior in your daily life.

2) Accepting and feeling compassion for the damaged, wounded child within you; noticing without judgment when your saboteur attacks your Inner Child; protecting your Child and stopping your Saboteur.

3) Nurturing your Inner Child with words of love, encouragement, and appreciation; strengthening your Nurturing-Enabling Self so it fills the space your Saboteur previously occupied; committing yourself to transforming your Saboteur by continuing to set limits with it so it learns to respect your authority over your own life.

4) Recognizing how your boundaries were violated when you were sexually abused and how you continue to allow similar violations of your boundaries in the present; learning to respect your boundaries and set limits for yourself and with other people.

B) Creating a healthy past reality for your Child-Self: A new past for her to occupy in a new home with new parents or in a transformed version of her old family. Allowing her to live there while you are involved in your current adult reality and the future you are designing.

C) Healing your damaged Child-Self and integrating her into your present life. Being her therapist and having regular session with her after she moves into her new home.

1) Assessing her difficulties through research and observation.

2) Understanding her needs, her feelings, and her impact on your life.

3) Embracing her in love.

4) Transforming her destructive unconscious program.

5) Integrating your transformed Child-Self into your transformed Child-Self into your daily life.

This Mastering The Fundamentals Stage of the Healing Process incorporates the Fundamental Model for Healing described in Chapter VIII. Remember that your basic goals are: 1) to expand your conscious awareness so you notice without judging your mental, emotional, physical, and spiritual processes; and 2) to shift your life out of the painful, Self-Sabotaging energy of fear into the powerful, healing, enabling energy of love.

You create your own reality. At each moment in time, you are choosing what you experience. You may choose to operate in the energy of love and feel the enabling vibrations of that energy. Or, you may step into the energy of fear and allow yourself to be caught up in its painful, negative vibrations. Moment by moment, you decide which reality you embrace. If at a given moment, you realize you have slipped into the clutches of fear, you can let go of that energy and shift your consciousness into the healing energy of love. It is a continuous discipline that requires practice, aware consciousness, and commitment moment by moment for the rest of your life.

Learning to recognize your Internal Saboteur helps you to practice this discipline successfully. The Internal Saboteur is the synergy of the personality patterns within you that operate in the energy of fear. With the help of its cohorts (your Inner Critic, your Worrier, your Pusher, your Martyr-Pleaser, your Judge, and your Distorted/ Adaptive Child), the Internal Saboteur constantly is busy helping you to doubt yourself and to fear your power. It is dedicated to destroying your life. Fear is the weapon it uses to control you.

When you learn to recognize your Saboteur, you gain a tremendous advantage. Seeing your Saboteur allows you to take charge of it. Ignoring the Saboteur empowers it. If you want to stop looking the other way while your Saboteur takes you over, here is a profile that will help you to identify it.

THE SABOTEUR: A PROFILE

ENERGY SOURCE: Feelings of isolation, abandonment, fear, sorrow, hurt, and anger that arise in response to "Don't be" and "Don't be who you are" messages. These messages are communicated, frequently unconsciously and early in life, by disowned and destructive energy patterns (the Saboteurs) in your parents.

MISSION: To do away with you so you won't threaten these neurotic, angry, destructive parts of your parents. To do this in both subtle and not-so-subtle ways, so you think it was your own idea in the first place.

METHODS OF OPERATION: Cynical, fearful, critical, pushy, worrying thoughts that undermine your self-confidence. Rebellious, negative suggestions that are calculated to defeat you and keep you from accomplishing your goals. Cunning, conning comments that are designed to confuse you and seduce you into going against your better judgment.

PERSONALITY TRAITS: Cunning, devious, clever, subversive, sneaky, secretive, conning, brilliant, convincing, and persistent. A fast learner who can take positive ideas and principles and give them a self-defeating, self-destructive twist. For example, "Let go and let God" becomes "Sit back and do nothing."

TACTICS: Uses stressful times to launch powerful attacks on your self-confidence, integrity, and commitment to yourself. Swings into action whenever you begin to be too successful or to enjoy being alive too much. Becomes very active when you make positive changes in your life. Doesn't like therapists or books that blow its cover. Will redouble its efforts to control you when you begin to recognize its activity in your life. In order to do this, becomes even more clever and subtle.

DISGUISES AND CLUES: May sound as if it is supporting your goals, but does so in a critical, heavy-handed way that actually encourages you to rebel and undermine yourself. May put a smile on your face when you are actually feeling sad or upset; may shake your head in a "no" gesture when consciously you want to say "yes" or vice versa. May give a cackling, raucous laugh about something which is not funny.

BASIC MESSAGES: 1) You can handle it by yourself. You don't need help from anyone else. 2) You don't have a Saboteur. You dealt with that years ago. This may apply to others, but it's not relevant to you. 3) You should be perfect and you can't trust yourself until you are. Don't succeed; you'll just be criticized. Don't take risks; you might make a mistake. 4) Everything right is wrong; everything wrong is right. (Your Saboteur lies to you.) You are better than this person; worse than that one.

Your Saboteur tells you that you are a victim; it insists that your problems really are someone else's fault. It encourages you to believe you can never change and have what you want. Instead, you must reconcile yourself to suffering as you always have. When you are confronted with the truth about yourself, your Saboteur steps in to deny it. It defends you and excuses you for your responsibility for your plight.

The object in recognizing your Saboteur is to take

charge of its energy, power, creativity, and determination so you can use these potent attributes to enhance your life, not to destroy it. Your goal is not to get rid of your Saboteur. Rather, it is to teach your Saboteur to respect you and your authority over your life. Eventually, when you consistently and effectively set limits with your Saboteur, you will transform its energy into a positive force in your life. However, its potential always exists within you. Especially in very stressful times, it may raise its head to test you once again.

The Internal Saboteur is extraordinarily potent in people who were sexually abused as children. It plays on their guilt and abuses them emotionally, long after the sexual abuse is ended. Because parents are role models for the Internal Saboteur, sexually abusive parents present a powerfully destructive model for their children. They teach them to disregard their needs and feelings in order to satisfy inappropriate, invasive demands other people make of them. When these children become adults, their Internal Saboteurs carry out the lethal internal programming that they absorbed. The destructive behavioral patterns that are common in the lives of sexually abused women are the result.

With fear as its weapon, the Internal Saboteur reminds women who were sexually abused of all their imperfections. If you were sexually abused, your Saboteur assures you that you don't deserve love and probably never will experience happiness. You are different from other people; guilty, bad, and doomed. You will be punished sooner or later, so you might as well punish yourself and at least feel in charge of this painful process. It encourages you to doubt yourself, to trust other people who don't deserve your trust, and to sacrifice your best interests. As a result, you engage in painful attempts to gain the love you so desperately need from abusive people who can't or won't give it. They are stand-ins for your parents as you compulsively re-enact your issues with them in your adult life.

You must learn to stop your internal self-abuse in order to stop these painful patterns in your outer life. When you identify your Internal Saboteur, you can also tune into the plight of your Inner Child-Self. Your Child-Self lives in the presence of your Saboteur's abuse and is the object of its attacks. In the past, you have listened to your Saboteur and ignored its impact on your Inner Child. Now you must let your Inner Child know you are ready to be aware of its feelings. You will no longer ignore its plight while allowing your Saboteur to run rampant with its abusive comments and suggestions. You will set limits with the Saboteur and stop its attacks on your Child-Self, which is the essence of who you are.

Stopping your Saboteur's abuse of your Inner Child is like stepping into the abusive situation you endured as a child and putting a stop to it. When you were a child, you didn't have the wisdom, strength, and experience to stop your abuser. Now you do. By stopping your Internal Saboteur, you declare that you no longer will allow yourself to be a victim. You claim charge of your life and start creating a new, nurturing reality for yourself. When you have mastered your Internal Saboteur, you can be sure you won't allow anyone else to abuse you. Setting limits with your Saboteur and protecting your Inner Child is analogous to confronting your abuser and stopping his attacks. Once you make and keep this commitment to yourself, you won't be likely to allow abuse of any kind to continue in your life.

The part of you that steps into your internal process and stops your Saboteur is your Nurturing-Enabling Self (NES). Here is its personality profile to help you strengthen and develop this dimension of yourself.

YOUR NURTURING-ENABLING SELF (NES):
A PROFILE

ENERGY SOURCE: Your loving relationship with God and with your Higher Self.

MISSION: To encourage, affirm, and accept your Inner Child; to assist you in facing your challenges and exploring your issues without judging yourself; to set limits with your Internal Saboteur and with other people.

METHODS OF OPERATION: Words of loving encouragement that enhance your self-confidence and self-esteem. Your NES affirms your successes and helps you realize your goals. It recognizes that you create your reality and expects you to create a joyous, fulfilling life for yourself. It supports you with honesty and commitment. Your NES genuinely loves your Inner Child and is devoted to creating a nurturing environment in which your Child-Self can thrive. It helps you feel safe and secure with yourself and with others.

PERSONALITY TRAITS: Warm, loving, genuine, intelligent, straightforward, honest, responsible, clear-thinking, and quietly confident. Always present and available, but not manipulating or controlling. Releases you to live in love, trusting the inner guidance that is always available to you.

TACTICS: Steps in to set limits with your Saboteur and to encourage your Inner Child to express her needs and feelings. Helps you accept success as your natural state of being; reminds you that there is an abundance of love, time, money, and support for all your needs when you actively use your creativity. Supports your reading books that inspire, educate, and entertain you. Also supports your asking for help and seeking teachers to assist you in your growth. Trusts you and lets you know you are appreciated. Encourages you to play and have fun.

BASIC MESSAGES: 1) You're OK. You are innocent and you deserve love. 2) Tell the truth. Express your needs and your feelings, appropriately and quickly. Tend to them; then let them go. 3) Explore the world, discover what is most interesting and important to you. 4) Look for the resources you need. Ask for help. 5) Think for yourself. Evaluate what you learn; be discerning and discriminating about what you accept. 6) Face your problems and your challenges. Examine them. Embrace and acknowledge your Saboteur and all your selves. You can transform your life.

You develop and strengthen your Nurturing-Enabling Self each time you set limits with your Saboteur and replace its comments and suggestions with sane, clear, encouraging, and appreciative words. Gradually, your NES will occupy more and more space in your inner world as its loving energy overrides your Saboteur's fearful projections. The Saboteur will be left to occupy only a small corner of your inner world.

Let's take a look at an example of how this inner limit-setting process works.

You have attended a therapy group for sexually abused women for three months. During the last session, one of the members worked through an especially angry confrontation with her father who began abusing her sexually when she was five years old. Her strong feelings stirred your buried rage. You've been somewhat uncomfortable all week with angry feelings that need to be expressed. You have done your best to ignore these feelings, but you have lashed out at your husband and your five-year-old daughter several times. Group meets again tomorrow. You're driving home from work. This is your internal dialogue.

Your Saboteur: *You know, that therapy group isn't doing you a bit of good. Look at how yucky you've been feeling all week. You've been terrible to Hank and Caroline. The truth is you're getting worse, not better. And look what it's costing you. It's much too expensive. You really can't afford it anyway.*

Your Rebellious Child: *I sure would like to quit. I don't like having to go anywhere at the same time every week, and I get real tired of hearing about everyone else's problems. I've got*

*enough of my own. I really like individual therapy better or no
therapy at all.*

Your Saboteur: *You ought to just quit both. It's not doing
you a bit of good anyway, dredging up all that old stuff from the
past. Just put it out of your mind and forget it. There's no point
in dwelling on it now. You'll feel better when you quit.*

Your Rebellious Child: *I'm going to quit. What a relief! I
didn't want to go tomorrow night anyway. I'll call in the morning and tell the secretary I can't afford to come anymore.
Wonder if she'll let me get away with that?*

Notice how the Saboteur begins its attack with what
sounds like concern for your feelings and your behavior.
But what it is saying is a discount to both you and the
group. The group isn't doing any good (implying that the
group should be working magic for you) and you're getting
worse, not better (judging your emerging anger which has
spilled out at Hank and Caroline as bad, and discounting
that you are in charge of what you get out of group). This
line of reasoning is quite seductive, however. Your Child-
Self is frightened of the anger that came out in the group
last week and would love to escape tomorrow's session. It
is also feeling the stirrings of its own deeply buried rage
and is terrified of what may emerge. So, it is glad to turn
that long-suppressed anger into rebellious behavior, agree
with the Saboteur, and quit group. But, notice its last
comment. The rebellious child wonders if she will get away
with the excuse she plans to make. Will her therapist confront her avoidance or will she get by with making a money
excuse to the secretary? Secretly, she hopes the therapist
will set limits with you and your Saboteur since you are
not doing so. Though your Child-Self is frightened and
thinks she wants to run away, she will be relieved if there is
a loving voice that is not swayed by her fears. For, deep
down, she wants you to acknowledge her anger, accept her
rage, and help her express and release those strong feelings
you've rejected for years.

Let's look at the same situation again. This time, you

have developed your Aware Consciousness and have become skilled at recognizing your Saboteur.

Your Saboteur: *You know, that therapy group isn't doing you a bit of good. Look at how yucky you've been feeling all week. You've been terrible to Hank and Caroline. The truth is you're getting worse, not better. And look what it's costing you. It's much too expensive. You really can't afford it anyway.*

Your Aware Consciousness: *That's your Saboteur, discounting you and the group, too.*

Your Nurturing-Enabling Self: *You don't have to get hooked by this. You know you're frightened about the anger you felt last week and the rage that has been stirring in you since that session. And playing on your old fears about money is a great strategy for seducing you. But, you don't have to play this deadly game. I know you're going to keep your commitment to finish your therapy and heal yourself.*

Chairman of Your Internal Board of Directors: *You're right! I'm not about to quit now. I'm just getting to the crucial issues.*

Your Internal Child (relaxing): *I feel better just knowing she's not going to listen to that voice that doesn't want me to feel anything. I'm frightened, but I'm also angry and I want her to pay attention to me. She's kept me locked in the basement long enough. I like being accepted and listened to for a change.*

This time, the Chairman of Your Internal Board of Directors, with the help of Aware Consciousness and your Nurturing-Enabling Self, stops your Saboteur and keeps your commitment to yourself. Your Internal Child is relieved and delighted to be taken into account. However, your Saboteur probably won't stop here. Be prepared for more subtle, and not-so-subtle, suggestions designed to hook your Rebellious Child and get you out of therapy. The closer you get to the real issues and to your long-buried feelings, the stronger your Saboteur's attacks will become. It doesn't want you to complete your healing process. It is afraid, because it knows that when you do, it will have lost its hold over you.

Remember, your challenge is to transform your Saboteur, not to get rid of it. You want its determination, creativity, brilliance, and dedication available to you for accomplishing, rather than sabotaging, your goals. Each time your Internal Board Chairman makes a conscious choice to stop your Saboteur's attack, you teach it to respect your authority over your life. It's a lot like teaching a destructive, two-year-old child to respect his parents' direction. Gradually, as they consistently and effectively set limits with him and enforce consequences for the choices he makes, he learns that what they say to him counts. They hold him accountable for his choices. Eventually, he learns how to be responsible for his own behavior. By the time he is a teen-ager, he will be able to say "no" to himself and to other people. But, he won't be perfect. There will be many times in the course of his years growing up when he will make mistakes, when he will test his parents' authority, and when he will be rebellious. When these incidents occur, his parents don't give up on him. They simply step in one more time and make sure he experiences the consequences of whatever choice he has made.

Your work with your Internal Saboteur will follow a similar pattern. You set limits with it or you allow it to dominate you. You experience the consequences of the choices you make. When you allow your Saboteur to prevail, you pay the price. When you refuse to play its games, you reap the rewards. You learn with every experience. You won't be perfect either. But, you will become stronger and stronger and more and more consistently in charge of creating a loving, rather than a fearful, destructive reality in your life.

The more effective you are in setting limits with your Internal Saboteur, the more effective you will be in setting limits with other people. If you were sexually abused as a child, this is a special challenge. Sexual abuse is a profound violation of limits. As an abused child, you learned to submit to this intrusive disregard for your needs, your feelings, and your body. Your boundaries were violated by a person you should have been able to trust, an adult who may have been one of your parents. He abused his power over you with no concern for the impact of his impulsive behavior on you. He made choices for you that you were not old enough to agree to or to understand. He acted as if you were not a being who is separate from him. He treated you as if you were an extension of him.

You, in turn, came to accept such intrusive behavior as part of the price of love and relationship. If your abuser was your parent, you also had a deep need for his presence in your life. Your physical and emotional survival seemed to depend on him. You learned that you must sacrifice yourself and allow yourself to be used in order to have your needs met for what you thought were love and security. When you became an adult, you continued to operate from this assumption. As a result, you now find yourself caught up in the painful, destructive patterns of behavior common in the lives of women who were sexually abused.

In order to stop these destructive patterns, you must reclaim your boundaries and learn to keep them intact. Your boundaries define and separate you from other people. You have both physical boundaries and emotional boundaries. Your physical boundaries are clear, defined as they are by your body. Emotional boundaries are more complex, especially in intimate relationships.

Transactional Analysis provides an excellent model for

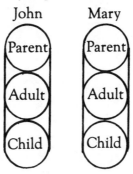

John   Mary

understanding how boundaries work. A person is drawn with three distinct ego states: the Parent, the Adult, and the Child. The line enclosing these three ego states and defining this individual is his boundary.

Since boundaries define our uniqueness, they are part of what makes us interesting to other people. Notice that John and Mary both have clear, strong boundaries that separate them from each other. Since they have just met for the first time, both their emotional and physical boundaries are quite clear. Given this clarity and definition, they may feel strong energy and excitement moving between them. They are strangers, a mystery to each other. Will they become more involved? Is this to be an important relationship, or a casual relationship? Or, will they never cross paths again?

Let's assume that John and Mary are strongly attracted to each other. They decide to meet again to become better acquainted. It's not long before they are dating steadily, and within a year, they are married. As they become closer and closer to each other, their emotional boundaries become less clear. Both John and Mary learned as children that in a close relationship they should take care of the other person's needs and feelings before considering their own. As a child, John was physically abused by his father. Mary experienced both physical and sexual abuse. Neither of them has dealt with the impact of their abuse experiences.

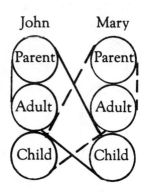

Each of them believes this relationship is very special so that each one's needs for nurturing and understanding will be met. The Child in each of them is starving for love and affection and secretly wants the other person to be the loving parent he has never had. These beliefs and expectations are basic to creating the symbiotic relationship they develop as their marriage evolves. Notice what happens to their boundaries.

John discounts the Child in himself to look after the Child in Mary. He uses his Parent and Adult ego states to take care of her. At the same time, he discounts the Parent and Adult in Mary that she could use to take her own needs and feelings into account. The two of them function with only half of their available parts now. Their relationship is based on discounting both of them. But, it is a relationship that is congruent with what they have been taught about how they should take care of each other. It also attempts to meet the deep needs of both of them for adequate parenting.

At other times, their roles reverse (see dotted boundary line in the diagram above). Now, Mary discounts her Child-Self and uses her Parent and Adult ego states to take care of the Child in John. The clear boundaries that used to exist between them are lost. John and Mary are trying to behave as if they were one person. The problem is that they can't read each other's minds. Mary doesn't always guess correctly about John's needs and feelings. So she isn't always able to satisfy him. When she fails, he resents her insensitivity. He may or may not tell her how he feels, because he secretly expects her to know what he wants without his having to say. Nor is John consistently able to satisfy Mary. She feels resentful when he doesn't do for her what she wants him to do. But, much of the time, she doesn't tell him what that is. He should know her well enough to know what she wants without her having to communicate.

Unacknowledged resentments mount between them.

Their verbal communication is inadequate, and their sexual relationship becomes almost non-existent. With their boundaries overlapping as they do now, the natural flow of loving energy between them is blocked. Lack of verbal and sexual communication breeds more resentments. They have created a vicious circle that becomes more and more destructive to their marriage.

Both John and Mary are afraid to acknowledge their anger with each other. Anger threatens them because they try to avoid anything that might sever their symbiotic attachment to each other. But their repressed feelings break through anyway in fights that become more and more abusive. They are terrified of breaking their symbiosis, because they feel as if their survival depends on sticking together. Yet, John does his best not to let Mary see how important she is to him. He acts out his buried anger with her in indirect ways, coming home from work late, forgetting to call, acting as if he doesn't care about her, and flirting outrageously with other women when they go out socially. He also threatens to leave her when they fight. Mary feels angry and abused by his behavior, but she buries her anger and has no idea how to set limits with John. She is afraid of upsetting him, provoking another fight, and risking abandonment.

If John and Mary get help early enough in their marriage, they may be able to interrupt these destructive patterns, which will destroy their relationship if they are left unchecked. Let's assume that they decide to see a therapist. In the safety of the structure their therapist creates, they begin learning to express their feelings honestly and in sane, constructive ways. They explore the beliefs and expectations that led them into their dysfunctional symbiotic relationship. They also begin restoring the healthy emotional boundaries each of them needs if their marriage is to succeed.

Both John and Mary need individual therapy as well as the couple's work they have begun. They must learn to nurture themselves as individuals and face their rage and sorrow with their parents who abused them. Because their parents violated their physical and emotional boundaries when they were children, they have re-enacted the same kind of boundary violations and abuse in their marriage. This re-enactment is an unconscious effort to resolve their old pain and hurt. Just as children try to master their emotions through their play, adults try to master their childhood issues through their relationships and marriages. But, such re-enactment rarely solves the underlying problem. Instead, it continues, sometimes through sequential relationships, until the old pain and hurt finally are faced, acknowledged, and released.

If John and Mary choose to do the individual healing work each of them needs, they will reap dividends for the rest of their lives. Each will free himself to be the person he really is, as an individual and as a marriage partner. Their relationship will deepen and mature as each of them grows. But, if one of them decides not to face what he has to face, while the other continues to grow; or, if they find that as they both grow, their needs and interests are no longer compatible, their marriage will have to change or come to an end. Once they begin the healing process and the energy of transformation is set in motion, they are committed to a growth path that may lead them into territory beyond what they can envision in the beginning. They will have to release their preconceived notions about how things in their lives ought to be and stay open to what they learn and how they grow as they evolve. Certainly, their marriage is at risk; but, remember that the alternative is continuing to live in the destructive, dysfunctional symbiosis they have established, and passing on the abusive patterns in their lives to their children, whom they also probably will abuse.

As John and Mary reclaim the boundaries that separate and define them as unique individuals, they discover what they can and cannot do for each other. One cannot be responsible for the other. John cannot change or fix Mary so she becomes the person he wants her to be. Mary cannot change John. But, if each chooses to do so, Mary can change Mary and John can change John. Each can express himself honestly, without blaming and attacking the other. Each can allow the other honest self-expression without becoming defensive or arguing about the validity of his experience. When they accept the boundaries that separate them and define their individual uniqueness, they realize that each of them may experience and perceive the same situation differently. The question is not who is right and who is wrong. Their different points of view are a function of their different ways of experiencing, their unique histories, and their individual perceptions. Having a difference of opinion has nothing to do with their loving each other. Instead, differences are an inevitable and fascinating dimension of sharing their lives. They can understand and accept their differences without feeling bad, wrong, or defensive because they disagree.

Healing their boundaries also requires that John and Mary set limits with each other. They must say "no" when "no" is their honest response, without being afraid of angering or upsetting the other. If John says "no" to Mary in an honest, straightforward way, Mary has many choices about how she responds. She may feel angry with John and tell him so in a healthy, non-blaming way. She may feel angry and pretend she doesn't. She may pout for the rest of the day. She may be angry and attack John in a destructive outburst. She may accept his "no" and be gratified that he is honest with her. She may refuse to give up, and pester him for a while in an effort to get him to change his mind. Whatever choice Mary makes, she is responsible for her response. And, John is responsible for his.

Frequently, when Mary sets limits with John, he becomes angry and defensive. Let's look at an example of such an interaction between them.

Mary: John, I was angry last night when I had prepared a special dinner for us only to have you arrive home two hours later than usual without calling to let me know your plans had changed. I've decided that in the future, if I don't hear from you, I'll go ahead with dinner at the regular time. You can fix something for yourself when you get here. That way, I won't be so angry and feel so discounted.

John (becoming defensive): Mary, you know I can't help it when I'm late. The boss expects me to work until we've finished a project. I can't just walk out. What do you expect me to do? You're always getting mad about stuff that shouldn't bother you. You really upset me. I don't want to have to fix my own dinner and end up eating by myself. I'm just out there trying my best to make a living for you.

Mary: John, you don't have to defend yourself. I understand that sometimes you have to be late and that you're angry about what I've said. That's OK. But, I'm not going to hold dinner if I don't get a call from you telling me what to expect.

John: Well, I don't like that. You're trying to control my life. And I won't check in with you or anyone else.

Mary: Just give me a call if you're going to be late and I'll hold dinner.

John: You're being a real bitch. I don't have to put up with this.

Mary: I'm going to take a walk now. You can join me if you like.

John: Don't you dare leave until we get this settled.

Mary: I'll be back in about an hour.

In this exchange, Mary shares with John how she feels about his discounting her by not letting her know he will be late for dinner. She then states that in the future, she will go ahead with dinner if she hasn't heard from John. She lets him know that this is a limit she is setting. If he expects to have dinner with her, she expects him to let her know if there is a substantial change in his schedule. If not, she will dine alone, and he will be responsible for his own meal whenever he arrives.

John responds angrily and defensively. He tries to pick a fight with Mary by defending himself and attacking her. But she is able to stay centered and simply stick to her original position. She declines the bait he offers to get her embroiled in a battle with him. When he continues to try to escalate the situation, she calls for time out by announcing that she is leaving to go for a walk. John can join her if he chooses. He declines, but by the time she returns he has had time to settle down and think about what she said. Whether or not they discuss the issue again, John now knows where Mary stands and what she expects. He can choose to call her or not when he will be late in the future. If he doesn't call, he knows what to expect when he gets home.

Let's explore what happens if John does not respond defensively when Mary states her limit.

Mary: John, I was angry last night when I had prepared a special dinner for us only to have you arrive home two hours later than usual without calling to let me know your plans had changed. I've decided that in the future, if I don't hear from you, I'll go ahead with dinner at the regular time. You can fix something for yourself when you get here. That way, I won't be so angry and feel so discounted.

John: You were angry last night when I was late and didn't call. Thanks for telling me how you feel. And I think your plan is fine. If I can't get free to make a call, you go ahead and eat. Then we can enjoy each other when I do get home without either of us feeling angry, discounted, or guilty. I don't much like to eat alone so I bet I'll remember to make that call. I really don't want to discount you.

This time John tells Mary what he heard her say and thanks her for being honest with him. He acknowledges her plan and accepts what she has told him. He even lets her know he will do his best to call in the future. They settle the matter in a simple exchange that takes little time or energy. John accepts Mary's limit and feels secure enough about himself that he doesn't choose to feel attacked and defensive about what she says.

As they become skilled with being honest and clear about their boundaries and limits, their relationship will be much more pleasurable for both of them. There is a wonderful freedom in a relationship when you can share honestly and appropriately without being afraid of your partner's reaction. Such sharing isn't always about conflicts. It is just as important to tell your partner about what you are interested in and excited about without getting a lecture in return or advice about what you've done wrong or might have done differently. Sharing the interesting details of your separate lives is an opportunity for lots of stroking and support for each other when you simply listen and respond without judgment, criticism, or advice. The capacity to share in this way is a function of being clear about the boundaries that separate you. You know and accept that you are two different people who do things in different ways. You are not therapists or counselors for each other. (You can hire someone who is an outsider to your relationship to fill that role.) You are peers who like and respect each other. You cherish the differences between you, because those differences keep your relationship interesting and challenging.

You won't be perfect in your sharing with each other. Sometimes one or the other of you will become threatened and allow his Frightened-Child part to take over. If the other person stays centered in the energy of love, the two of you will get back on track quickly. But, even if you both get caught up in fear and anger, you will live through your conflict. The key is being willing to accept your mistakes and learn from them, without condemning yourself or your mate for failing to be a perfect person.

Here are some tips to help you keep your boundaries strong and healthy so your relationships will be healthy, too.

1) Recognize that you are a separate being, unique and different from all others. Realize, however, that you are

also part of a much larger whole that links you with all other living beings and connects you with God. You are like an individual leaf on the magnificent tree of life. You are separate from the other leaves, yet all the leaves are part of the much greater whole that is the synergy called a tree.

2) Be clear with yourself about what you can and cannot be responsible for; you are responsible for yourself and the reality you create in your own life. You are not responsible for other people and the realities they create. (The exception is with your children. You are entrusted with the responsibility for caring for them, nurturing them, and, ultimately, teaching them to be responsible for themselves. In the end, you must release them and accept their separateness, too. You know you have done your job well when they take hold of their lives, creating successful realities for themselves.)

3) Recognize that because you were sexually abused as a child, you have a tendency to be drawn into situations where you may allow your own boundaries to be violated or may try to violate someone else's. Make a commitment to yourself to practice and work to become clearer and clearer about boundaries and limits and how to set and respect them.

4) When you set limits with others:

a) Do your best to stay centered in love and refuse to be drawn into their defensiveness.

b) Stick to your point. Don't be drawn off into defending yourself or debating the merits of your position.

c) Let go of your fear of anger, whether it is of your own or of someone else's.

d) Be responsible for expressing yourself in ways that are clear and loving rather than fearful, blaming, and attacking. Be aware that the quality of your communication affects the person you address.

e) Speak in an honest, sane, appropriate manner without attacking. Then release the other person to be

responsible for his response to you. He has many
choices about how he reacts to what you say.

f) Take full responsibility for the reality you create
for yourself.

g) Be responsible for nurturing and loving yourself
beautifully and adequately. Don't expect others to
love you more than you are willing to love yourself.
Remember that loving yourself includes setting limits
effectively within yourself and with other people.

(For more on boundaries and limits, please see
Nurture Yourself To Success, Chapters 15 through 22.)

LOVING AND NURTURING YOURSELF

The fundamentals of the healing process are all about
taking responsibility for loving yourself as you deserve and
need to be loved. Love is a skill which you can learn and
practice. If you were sexually abused as a child, you are
afraid of love because you don't know what love really is.
What you were told was love was instead a distorted, destructive experience that included serious violations of your
physical and emotional boundaries, your needs, and your
feelings. Now, as an adult, you must discover what love
really is so you can practice both giving and receiving it.

The teachings of Lazaris have been especially helpful to
me in learning to love myself. [For more information
about Lazaris, write or call Concept Synergy, P.O. Box 159
(M), Fairfax, CA. 94930, (415)-456-4855.] The section
that follows is a summary of some of his concepts and
understandings that are important for me. I have attended
several of his weekend workshops and have listened to and
watched many of his audio and video teaching tapes.

Lazaris speaks of seven levels of love. These steps in the
evolution of love show how we develop the capacity to
love more and more of God's creation. As you read, ask
yourself where you are in this process of realizing your
potential for living in love.

The first experience of love is for security. This is the love an infant feels for his mother. She meets all his needs for survival. She is the center of his world. He loves her because she cares for him and because he needs her care in order to survive.

Love for pleasure is the next experience of love. This is the love the young child feels when he discovers the joy of exploring the world and tasting its delights. He loves the fun he shares with his parents and his playmates. He revels in the pleasures of living and learning, and he loves the ones with whom he shares his adventures.

The third step in developing our capacity to love is loving for sensual pleasure. This is what the three to five year old, and later the teenager, discover. At this level, love is based on sensual, sexual pleasure. This is where many people get stuck in developing their potential for love. (If you were sexually abused, you are vulnerable sexually and particularly likely to get stuck at this developmental step. It is especially potent for you since your normal sexual development was distorted because of the abuse you experienced.)

The fourth developmental step is self-love. This level is of prime importance since all that follows is built upon this foundation. Self-love means giving to yourself and caring for yourself with a deep commitment to your responsibility for your life. It includes valuing yourself and respecting your feelings while striving to know yourself honestly and with humility. Truly knowing yourself and being honest with yourself about yourself are the greatest challenges of all. When you love yourself, you feel safe and secure and you experience the pleasure of being who you are. You are honest with yourself, and you accept your vulnerability, trusting that you will be able to care for yourself, no matter what challenge you encounter. This self-trust enhances your feeling of security and allows you to live with less fear of loss and hurt. Loving yourself is the ultimate technique. If you loved yourself fully, there would be no need for anything else. All you need to know you could learn and gain from within yourself. The more you love yourself, the more quickly all other techniques work.

Societal love is the fifth developmental step. When you love yourself well, you have abundant love to share with others — your mate, your family, your friends, your community, this nation, and our planet. Rather than sacrificing yourself for others, you give to others from the abundance of self-love that empowers you. The more love you give, the more you receive in return.

The sixth developmental step is humanitarian love. At this level, you love the nature and potential of human kind. You love and value your connection with all other beings and your connection with the planet and the universe we share. You feel the love energy that links you with All That Is.

The seventh and highest level of love is spiritual love; loving your Higher Self and the connection you experience with Source, God/Goddess/All That Is. Your spiritual life is your relationship with God/Goddess/All That Is. This is the ultimate expression of love which flows directly out of loving yourself completely and accepting yourself as a part of God/Goddess /All That Is. Just as the cells of your body are integral parts of the whole of your physical being, you are a cell in the body of God. Because you participate in the whole of creation, you are a creator, too. You take full responsibility for the reality you create, knowing that it is a mirror of the depth of your love of yourself and an expression of your love of God.

Love is a skill you can learn and practice. Your Saboteur would have you think that love is bells ringing and endless excitement that comes automatically. This is not so. You must practice the doing and being of love with yourself, with your friends, and with your family.

Love requires responsibility. When you love, you are responsible for what you do, what you feel, what you say, and what you think. You are responsible for both giving love and allowing yourself to receive love, too.

Love is an imperative. You must love. There really isn't a choice about love, because it is the truth about who you are.

Love is all there is and love is real. It is the only thing that is absolutely real. Everything else is an illusion. Love can hurt and *it can heal. You can use it either way. Love which is unexpressed or expressed in a manipulative way hurts. Love expressed honestly and openly heals.*

When you love yourself and value yourself, you own your tremendous creative power. This creative power includes the recognition that you have impact on others.

How are you affecting others? When you take responsibility for your impact on other people, you must look honestly at the games you play. How have you been punishing, rather than loving, with other people? How do you play the martyr? Though we don't like to notice or admit it, martyrs are mean, punishing people. Ask yourself who is the most punishing person in your life. Chances are that person is a martyr. Admit to yourself the truth that you play martyr, too. Odds are that you have been a major obstacle for at least one other person. When you can really let that truth in and feel its impact, you will transform yourself and stop being a martyr. Then you can forgive yourself for the pain you have caused in the past and release it. You can lovingly accept the power of your impact, the value of your life, and the creative nature of your being.

When you love yourself, know yourself, and trust yourself you can choose to need other people. You don't need them just for survival, pleasure, and sex. You choose to need them in your life because they enrich your life and help you reach beyond yourself into higher dimensions of love and spiritual consciousness. Your relationships expand your reality and bring you closer to God/ Goddess/All That Is.

Your outer relationships reflect the quality of your inner life. As you develop your relationship with your Higher Self and with God/Goddess/All That Is, you open yourself to love that is always present for you. Rather than desperately seeking love from other people to meet your needs, you learn to trust and rely upon your spiritual resources for love that never fails you. As you release your struggle to get love from parents, mates, or children who cannot ever give you all you yearn for, you free yourself to love these important people in your life out of choice, not needy desperation.

While you deepen your relationship with your Higher Self and with God/Goddess/All That Is, you also expand your Aware Consciousness which flows from Unconditional Love. You take your place as Chairman of your Internal Board of Directors, assuming that position of responsibility and authority that previously was not occupied. From this position of informed authority, you listen to what your various board members have to report and suggest to you. Then you make conscious choices that take the interests of the whole of you into account. You no longer allow your Internal Saboteur and its cohorts to dominate your thinking and control your life as they were able to do when no one occupied the Board Chairman's place at the head of the table. As Board Chairman, you are aware of what all your board members contribute. But you do not allow any single director to make your choices. You take advantage of the perspective you possess and the capacity you have to see the larger picture of your life purpose. Attuned to the guidance, wisdom, and love of your Higher Self, your Internal Board Chairman directs your mental, emotional, and physical reality in harmony with your highest good.

The chart below shows how your Internal Board of Directors functions. Your Board Chairman uses Aware Consciousness to make conscious choices. One side of your Inner Board is dominated by your Saboteur, operating in the energy of fear and feeding on repressed feelings. It relates to your Distorted/Adaptive Child and your Disturbed Adolescent Self. On the other side of your Internal Board, your Nurturing-Enabling Self, operating in the energy of love and generating joy and happiness, relates to your Natural Child and your Healthy Adolescent Self.

GOD/GODDESS/ALL THAT IS
↑   ↓
HIGHER SELF
↑   ↓
CHAIRMAN OF YOUR
INTERNAL BOARD OF DIRECTORS
USES AWARE
CONSCIOUSNESS
TO MAKE
CONSCIOUS CHOICES
↙   ↘

INTERNAL SABOTEUR	NURTURING-ENABLING SELF
(ENERGY OF FEAR)	(ENERGY OF LOVE)
Critic	Encourager
Judge	Limit-Setter
Worrier	Accepter
Pusher	Explorer/Seeker
Pleaser	Researcher/Questioner
Martyr	Clear-Thinker

DISTORTED/ADAPTIVE CHILD	NATURAL CHILD
Low Self-Esteem	Self-Confident
Controlled	Spontaneous
Shy	Playful
Destructive/Rebellious	Creative
Depressed/Blocked	Expressive
Passive	Active/Curious
Frightened/Rejecting	Loving/Lovable
Conforming	Experimenting
Apathetic	Energetic

DISTURBED ADOLESCENT	HEALTHY ADOLESCENT
Blaming	Powerful
Rebellious	Enthusiastic
Passive	Ambitious
Don't Care Attitude	Committed/Involved
Macho/Tough	Tender/Expressive/Sensual
Destructive	Creative

Suspicious	Trusting/Risking
Closed/Noncommunicative	Expressive
Failing	Succeeding
Frightened	Loving
Feeds on Repressed Anger and Sadness	Generates Joy and Happiness

BASIC MESSAGES:	BASIC MESSAGES:
1) You don't need help.	1) You're OK.
2) You don't have a Saboteur.	2) Express yourself.
3) Don't.	3) Explore.
4) Everything right is wrong; everything wrong is right. (Always tells lies.)	4) Ask for help.
	5) Think for yourself.
	6) Face your challenges.

As you develop your relationship with your Higher Self, your Nurturing-Enabling Self becomes stronger and stronger. It occupies more and more of the space in your inner awareness that once was dominated by your Internal Saboteur. Your Child-Self thrives in response to the love she experiences in this new internal environment. She is free to express her feelings without fear and to release her creativity. There are lots of strokes for her, too. She is appreciated, encouraged, and valued for being exactly who she is. Your Nurturing-Enabling Self cares for your physical well-being also. It makes sure you are well fed, get the exercise you need, and achieve a balance between work and play.

But even with a strong Nurturing-Enabling Self functioning well and loving your present day Inner Child, your damaged, abused Child-Self still slips back into the pain of your past. Though she is healing slowly in the loving environment you create for her now, her wounds are deep. She requires a great deal of love and attention to learn to trust again. She has a tendency to slip back into her old pain and hurt. When she does, she intrudes on your present reality. Just when you least want to be interrupted and distracted from your current experience, there she is feeling frightened, shy, unworthy, and different from others. Obviously, this is not how you want to feel when you are in the midst of an important business or social situation.

In order for your damaged Child-Self to receive all the healing love she needs, you can structure a new past reality for her to occupy. This may sound impossible, but remember that we are locked into perceiving time and space as linear. Beyond what we can comprehend within our physical form, everything is simultaneous. This means that your Child-Self is as real today as she was when you were three, four, or five years old. She lives in the past you remember where you experienced abuse. While you must deal with and release your feelings about that painful past, you don't have to leave your damaged Child-Self stuck there. The past is no more set in stone than the future is. You know that you are creating your future out of what you are doing today. Why not create a favorable past for yourself as well so you can drop the painful burdens you have been carrying?

Through meditation, you can lift your damaged Child-Self out of that old situation and set her down again in a new environment where she will have all the love she needs to thrive and grow. The new past you create for yourself will change you in the present and for the future. [For a discussion of these concepts, listen to the audio tape by Lazaris, *Your Unseen Friends*, published by Concept Synergy, P.O. Box 159 (M), Fairfax, CA. 94930, (415)-456-4855.]

In the meditation that follows, we will go to a place that is safe for you. There you will meet your damaged Child-Self and create a new reality for her. When the meditation is complete, she will have a new environment where she receives the healing love she needs. This will free you to express yourself in your adult reality without her pulling on your skirts. She will no longer need to vie for your attention, constantly looking for love and reassurance.

To understand how this change will affect you, imagine that you go to visit a friend, taking along a happy child who is at peace with herself. She is content to play quietly by herself while you and your friend talk. She doesn't disturb you or make annoying bids for your attention. You and your friend are free to enjoy each other and enjoy the child's presence as well. Contrast this picture with one in which you take along a child who feels unloved, unhappy, anxious, angry, and frightened. You and your friend won't be able to enjoy each other for the child's agitated, disruptive behavior.

During the meditation that follows, you will have an opportunity either to change the parents you had or to create new parents for yourself. Think about which choice fits best for you. If you elect to change your parents, visualize them as the most highly evolved people you can imagine them to be. See them getting along well with each other and having a truly healthy relationship which they cherish and enjoy. Notice how delighted they are with you, their child. They prepared themselves for your birth by healing their old hurts and pains. They study and learn all they can about children and how they grow and develop. They want nothing more than to be truly loving, enabling parents who help you develop your potential and express your creativity. They want you to learn to be responsible for yourself in healthy, appropriate ways, and to enjoy life being exactly who you are.

If you choose to create new parents for yourself, let them be exactly as you want them to be. Imagine them in great detail and make them as attractive, loving, successful, and happy as the parents you deserve to have. Whether you restructure your parents or create new ones, you can give your Child-Self whatever she wants in her new reality. Whatever went wrong in your life, fix it. If a parent died, bring him back. If you didn't have enough money, make sure there is plenty. Give yourself your dream of an ideal childhood and make it real for you.

When you are ready, move into the meditation. Read through it first and then close your eyes and experience it for yourself. If you have trouble remembering the details, tape record the directions and then listen to your tape to guide yourself. Be sure you read slowly and give yourself plenty of time to go through each step in the process. (Or, you can order audio tapes of this and the other meditations that I have recorded for you. There is an order form in the back of this book.)

Close your eyes and let yourself begin to release all your concerns and all your worries. Just imagine that you are putting them into a package which you can leave outside for now, knowing you can pick it back up later if you so desire. (Pause.) As you move inside yourself, become aware of your breath. Watch quietly as your breath moves in and out, in and out; be aware of the miracle of your body; how it functions so beautifully without your having to pay any conscious attention at all. Visualize your lungs as they fill with air each time you inhale; then see them as they empty completely with each exhalation. As you breathe in, you are breathing in the energy of love. As you breathe out, you are releasing the energy of fear. Breathing in love, breathing out fear; this is the rhythm of life; breathing in all that you need to nurture your body, breathing out all that is toxic that you need to release. Breathing in and letting go; breathing in and letting go.

Feel your body, relaxed and comfortable. If you are aware of any places that feel tight or painful, breathe into the tightness as you inhale and release the pain as you breathe out. Breathing into the tightness and letting it go; taking all the time you need to allow your body to feel completely relaxed and quiet. In your mind's eye, visualize a beautiful beam of pure white light, streaming down from above your head, and entering your head through the crown. Watch as this white light fills your head and moves down through your neck and shoulders, down your arms and into your hands where you can feel it pulsing and tingling.

Bring the light down your spine, through your chest, and into your heart. Feel into the energy of your heart, the energy of unconditional love. Let this love energy radiate out to encompass your whole body, moving through all your internal organs, filling you with love and healing all there is within you that needs healing and release. Let this light and love stream down through your legs, into your feet and toes, and visualize it moving out through the soles of your feet, into the earth beneath you. Bring your focus back to your heart as you feel your body relaxed and balanced, resting comfortably wherever you are, and in your mind, affirm, "I am centered in the energy of love."

Watch this radiant light fill your entire body and feel yourself a light being, glowing with love and peace. See the light moving out through the soles of your feet as it reaches into the earth and spreads beneath you, forming a beautiful system of roots; roots that nurture you, that give you support and stability; roots that connect you with the earth and keep you grounded. In your mind, affirm, "I an centered and grounded in the energy of love."

Now, see this clear, pure light radiating throughout your body, filling you and extending out and around your body, forming a beautiful chrysalis of love which protects and shields you. Visualize yourself within this cocoon of light, and again, affirm, "I am centered, grounded, and shielded in the energy of love."

Feel your whole body relaxed, heavy, and comfortable. Your scalp is relaxed, the muscles in your face have let go, your jaw is loose and easy. Notice your neck and shoulders, releasing them, relaxing them, and feel the relaxation spread down your arms into your hands and fingers. Your elbows are loose, your arms are heavy. Your chest is open so your breath flows even more completely than before. Relax your hips and thighs, your legs, your knees and your feet. You are filled with light; feeling loose, comfortable, and easy.

Take a nice deep breath now and as you exhale, visualize the number three and say it to yourself three times. (Pause) Take another deep breath, and on this exhalation, visualize the number two and say it to yourself three times. (Pause) On your next deep inhalation, see the number one, saying it to yourself three times as you exhale. As I count back from ten, you can relax and go deeper inside yourself with each descending number. Ten, nine, eight . . . seven, six, going deeper, five, four, three, two, and one.

Visualize yourself standing in front of a door, a door that is familiar, a door you've seen many times before. And, reaching up, open the door; feel yourself moving quietly through it, closing it gently behind you. You are standing at the top of a stairway, a beautiful, old stairway, built of stone. Feel yourself beginning to move down the stairs, moving easily and gracefully, moving down step by step, one step at a time, going down deeper and deeper. Your hands feel the coolness of the stone as they lightly touch the stairway wall. Your body is moving, you are very relaxed. Ahead of you at the bottom of the stairs, you see a place that is very special to you, a place where you feel safe, a place you liked to visit as a child; a place that is real or a place you visited in your imagination. As you move down the stairs, you are coming closer and closer to this familiar place. Take a deep breath and smell the richness of this place as you reach the bottom of the stairs now and step into your safe world. Let your eyes take in the visual beauty that surrounds you, noticing wondrous details you may never have seen before. Hear the sounds that are part of this experience and feel yourself here, completely present, moving around in this place, delighted to be back again. Find yourself a comfortable place where you can sit down and relax while you wait for your Child-Self to arrive. You're feeling very peaceful and centered as you gently invite the Child that is you to join you now in this special, safe place. Do not rush her or push her. Just let her know you are here and you are open to her.

Visualize her surrounded in light and love as she approaches you. Be aware of how she comes toward you. Is she excited to see you? Is she shy and afraid to come too close? Does she look very serious and too old for her years? Is she angry and defiant? However she appears, let her come as near you as she will. She needs to feel in charge of the space between you. She may sit in *your lap or she may keep some distance between you. It may or may not be hard for her to trust you.*

Wherever she chooses to be, greet her gently and lovingly. Let her know how glad you are to be here with her. Explain to her that you are here from her future and that you bring with you all the strength and wisdom you have acquired over the years. You are here now to help her and to heal her hurts and wounds. You are here to listen to her. Invite her to share with you anything she wants to tell. Tell her it is OK for her to cry or to be angry or frightened. You are here for her and she is safe. Give her all the time she needs. Follow her lead. Let her be in charge of how she shares. (Pause on your tape.)

When she has had plenty of time to share with you, invite her to sit in your lap if she will. Always be aware of keeping her surrounded in white light as you talk with her. When she is settled comfortably near you, tell her that you have come to take her out of the home where she has experienced so much hurt and pain. Have her watch with you as you surround her old reality in white light and pure, clear quartz crystal. Create a crystal shield that encompasses her old reality; a shield that prevents her re-entering that old reality unless you are with her so you can enter together in order for her to deal with any still unresolved feelings that she may need to face and release in the future. Tell her that every day, as you meditate, you will see that old reality surrounded in the healing energy of love, until it is completely dissolved and completely released. And explain to her that now you and she are going to create a new, safe, loving family for her; a home for her where she will be cared for as she needs and deserves to be; a home with parents who love her unconditionally and who know how to care for her so she can grow and thrive and be healed. Tell her about her new parents (or about how her old parents are now changed) and about the beautiful home they will share. Ask her if there are any special things she wants to have that will help her feel safe and comfortable in her new home. Put in as much detail as you can so you both have a clear picture of her new reality. Ask her what age she wants to be when she enters this new environment. If she wants to be younger than she is now, let her become that younger age as you continue to hold her in your arms. (Pause.) When she is ready, invite her new parents to join you. See them clearly as they approach the two of you. When they are seated, talk with them and tell them about this precious child who is about to become their own. Tell them all that you think they need to know about who she is, what she has experienced, what she needs now, what she likes, and how she wants to be cared for. When you feel ready, gently hand her to them and watch as they become acquainted. Assure your Child-Self that you will contact her regularly each day. Watch the three of them surrounded in light and love as they begin their bonding process with each other. Join hands with your Child-Self and her parents, forming an energy circle of love. When you feel ready, squeeze hands, release them and say goodbye, knowing you can return to this special place to join them at any time you choose, simply by taking the time to come inside yourself and enter this reality. Watch while they enter their home together as you move back toward the stairway and make your way easily and effortlessly back up the stairs. You are moving up the stairs, step by step, feeling very warm and peaceful, knowing your Child-Self is safe and happy, as you begin to return to the reality of the place where you are. Coming now to the top of the stairs, open the door, and feel yourself moving through to the other side. Listen as I count from one to five as you come back gradually, integrating what you have learned and created, feeling much better than before, feeling in perfect health and harmony. One, two, coming back gradually now, three, integrating what you have created, four, feeling much better than before, feeling in perfect health, and five, opening your eyes.

Take the time to write about this experience in your journal so you will have a record of this important healing event in your life. Each day, take the time when you meditate, to visit your Child-Self in her new home to make sure she is happy and to be aware of what she wants to share with her new family on that particular day. During the day, check in with her periodically, as you become accustomed to knowing that your Child-Self is safe and beautifully cared for in her new home.

Once you have taken this critical step of removing your damaged Child-Self from the home in which she was abused, you know that she is out of danger. Yet the scars from her past are still with her. The love she receives from you and from her new family will hasten her healing. But she also needs help to overcome the impact of the abuse on her personality and her behavior.

For this part of the healing process, imagine that you are a skilled therapist for children and adolescents. You are assigned to work with your damaged Child-and-Adolescent Self. You have removed her from her old, abusive environment. Now you are to see her each day and work intensively with her in your meditations. Your Higher-Self will always be available to consult with you and to guide you in your contacts with her. And the steps outlined below will help you with a specific program to follow.

1) Do an extensive assessment and history taking with her. What exactly do you know about her? Do some research by talking to family members and friends who knew you when you were a child. Check to see what documents are available from your childhood. Perhaps there are old school papers, drawings, or report cards. Look at picture albums and home movies, if there are any. Get a clear picture of how your Child and Adolescent look. Notice all you can about the pictures you examine. (It may help to take your albums with you to one of your therapy sessions so you can have the benefit of another person's perspective on what the pictures reveal.) Who appears in the pictures? Who is missing? Who stands next to whom? What patterns emerge as you look through the pictures? See if you can tell where big changes happened in your life (and when the abuse began) by looking at your eyes and your expressions and how they change over the years. For some people, these changes are remarkably obvious. Others learn to act for the camera and cover their pain in the pictures.

2) How does your Child-Self feel? What is the core of
her pain? After releasing her rage and sorrow, what is left
to be healed?

3) What is her personality like? Look at her as a child,
trying to smooth over her pain. Watch her as an adolescent, blaming others for her problems, but feeling helpless
and terrified still. What are her goals? What are her ideals?
What does she expect? What is her impact on your life?
Remember what you know about the differences between
healthy children and adolescents and those who are
depressed and disturbed. (See the chart below.) Use this
knowledge to help your Child-and-Adolescent Selves
access the loving, creative, positive dimensions of themselves. Introduce them to dolls, stuffed animals, music, all
kinds of art materials and projects, and let them dance. If
necessary, take lessons yourself to facilitate the healthy
development of their creative potential.

HEALTHY, LOVING CHILD	DISTORTED/ADAPTIVE CHILD
Playful	Quiet
Spontaneous	Reserved
Loveable	Has an Emotional Wall
Loving	Frightened
Creative	Depressed, Destructive
Curious	Shy
Sensual	Tense
Aware of Sexuality	Denies Sexuality
Aware of Feelings	Disconnected from Feelings
Expressive	Non-expressive or Misbehaving
Adventurer	Adaptive Pleaser

HEALTHY/LOVING ADOLESCENT	FRIGHTENED/DISTURBED ADOLESCENT
Powerful	Blaming
Enthusiastic	Rebellious
Ambitious	Passive

Energetic	Don't Care Attitude
Tender/Sensual	Macho/Tough
Experimenting/Exploring	Conforming
Creative	Destructive
Risking	Suspicious
Expressive	Closed/Noncommunicative or Acting Out

Now ask how your Child-Self feels about her sexuality? Contrast her feelings with those of the Adolescent in you. Your sexuality is a dimension of your being that was distorted by the sexual abuse you experienced. You were not ready for sex when you were forced to first experience it. The feelings you discovered were powerful ones, ones that were too big for the small body you occupied. In addition, you sensed the guilt your abuser felt. Guilty feelings became associated with sex for you. You knew this was something that was forbidden and was supposed to be kept secret. Sexual arousal became linked with guilty, forbidden behavior.

You may have dealt with your sexual abuse by cutting yourself off from the experience. Many children leave their bodies and watch what is happening to them from a vantage point outside their physical being. This enables them to avoid the pain and/or the uncomfortable arousing feelings they encounter. The child may sense that she is not supposed to show any emotion at all while she is being abused. Or, she may discover that her abuser is pleased if she responds to his touch and likes what he does to her.

If you blocked your feelings during your abuse or disassociated yourself from them, chances are that you may still cut yourself off from your sexuality. You may be afraid to flirt with men or to take the initiative sexually with you mate or partner. You may have learned to act as if

you are not a sexual being. This does not mean you don't
have sexual relationships. But, you are probably most comfortable and aroused when the lights are out and you
feel very secure with your partner. You may also enjoy
relationships that are very new or secret and forbidden.
The daring, risk-taking behavior involved taps back into
the guilty, forbidden feelings you first associated with
sexual arousal.

If you found that your abuser liked your responding to
him, you may have become overly identified with your
Sexual-Self. You may have decided that your sexuality is
your major attribute. It may be your primary means of
relating to other people. If this is your pattern, you may
engage in promiscuous sexual behavior, taking risks that
are dangerous to your safety and well-being. You may lead
a double life, appearing to be a reliable, responsible person
much of the time while visiting bars and picking up strange
men for one-time encounters at other times. In this
way, you re-enact the secret abuse you experienced
in childhood.

Ask yourself how your sexually-damaged Child-Self is
impacting your life in the present. What is she trying to
accomplish? How does she take you over? How are you
rejecting her? How does she feel about that rejection? How
is she trying to get your attention? How does she manipulate you and outsmart you? To answer these questions,
let yourself write and be open to whatever comes when you
ask your Child-and-Adolescent Sexual Selves to communicate
with you in this way. You may be surprised by what unfolds
as you write. As you get to know your sexually-damaged
selves, appreciate them for sharing with you and being willing to let you know them better. Spend some time during
your daily meditation connecting with your Sexual-Selves
(the Child and the Adolescent) and integrating them into
your life. You want them to be beautifully visible dimensions of your being and you want to be in charge of their
behavior. Indeed, as you take them into account, love and

appreciate them, they will have no reason to continue to repeat rebellious, destructive behavioral patterns.

The next area to explore is how you can create assets for yourself from your hurts. How can you take advantage of what your damaged Child-and-Adolescent Selves experienced to enhance your life now?

Allow yourself plenty of time to explore these questions and to complete your assessment of your Child-and-Adolescent Selves. Be sure you feel a genuine understanding of these parts of you and embrace them in love that is deep and unconditional. All of this will prepare you to transform the destructive unconscious programs your damaged-selves created as a result of the sexual abuse you experienced.

Now you are ready for a transformational journey into your unconscious mind. Follow the steps outlined below. (This material and the suggestions that follow are adapted from the Lazaris workshop titled "Vision Quest" which he presented in Atlanta in November, 1987.)

1) Prepare for your transformational meditation. You can begin by appreciating the power of your unconscious mind. Your unconscious mind gathers and stores all your experiences and your learning and keeps these resources available for you. It also provides balance, harmony, and consistency in the ways you function. Your unconscious mind makes sure that what you believe and what you create in your life are consistent. If you believe you always succeed, you always do. If you believe you always get hurt in relationships, your unconscious mind makes sure that belief goes unchallenged. It also filters all the information you receive and translates it so it fits into the life programs you established long ago.

Obviously, your unconscious mind can be your best friend or your worst enemy, depending upon the belief systems and unconscious programs you have adopted. In order to create lasting change in your life, you must reprogram your unconscious mind so that its programs and beliefs are congruent with your current level of wisdom, understanding, and loving acceptance of yourself.

Reprogramming your unconscious mind requires that you get into its control center. We will call this control center the core of your unconscious mind. You have discovered through meditation and hypnosis that it is easy enough to enter your unconscious mind. But getting into its control center is another matter. Long ago you established your unconscious programs, entered them into your computer center located at the core of your unconscious, and then locked them in. When you set these programs, you also left instructions that under no circumstances were you to be permitted to re-enter your control center and make changes in what you had established.

In order to get into the core of your unconscious mind now, you must bypass these old instructions. Two elements are necessary to accomplish this mission. First, you must appreciate your unconscious mind. Feel your gratitude for all it does for you; for how well your life has evolved despite your hurt and pain. Appreciate all the resources you possess because of your experiences. Surround your unconscious mind with gratitude and genuine thanks for all the incredible ways it serves you. Communicate with it and tell it that you want to update some old programs. Again, appreciate how faithfully, consistently, and perfectly it has carried out all your programs. Explain to it what you want to accomplish now. Then, you must call upon an ancient, wise man or woman to guide you and protect you as you enter to make the changes you desire.

But before your ancient wise one joins you, create your own mental picture of how your unconscious mind looks and works. Perhaps the image of a huge bank of computers will work for you. Or, it may be like a gigantic switchboard with thousands of plugs and connections. It could be like a vast library. Intuitively, select an image that feels right for you.

Invite a guide to accompany you on your journey to the

core of your unconscious. This guide can be a librarian, a computer expert, a spiritual entity, or a friend. Explain to your guide that you want him to join you as you enter your unconscious and as you come back out again after your mission is completed. He is to wait for you while you enter the core of your unconscious with your ancient wise one.

2) Enter a relaxed state of consciousness, using the methods for centering and releasing tension that you like best. When you are ready, bring your guide into your awareness and travel with him toward the core of your unconscious. It may help to imagine yourself entering a cave or traveling to the center of the earth to symbolize this journey you are making inside yourself. Take plenty of time for this phase of your meditation.

3) When you arrive at the outer wall of the core of your unconscious, go through your appreciation process. Surround the core of your unconscious with gratitude, expressing your thanks for all it gives you and accomplishes for you. Remember that this is an essential phase of your mission. Do not hurry yourself. Feel your appreciation and stay with this experience until you sense that it is now possible for you to enter the core.

4) Invite your ancient wise man or woman to join you. Visualize your old one, realizing that this archetype of wisdom and experience has existed through all time. Feel the strength and serenity of his presence. Join hands with him and let your old one wrap you in his cloak. Thus protected and guided, you are ready to enter your unconscious control center.

5) As you enter, visualize your control center as clearly and vividly as you can. Once you are inside, make the changes you need to make. Unplug or de-program each aspect of your old system that you want to disconnect. You are re-wiring your unconscious mind, disconnecting your old, self-defeating patterns and beliefs and connecting your new, enabling beliefs. You are disconnecting your sexual confusion and re-connecting a new healthy sexuality and

sensuality. Dispose of the debris of your old beliefs. Burn them or drop them into a great void. Now make the new connections that are necessary for you. Stay open to the guidance you feel about what you may have missed that still needs to be tended to and changed. When you feel that you have completed your project, take one more opportunity to look around you to see if there are still stray details that you must handle. Are there any last plugs you need to pull; any remaining connections that need to be switched? Continue to unplug and re-connect your new system until you know you have accomplished your mission. Then step back and watch the new program you have created as it functions for you for the first time. Take plenty of time to appreciate your work and what it will mean to you in the future. Program in one last instruction that locks your changes into the system. These changes cannot be tampered with or modified unless in the future you decide to return to the core of your unconscious mind with your ancient guide to make new adjustments. Look into the eyes of your ancient one now, expressing your gratitude without words as you leave the core of your unconscious mind together. Close and lock the door again when you have made your exit.

Once again, take the time to appreciate all of what you have done and accomplished. Appreciate yourself and the ancient one. Then watch as he slips quietly away. Rejoin your original guide and prepare to return to your present reality. Thank your guide for accompanying you and for waiting for you while you went into the core of your unconscious mind. Feel the joy of knowing that you have healed your unconscious mind and healed your damaged Child-Self. Feel the joy of knowing that now you are free.

Over the months and years ahead, all of you will thrive in the new reality you have created for yourself. As you grow and experience how well your new unconscious programs work, you will feel more and more freedom, spontaneity, wonder, excitement, and creative power. And you will be free in your adult reality to function with the energy of your Child-and-Adolescent Selves aligned with you in a partnership of love, confidence, and genuine support and self-acceptance.

If you don't allow the meditation process to work for you, look for the payoffs you cling to by holding onto your old pain. Some people are forever poised on the brink of success but are afraid to take the final leap into a new reality. It is as if they stand on the edge of a deep abyss. Though this abyss is quite deep, it is also very narrow. One step across is all that is required to move into a totally new world of love, joy and success. But taking that one step across that incredibly deep chasm looks terrifying, especially if you look down and imagine you will fall into nothingness if you dare to make a move. Try looking ahead of you at the land on the other side. See how inviting and beautiful that territory really is. Be aware of the hands that reach out to encourage you to come across the great divide. Notice that only one step across is required. You've made millions of longer leaps before. You can cross this chasm now — if you're willing to take the risk, to look ahead, and to reach out and accept the help that is offered you. You also must be willing to leave behind the place where you have been standing. You must let go of it and all the misery you are accustomed to and comfortable with. Are you ready to take the risk, to let go, to allow your rites of passage to begin?

CHAPTER XIV

FORGIVENESS

STAGE IV: FORGIVENESS AND CONFRONTATION

STEP ONE: Understanding the why and the how of forgiveness. Beginning the process of forgiving and releasing your abuser and yourself.

STEP TWO: Recognizing and taking responsibility for the burden you have carried by keeping the incest/abuse secret and thus protecting yourself, your abuser, and your family from facing what happened.

STEP THREE: Preparing for the confrontation; continuing to face your rage, express your feelings, write in your journal, and work with your dreams. Working through your fears of confronting and facing conflict by practicing simulated confrontations with your therapist and in your therapy group.

STEP FOUR: Accepting that parts of the incest/abuse experience may have been pleasurable. Forgiving yourself for any pleasure you felt when you were abused and releasing your guilt for feeling pleasure in the present. Affirming, "I now allow myself to experience pleasure without guilt."

STEP FIVE: Confronting your abuser and your family.

STEP SIX: Completing the forgiveness process.

(Stage Four of the Healing Process includes forgiveness and confrontation. I will discuss the why and the how of forgiveness in this chapter. Chapter XV will deal with confrontation and completing the forgiveness process.)

Let's go back to the women's group now as we move into forgiveness, the most essential stage in the healing process. Each member of the group is working with the fundamental model for healing. She recognizes her Saboteur, is developing her Nurturing-Enabling Self, and learning to set limits within herself and in her relationships with others. She has created a new past reality for her Child-Self to occupy. Each woman is in her own unique process of releasing rage and sorrow. In order to help everyone take a giant step forward through this stage and on into forgiveness, the group, through its own creative process, developed an idea we dubbed "the great fence-and-bottle caper."

During a group session, Jan remembered a time when her mother threw a glass at her, shattering the glass against the wall and drenching her with milk. As she talked about this experience, she realized how much she would like to throw glasses and to break them herself. "It would be so satisfying, just to watch them break and not care about anything but getting to throw another one," she commented. Several people responded to what Jan said. Melissa, with a mischievous look in her eyes, mentioned that she knew where she could get lots of old glass bottles. It didn't take long to concoct the caper; we would have a rage session. There is a private grassy area outside the group room that is enclosed by a weathered cedar fence. Melissa offered to bring a supply of glass bottles. We also planned to cut a garden hose into short sections ideal for hitting the fence. On the appointed day, we would gather outside and encourage each other as everyone who chose to had a turn hitting the fence and throwing bottles at it.

Early on the appointed day, I meditated to prepare myself and ask for guidance in structuring this experience so it would be productive and positive for all of us. The plan I devised began with a group meditation. Each member would select a partner to work with during the rage release. After we completed the release, we would return to the group room to process the experience and deal with the feelings that needed to be faced. We would close with another short meditative sharing.

Everyone was dressed in "smashing clothes" — jeans and T-shirts. When we gathered in the group room to begin our session, some were eager to begin. Others were apprehensive. We joined hands to begin the group with our usual energy circle. After the energy exchange, I stated that I would structure the experience to make sure we were all prepared and adequately protected during the fence beating and bottle throwing.

Then I began the meditation, inviting each person to go inside herself to relax and release her everyday concerns and worries. After a period of breathing and body relaxation, I suggested that each member go to her own safe place from childhood to prepare to meet her angry Child-Self. When the angry child entered her reality, I asked her to greet this part of herself and explain to her that she was about to have an opportunity to express some of her long-buried rage. She told her child that she would be present to encourage and protect her as she let these feelings emerge. (In effect, her partner would play the role of her Adult-Self while her Child-Self got to beat the fence with a hose and then smash bottles.)

I also asked her to invite her Protector-Controller part to enter this scene. When the Protector-Controller was present, she asked that part of herself for permission for her Child-Self to participate in the rage release experience. She assured the Protector-Controller that her intent was to make its job easier by releasing some of the burden she had been carrying since childhood. She asked the Protector-Controller if it had any objections, and requested its permission to participate in the group process. If at any time during the experience, the Protector-Controller wanted to stop her participation, she acknowledged that it could do so. When she had its agreement, she again encouraged her Child-Self to join in the rage release and invited her to come with her back to the reality of the present moment.

When the meditation was completed, I asked if there

was anyone who did not have permission to participate. No one declined. We gathered our tools and went outside.

The next few minutes were spent preparing the area for the bottle smashing. We spread out old sheets on the ground and tacked them to the fence to catch the broken glass. Bricks were piled against the fence to provide an effective target point for the bottle throwing. When all was ready, we paused to determine who wanted to go first.

Katherine was ready to begin. With her partner encouraging her, she took a section of hose and began hitting the fence. Each blow left a mark on its weathered wood surface. We watched, fascinated, as a sunburst pattern of licks started to emerge. Seeing the mark left by each blow added a powerful touch to the experience. We all knew the marks we each carried from our own abuse experiences. Now we could transfer those scars to the fence and symbolically free ourselves from them. Hitting the fence turned out to be much more satisfying than we had anticipated. We took turns beating it and cheering each other on.

Smashing bottles was the next step. Katherine surprised everyone with the power of her throw. She began with an old Ragu spaghetti jar, which turned out to be sturdier than expected. It survived several vigorous tosses. More bricks were added to the target point, and Katherine selected a different object to smash. This time she found an old Gordon's gin bottle. Holding it by its neck, she took aim and unleashed a potent shot. A loud pop and flying glass proclaimed her success. The group cheered.

Elaine was reluctant to begin. I stood next to her, hitting the fence myself, and encouraging her to breathe and let go as she pounded. Gradually, she relaxed. Soon she was enjoying herself, alternating between beating the fence and smashing bottles. Melissa was cautious at first, too. But, the group energy was powerful and soon she was pounding and throwing freely. Jeanette videotaped our event. When Melissa took over the camera duties from her, Jeanette had fun clowning, delaying her participation even more. When she finally let go with her rubber hose, she allowed her anger to come. Afterwards, she was radiant from the energy release she experienced.

When we had broken all of our glass supply, we concluded that old liquor bottles were best. They held powerful associations for those who had an alcoholic parent, and they were great for smashing. With more comments about how to improve the logistics next time, we returned to the group room to process what had happened. The women I saw around me now presented a striking contrast to those who had gathered here an hour earlier. Eyes sparkled. Skin glowed. There was a new aura of confidence. They had owned the power of their rage. Each, in turn, described her own feelings now and during the release. Having faced these monster emotions, they knew they were ready for the rest of the healing work that lay ahead.

When it was time to close the group, we joined hands once more. With eyes closed, I asked each woman to center herself and reconnect with her Angry Child-Self and her Protector-Controller. She thanked them and checked to see if these parts of her had any comments she needed to hear. She then embraced them both and brought them back inside her, welcoming her angry self that had been so long denied and rejected. We squeezed hands, released our circle, and trooped outside to clean up the broken glass. The great fence-and-bottle caper was completed.

As I reflected on our experience later, I marveled at how satisfying it was to let go in this way. This went much deeper than hitting with padded batacas. With the rubber hoses, we could hear the impact of our blows and see the marks they left. The power of the group energy allowed us to go more deeply into our rage than one person working alone would have done. Smashing the bottles was especially potent. The shattered glass symbolized the shattering impact sexual abuse had made on our lives. Letting our rage go in this way, we knew we were not passing the damage on to other people. We were cleansing ourselves in order to heal our lives. We could leave our marks on a fence and our broken shards of glass in a garbage container. But we wouldn't keep repeating our old abuse patterns within ourselves and in our families.

The fence-and-bottle caper was an enormous release for everyone. At the next group session, three members reported new memories they had recovered in the intervening week. Others were ready to move on into forgiveness, confrontation, and transformation. Though they knew more anger and sadness would emerge in their work, they also knew they would express and release their emotions without staying stuck with them. They could move ahead, backtracking whenever necessary to deal with deeper levels of rage and sorrow when they encountered them.

Releasing rage releases guilt, a crucial step in forgiving yourself and forgiving your abuser. When you let go of rage, you free yourself from a self-imposed prison of guilt and self-punishment. Fritz Perls, father of Gestalt Therapy, liked to point out that guilt is "unexpressed resentment." Lazaris states that guilt is not a true emotion. Real emotions have both a positive and negative polarity. Love can hurt and love can heal. Fear warns us of dangers that are real. It can also consume us in self-sabotage. But, guilt has no positive attribute. It is not the source of our moral and ethical imperatives. Conscience is. Guilt is a synthetic emotion that serves no useful purpose.

Bob Mandel in his book, *Open Heart Therapy*, states:
> *Often we confuse guilt and conscience, thinking we should listen to the voice of guilt in order to live a life of integrity. Guilt is your mind disapproving of your heart. Conscience is your heart reminding your mind of what you really value. They are quite opposite states, though your ego can confuse you into thinking you have a "guilty conscience."* (Mandel, Bob, *Open Heart Therapy*, Berkeley, CA., Celestial Arts, 1984, p. 73.)

Conscience keeps you connected with your spiritual

nature and your moral imperatives. If you feel guilty about cheating someone else, forgiveness is not enough. Cheating is a matter of conscience. You must make restitution and honor your moral principles. But, when you feel guilty about having pleasure, forgiveness is all that is necessary. This is not a matter of conscience. Instead it reflects lack of self-love and self-acceptance, coupled with buried feelings of rage and sorrow.

Forgiveness is the most critical aspect of healing. But forgiveness is not real until rage and sorrow are recognized, acknowledged, and released. Unfortunately, phony forgiveness often is substituted for real release. Instead of being honest about their anger, martyrs make statements like, "I can forgive you but I can never forget what you did." That's not forgiveness. It's a nasty manipulation from an assumed position of superiority which rests on unacknowledged rage. True forgiveness comes after rage is recognized and released. It flows from the heart and is the fruit of self-love.

Only when we love and accept all of ourselves, including the parts that feel rage, hurt, and sorrow, can we truly forgive ourselves and others. Forgiveness is "giving for." It is giving for me and giving for you. It frees me from the pain and hurt I cause myself when I hang onto resentful feelings I need to release. It is a gift for myself. Forgiveness also clears my relationship with you, whether or not you release your resentments of me.

Forgiveness frees you from the past. Until you forgive your abuser, you remain stuck in the abuse with him. You carry him about within you, day after day. Your energy is spent bearing the burden of your pain and trying to contain it so you can function with part of your resources available in the present.

When you forgive your abuser, you set your burden aside. It is like putting down a huge sack of heavy rocks you have been carrying about on your back. What a relief! Before you let go of your load, you have no idea how you will feel without it. Once you release it, a delightful surprise is in store for you. Then you must forgive yourself for carrying this burden for so many years.

Why is it so hard to let go? Why is pain so precious? The burden you carry is a familiar companion. You know what life is like when you keep it with you. You don't really love yourself, so you think you don't deserve life without hindrances. You are into judgment and condemnation of yourself and of others. You want to feel self-righteous so you can have someone to hate, someone who wronged you. You want that person to be someone outside yourself, an external force you can't control. You want to remain a victim and reap the destructive payoffs that accompany that position.

You are not clear that you are the one who creates your reality. You are the one who is hurting you, refusing to love you, clinging to your burden. You are allowing your fear of letting go to sabotage your life. You don't let yourself see that you have a choice.

If you were abused as a child, you decided in your child's mind that you were bad. "I must be bad," you thought. "They wouldn't do these things to me if I were good like other children. This is because there is something wrong with me." And so you tried to be good. "Maybe if I'm good enough, if I try hard enough, I can get them to stop." You would prove your worth if you ever could get your abuser to stop. When you became an adult, you found other abusers to help you continue your quest for your self-worth. Now you say to yourself, "If I can just make him be the wonderful person I know deep down he really is, he won't treat me so badly. If I can be a good enough woman, he will love me and not want to hurt me." And then you will know, finally know, that you are OK. You will have become so good that your abuser will have no cause to hurt you.

Your Child-Self knows no boundaries between you and other people. It imagines you control others with your goodness or your badness. This is your Child's defense against recognizing your vulnerability and taking responsibility for taking care of yourself. As long as you try to love others enough to make them change, you ignore reality and reject your own needs and feelings.

The person who abuses you chooses to do so. He abuses you because he does not know how to love himself or anyone else. He has many deep issues he must face within himself before he will be different. Though he may promise that never, ever again will he hurt you as he has done in the past, he will not be able to perform on that promise unless he invests his time, his energy, his money, and himself in an intensive therapeutic program over an extended period of time. Otherwise, though his intentions may be good, he will continue to be subject to outbursts of his rejected rage and sorrow from childhood. During these outbursts, he allows his rejected feelings to take him over completely. Both of you are at the mercy of his destructive rage.

When you look honestly at your abuser and see him as he is, you realize that you cannot control his rages. Neither can he in his current state of emotional development. You can control yourself and decide to stop carrying your abuse burden. You can set your burden down, because you love yourself and know that your worth is real, no matter how you have been treated in the past. Your worth is given. It is a fact of your existence. You and everyone else are absolutely worthy, just because you are. You are a part of God. Your worthiness is a fact of your spiritual being.

Your task is to see the innocence and worth of your Child-Self and forgive yourself for your lack of power to stop the abuse. You must forgive yourself for participating in it and forgive your parents or abusers for their ignorant, insensitive, destructive behavior toward you. As you have discovered, by not forgiving yourself, you have continued to create similar pain over and over again. When you forgive yourself and your abuser, you will be free of that pain and ready for love to take its place.

Self-love is the key to forgiveness. It is the key to releasing your burdens of hurt, anger, guilt, and revenge. When you love yourself unconditionally, there is no room for clinging to your painful handicaps. Instead you lay them down, having faced them and cleared your emotions related to them. You forgive yourself and you forgive your abusers.

Sanaya Roman, in her book, *Living With Joy, Keys To Personal Power And Spiritual Transformation*, states:

> *Another quality of self-love is forgiveness. Some of you hang onto old issues, feeling the anger over and over. It is irritation at yourself, perhaps, or at another who let you down. The higher self knows forgiveness. If there is anything you are hanging onto, an anger, a hurt, a negative feeling about another, then you are keeping it in your aura. The person you are mad at is affected, but not as much as you will be. Anything you are carrying in you towards another sits in your aura and acts as a magnet for more of the same. There is most definitely a reason for forgiveness, for it cleanses and heals your aura.* (Roman, Sanaya, *Living With Joy, Keys To Personal Power And Spiritual Transformation*, Tiburon, California, H.J. Kramer, Inc. 1986, pp. 47-48.)

Visualize yourself forgiven and forgiving, free of your burdens. See your aura, bright and clear, radiating through you and all around you. Let yourself be the being of light that you truly are. Watch the abundance of love and prosperity you draw to yourself now. Remember how you used to be with your aura disturbed by the pain you clung to. Notice the difficulties, pains, and hurts you used to attract through the magnetic power of your burdens. Release that out-dated image and feel into the radiance that is you now. And give thanks.

Unconditional love is the key to valuing yourself and forgiving yourself. When you really value yourself, you create a reality for yourself that works. Even if you are in the midst of a reality that is negative, you can change that reality by forgiving yourself and valuing yourself. Lazaris describes seven essential elements in the experience of valuing and loving yourself unconditionally. I want to share them with you because I have found this model so useful.

UNCONDITIONAL LOVE

The Key to Valuing Yourself

1). *Self-Awareness. You must be aware of your thoughts, feelings, choices, and behavior and willing to look at yourself honestly and lovingly. You have impact, therefore, you must be aware of how you use it.*

2). *Self-Worth. You must accept your worth which is a fact of your existence. You are part of God; therefore you are 100% worthy. Period. There are no exceptions. No matter what mistakes you create, your worth remains intact. Everyone is equally worthy. A murderer and Mother Theresa have equal worth. The difference is that one is aware of his worth and the other is not. You cannot become more worthy than you've always been because you have always been totally worthy. When you realize your worth, you appreciate your spiritual nature.*

3). *Self-Esteem. Your self-esteem is determined by you from within yourself. It is a function of your honesty, integrity, trustworthiness, and personal responsibility. Your self-esteem is your validation of yourself which grows as you learn that you can trust yourself.*

4). *Self-Love. Self-love is also a given. You are born with it. Unfortunately, it may have been pounded deep within you and out of sight as you grew up. All you have to do now is to uncover it and let it shine through you.*

5). *Self-Confidence. Self-confidence is based on your ability to cope with life. It is learned as you develop the knowing that you can make it, that you can get through your challenges, no matter what they are.*

6). *Self-Respect. Self-respect involves appreciating your emotional nature. When you respect yourself, you honor your feelings, acknowledge them, and release them without clinging to them.*

7). *Self-Realization. Self-realization is directing your impact, using your talents, and realizing your goals. You recognize that you have impact and that you can direct it. You know yourself as the creator you are.*

(For further development of these ideas, see the video tape by Lazaris titled *Unconditional Love.* It is published by Concept Synergy, P.O. Box 159 (M), Fairfax, CA, 94930.)

The why of forgiveness is clear. How to forgive yourself and others is another question. Let's look now at the process of forgiveness. Again, I draw upon the teaching of Lazaris, specifically his video tape titled *Forgiving Yourself.* The outline that follows focuses on forgiving yourself. Once you go through these steps for yourself, use them also for forgiving your abusers, one at a time.

THE FORGIVENESS PROCESS

1). Get clear about what you want to forgive yourself (your abuser) for. The best way to do this is to write out your secrets, making a commitment to yourself to be brutally honest with what you say. As you write, you may remember more and more that you need to forgive. Give yourself plenty of time to really experience this crucial first step in the forgiveness process. It is healing in itself. When you have completed your inventory, ask yourself why you want to forgive yourself (him). Again write down your answer to this question.

(As we go through the forgiveness process, I will share with you my responses to these questions when I first watched the Lazaris *Forgiving Yourself* video tape. Because I was watching the tape with a group of people, we took only a few minutes to write during a pause in the lecture. So my responses are an abbreviated version of what you will want to do.)

I want to forgive myself for thinking I was bad because I had sexual experiences with my father and with my mother. I want to forgive myself for the ways I have used those experiences and my feelings of guilt to hurt myself, my parents, my children, and my husbands.

I want to forgive myself so I will be free from the pain, confusion, self-hatred, and self-destructive patterns I have used to punish myself over the years.

2). Take time now to feel your positive emotions about forgiving yourself (your abuser). Be aware also of your negative feelings: your fears, sadness, and anger. Write about all of what you feel.

I am excited about forgiving myself. I feel hopeful and loving. I want to forgive myself and release these old hurts. I feel peaceful and right about doing this.

Another part of me is frightened. I don't know what life will be like without my guilt. This will stop me from clinging to my parents with my resentments. I feel sad to let go of all of this. Somehow it makes me special. Who will I be without it? Maybe I don't deserve forgiveness.

3). Ask yourself what your Child-Self has to say about forgiving yourself (your abuser). What does she want and how does she feel? Consider also what your Adolescent-Self has to say. Write out your responses.

My Child-Self says; "Please take this burden away. I want to be free. I want to live. I want to feel love. I don't want to hurt like this anymore. I am innocent. I am not bad."

My Adolescent-Self says; "I'm afraid to let them (my parents) off the hook. Holding onto this gives me a feeling of power and control. But I also hate the pain. I want to be free, too. I don't want to live the rest of my life involved in this old mess with my parents. I want out of this and into the good things I know I deserve."

Ask yourself about the specific payoffs you will experience when you forgive yourself (your abuser). What have been your payoffs for not forgiving yourself (him)?

Payoffs for forgiving myself: I will be free to be who I really am, without feeling bad or different from others. I will feel confident and triumphant when I forgive myself and put sexual abuse behind me for good. I will be free to succeed, enjoy life's pleasures, and have happy, fulfilling relationships with others.

Payoffs for not forgiving myself: Not forgiving myself has given me an excuse for not succeeding in love and marriage. It has enabled me to keep punishing myself and spoiling my pleasure. It has kept me entangled in my parents' problems, a child clinging to the past rather than a grown-up living successfully in the present.

What are you going to do once you have forgiven yourself (your abuser)?

I am going to be totally successful in creating what I am here to create for my own growth and good and for a larger good as well.

4). Experience a meditation, forgiving yourself (your abuser) for the specific issue you are releasing. (There is a beautiful meditation on forgiveness on the Lazaris video, *Forgiving Yourself*. At the end of this chapter, you will find a meditation I have written especially for forgiving yourself and your abuser for sexual abuse. This meditation is also available on audio tape. See the order form in the back of this book.)

5). Ask yourself what you have learned from your meditative experience. What do you want to do now? *I have learned to reunite with myself, truly releasing what is past and welcoming and fully experiencing my new wholeness.*

Now I am ready to be completely successful; to use my talents to the fullest; to accomplish all that I have set for myself to do and to give. I also am ready to allow love in my life; to live one day at a time with love, patience, and trust as my highest good unfolds.

6). What does this mean now that you are (he is) forgiven? What can you do now? Where can you go from here?

Now I truly can help others heal themselves. I can program and manifest the reality I choose. I can solve the problems I face. I can fully and completely enjoy my life, feel loved and be loving.

7). Your challenge now is to be and do from your new position of forgiveness and inner peace.

I am free to live fully, forgiven fully, being all of who I am. I am joyous and grateful.

Forgiveness is an experience of transformation. It requires a profound letting-go that is like allowing your old, familiar, burdened self to die so your new, free, healed self can emerge. This may not be easy for you to allow. If you find yourself resisting the forgiveness process and the meditation, you may need to do more work with releasing anger and sorrow.

Another possibility to consider is that you may be fearful of such a deep transformation. Your Protector-Controller part, encouraged by your Saboteur, may be afraid to allow you to let go. If this is the case, talk with your Protector-Controller, assuring it that you are not trying to get rid of it. You will need its services after your transformation. Its job will be easier and more pleasant then, too. Be aware that your Saboteur is actively opposed to your healing. It will orchestrate your resistance to completing your forgiveness process. Your Saboteur will try to block you from releasing your feelings and from letting go of your burden of abuse. Notice the distractions it creates, the excuses it generates, the reasons it gives for not working through your healing. You may find yourself having a hard time completing this book. You may put off doing the meditations. You may go unconscious and fall asleep when you do set aside time to experience them. Recognize these patterns for what they are: your Saboteur's activities designed to keep you stuck in your pain where it can control you and continue with its plans to destroy you.

Your Saboteur needs forgiveness, too. Healing your life requires that you forgive your external abuser. Your internal abuser must also be forgiven and released.

When you were a child, your Saboteur developed within you in an effort to please the destructive parts of your parents. The verbal and nonverbal messages you received from the Saboteur parts in your parents fell into two categories: either "Don't exist" or "Don't be who you are" or both. Your sensitive Child-Being sensed these injunctions or heard them directly. She was hurt, devastated, and terrified in response. She wanted and needed love and some of the time she felt it. But, when she felt her parents' destructive, fearful energies instead, she still wanted love. How could she get it from the abusive parts of her parents who attacked her with lethal messages and destructive behavior? Maybe if she did as they said, they would love her someday. Maybe if she destroyed herself eventually, they would appreciate her in the end. And so your Saboteur evolved. It hid your hurt Child-Self, fed on your buried rage and sorrow, and set out to abuse and ultimately destroy you as your parents, consciously or unconsciously, had suggested that you should.

You have learned to recognize your Saboteur and to set limits with it. You have been teaching this abusive part of yourself to respect your authority over your own life. At the same time, you have learned to love and nurture yourself. Your new Nurturing-Enabling Self now is a much more powerful force in your life than your Saboteur is. But your Saboteur still exists, trying to get love through self-destruction for your wounded Child-Self that it covers. Are you ready to lovingly forgive this part of yourself that you created to solve a love dilemma in the first place? Are you ready to acknowledge that its destructiveness flows out of the pain you have not yet completely released?

If you are, go through the forgiveness process again with the intention now of forgiving your Saboteur. Elaine decided to forgive her Saboteur, working with the Lazaris forgiveness meditation. She followed his instruction to visualize her Saboteur as vividly as she could. When she had the picture clearly in mind, the meditation suggested that she make this part of herself as ugly and disgusting as possible. She did this, and then visualized a bubble of violet light enveloping the hideous image of her Saboteur. As she watched, she was amazed to see her Saboteur crack open and fall away, leaving her to face her hurt Child-Self instead. She immediately approached her Child to hug her. When she touched her, she realized that her Child was in great physical pain so it was necessary to hug her very gently. (It is interesting to remember that when Elaine came to her first therapy session with me, she asked me never to touch her or hug her. I honored this request until about eight months later when she changed her mind and allowed me to hold her while she cried. Since that time, she has been more and more comfortable with allowing other group members to touch her and hug her. Now she could clearly see the origin of her fear.) Elaine's commitment to herself is to listen to what her wounded Child-Self has to tell her. Now that she has forgiven her Saboteur, it is much less active within her. Whenever she does hear fearful, negative comments from it, she knows she must look deeper within her. Her Saboteur signals her that she must make contact with her Child-Self so she can tend to her pain, anger, and sorrow and further her continual healing process.

In addition to the meditative process of forgiveness, you can use affirmations to reinforce your release of old burdens of guilt. Affirmations also will help you expose and clear away your Saboteur's fearful objections to your letting go of guilt.

Sondra Ray suggests in her "forgiveness diet" that you work with four basic affirmations: *"I forgive my father completely." "I forgive my mother completely." "I forgive myself completely." "I forgive God completely." (The Only Diet There Is* by Sondra Ray, published by Celestial Arts, Berkeley, CA., 1981.) Work with each affirmation for a full week, writing it 70 times a day. This satisfies the Biblical exhortation to forgive your brother 70 x 7 times for his failings. The commitment of time and energy that the "forgiveness diet" requires is part of its effectiveness. By the time you complete it, you will have thoroughly implanted your forgiveness affirmations and exhausted your resistance.

These are additional affirmations I find helpful in healing and forgiving sexual abuse.

I forgive myself for not stopping _____ from abusing me sexually.

I forgive myself for thinking I was bad because I was sexually abused.

I forgive myself for the pain and self-abuse I created before I decided to heal my life.

I forgive myself for the pain I caused others before I decided to heal my life.

I forgive myself for any sexual pleasure I experienced when I was abused. It is OK for me to feel sexual pleasure without guilt now.

I forgive _____ for abusing me sexually. I now release him completely.

I forgive _____ for his ignorant, infantile, insensitive, destructive behavior toward me.

I forgive my Internal Saboteur for abusing me. I now recognize that my Saboteur signals me that I need to make contact with my Child-Self and listen to her feelings.

I am innocent and I deserve love.

Subliminal tapes are a powerful resource for forgiving yourself and releasing guilt. You may want to try:

Midwest Research: Tape #6 — Sex/Loving Relationships, and Tape #19 — Mutual Sexual Pleasure

Potentials Unlimited: Overcoming Sexual Guilt

All these techniques prepare you for facing your abuser and approaching him in a spirit of love and forgiveness, rather than anger and revenge. In the next chapter, we move into confrontation, letting go of the secret you have guarded all your life. But, first, I want to share with you a meditation you can follow in forgiving yourself and your abuser.

Relax your body and allow yourself to clear your mind. Gently close your eyes and use whatever method works best for you to move inside and center yourself in the energy of love. As you release all your ordinary concerns and distractions, focus your attention on the rhythm of your breath, watching as you breathe in and out, nourishing yourself with each inhalation and cleansing your body, your mind, and your emotions each time you exhale.

When you reach your ideal place in consciousness, appreciate the joy of being exactly where you are, feeling the deep peace that is the core of your being. Rest here and allow yourself to go even deeper if you choose. Visualize yourself entering a place that is especially beautiful and satisfying to you. Let it be the loveliest scene you can imagine. It could be a room. It could be a place in nature. It could be a place you visited many times before. It could be a place you've always dreamed of experiencing. Tune into your senses and allow yourself to drink in all that you can see surrounding you and all the sounds your ears can hear. Feel the air touching your cheeks and smell its fragrant freshness.

When you find the special spot that invites you to sit down and relax, settle yourself into its embrace. As you feel the comfortable security that surrounds you, become aware of the richness of your being, contemplating the many different parts of yourself that you have learned to recognize. Imagine yourself asking all your Internal Selves to join you here. Bring them in one at a time, letting yourself get a clear visual image and feeling impression of each one as it moves toward you. One by one, have each of your selves sit before you and look directly into its eyes. Surround it in a beautiful bubble of violet light. Then tell that part specifically how it impacts your life. Share with it what you appreciate about it, what you resent, and what you are here to forgive it for. Take all the time you need with each of your selves. When you feel ready, affirm to each part of you, "I love you; I bless you; I release and forgive you. May my love, awareness, and acceptance allow you to become as beautiful and healthy as you are created to be." Gently release each part and invite it to take its place in the circle of parts that is forming around you.

When you have spoken with each of your parts, join hands around the circle of your selves. Then move yourself into the middle of the circle and visualize all of you, your entire synergy of selves, enveloped in violet light. Feel a new dimension of internal harmony emerging within you as you make this statement of affirmation:

I, (your name), love all of myself; I bless all of me; I release and forgive myself completely. I am free to be the whole of who I am. I am free to create a healthy, beautiful reality in every dimension of my life. I am free to find and fulfill my life purposes, enjoying every step I take along the perfect path I evolve for myself with loving guidance from my Higher Self and from God/Goddess/All That Is. I give thanks, I give thanks, I give thanks.

I appreciate and accept all the difficulties I have experienced to this point in my life. I take full responsibility for how I use those experiences now to transform my life and bring new meaning and new definition to my existence.

Gently bring your selves back inside you and feel the peace and harmony that fill you. When you are ready, allow yourself to return from your meditation, bringing the blessing of forgiveness with you into the new reality you are ready to create.

You may want to use this meditation for a number of days, working with a different part of yourself each day until you have met and forgiven all of your selves. If this is your choice, each day your circle of selves will grow larger until it is complete. Ask your Higher Self for guidance to be sure you don't neglect or omit a part, or parts, of you that you may hide from your awareness. Include your Saboteur and its cohorts: the Critic, the Martyr/Pleaser, the Pusher, the Judge, and the Worrier. Invite your Inner Child and its parts that are Frightened, Shy, Adaptive, Spontaneous, Creative, Expressive, and Sensual/Sexual. Also make contact with your Nurturing-Enabling Self and your Powerful

Clear-Thinking Adult Selves who know how to create choices for you and solve problems. Take as many days as you need to complete this internal forgiveness process. Then you will be ready to proceed to the next phase of the forgiveness meditation.

In this phase of the meditation, you will visualize yourself whole and healed, encompassing and accepting all of your selves. After you relax and enter the special place you have created for this forgiveness experience (you can use the introductory stages of the first meditation to take yourself there), invite your abuser, your parents, and other members of your family to join you. Have them sit in a circle surrounding you. Visualize an enormous field of violet light embracing the whole circle with you in its center. When you feel ready, move directly in front of your abuser and look into his eyes. Tell him what you are here to forgive him for. Let yourself be fully aware of the ugliness of the situation you are releasing. Tell him without minimizing how his abuse has affected you. Listen to anything he may say in response. Let him ask for your forgiveness. Allow yourself time to decide to take this step and to forgive him completely. When you are ready, see your abuser surrounded in violet light. Watch as it moves through his body and through his aura, cleansing and healing him. Continue to look into his eyes. When you see him healed and whole, cleansed and free from the past, take his hands in yours. Listen to anything he has to say. Then repeat your forgiveness affirmation to him, "(His name), I love you, I bless you, I release and forgive you. May my love allow you to become all that you are created to be." Release his hands and return to the center of the circle. Take the time to surround yourself in violet light. See your body and your aura clear and clean and pure. Watch as the one you have forgiven moves back into his current life. Notice that the cords that have bound you to him over the years have fallen away. As he moves away with nothing binding him to you, realize that you are no longer tied to him. You are free, and he is free. Experience this new freedom you have created for yourself and give thanks. Thank your other family members for their presence and ask them to continue to work with you in this way in subsequent meditations when you will encounter each of them individually to complete your healing process. When you are ready, bring yourself gently back to your current reality, knowing that you are released from the burden you have carried until now. Spend a few more minutes appreciating what you have accomplished.

Repeat this meditation with all of your family members and anyone else you need to forgive. Work with these meditations as often as you need to. Don't be discouraged if you find you must go through the forgiveness process more than once. The important thing is that you have the courage to continue with it for as long as is necessary and perfect for you. Don't stop short of complete release. You could sabotage yourself by settling for partial release, holding onto some of your anger and resentment because of your fears of letting go so completely. Remember that you deserve to be completely free. Take all the time you need, but don't stop before you've found your freedom and claimed it fully for yourself. Then you will know there are no more cords binding you to the pain of your past.

CHAPTER XV

CONFRONTATION

Your forgiveness process will not be complete until you confront your abuser and let go of the burden of keeping the abuse secret. But, I believe, you will be most effective with your confrontation if you are well into forgiveness when you face your abuser (or your surviving family members, if he is dead) with his responsibility for violating your sexual boundaries.

In my work with women who were sexually abused, I have found that confrontation before beginning the forgiveness process adds to destructive energy that is already powerful in dysfunctional families. Shortly after remembering her abuse, Alice insisted on confronting her father so she could "get it over with and be done with it." Despite warnings that she slow down and give herself time to deal with her feelings before taking this step, she went ahead with the confrontation. Though she appeared to be quite calm, she was denying her rage and trying to avoid her feelings by rushing the process. When her father denied that he abused her and her mother supported his position, she was not prepared for her own response. Within a week, she had a physically abusive fight with her husband, taking her rage out on him and frightening both of them with the intensity and destructive power of her long suppressed feelings. She escalated her distress until she made a suicide attempt and was hospitalized. The hospitalization gave her time and a safe place to face her feelings and her parents' reactions. Eventually, she recovered her balance, but she left therapy before she completed her healing process.

Though it is hard to be patient with yourself and give

yourself adequate time while you go through the healing stages, patience is essential if you want to free yourself from an abusive life-style. Impulsive behavior on the part of your abuser started the destructive cycle in your life. Impulsive behavior on your part, while understandable because of your past, is not a solution to your dilemma now. You must take the time to learn to think while you feel and take care of yourself wisely, too. That means you can't push the river and go faster through the healing stages than your own internal rhythm and needs allow.

When Lindsey introduced herself in group, she told about first confronting her father in rage soon after she remembered her incest experiences. That confrontation was followed by estrangement from her family which lasted for more than a year. When she next met with her parents, this time in my office after another year of therapy, she was well into the forgiveness process. This second confrontation was the beginning of healing her relationships with both her parents. Lindsey approached them in an attitude of forgiveness and healing rather than rage, blaming, and recrimination. Though her father still did not directly acknowledge abusing her, he did apologize for hurting her in any ways he didn't remember. But, no matter what his response might have been, Lindsey was relieved of the burden of keeping the incest secret and was ready to forgive both her parents for their behavior that had hurt her so deeply.

The timing of your confrontation and your decision to let go of the abuse secret are both crucial elements in your healing process. Keeping the secret is an overwhelming burden that holds you in the grip of the abuse long after it has physically ceased. It means that you choose to protect everyone else in your family from the truth while letting the secret you protect destroy your life. You may tell yourself that you are too embarrassed to tell what happened. Perhaps you were threatened as a child to impress you with the importance of protecting your abuser. Statements like,

"No one else must ever know. This is our special secret. No one else would understand;" or, "If anyone ever found out, I'd be ruined;" or, "If anyone ever finds out, I'll have to kill us both;" are powerful injunctions to keep silent. Breaking such an injunction feels like a life-or-death risk.

I found myself in just such a struggle while writing the final chapters of this book. My father's injunction was, "I'll have to kill us both if anyone ever finds out." When I publish this book, the secret will be out and out beyond my family whom I have already told. Though both my parents and most of their friends are dead and I have a very small family, the Healing Child in me was terrified that I would die if I carried this book to completion. I realized I must be very gentle with my Frightened Child, not allowing her to control me, but taking her fears into account and moving ahead at a pace she can tolerate. Breaking through my father's death threat injunction is terrifying to her even though the rest of me is clear that writing this book is a crucial part of my life purpose and my healing process as well.

So, I am acutely aware that confronting your abuser and your family is an enormous challenge. You may say to yourself that there is no point in stirring up trouble. Why hurt anyone else with what has already caused you such pain? Perhaps you think your parents couldn't handle your honesty. You believe your job is to protect them always, no matter what the cost is to you. Or, you may be afraid you will be cast out of your family and totally rejected if you dare to speak up. Your Saboteur will create endless reasons for you to continue to keep the secret, precisely because keeping it keeps you stuck in self-destruction. Or it may push you, as Alice's Saboteur did, to confront them before you are ready.

If you confront while still denying your anger or even in the midst of your rage, you increase the probability of a painful outcome for you and for your family. Your rage will get in the way, directly or indirectly, and you will be less likely to communicate effectively. If you confront after you have released your buried rage and sorrow, you will be free to speak honestly without undue fear of your family's rage in response to what you say. Because you have faced and expressed your own rage, you know that these powerful feelings will not destroy you or anyone else. You will also know that they are an inevitable, unavoidable part of the experience of facing the pain of incest/sexual abuse. Though your parents will be angry and defensive, and though they may deny the validity of what you say, you will stand on the firm ground of having thoroughly dealt with your feelings and will be much better able to accept theirs without getting caught up in fear and panic.

When you do decide and feel that you are ready for confrontation, you may want your therapist present when you talk with your family. A therapist can help structure the experience and keep order so that impulsive reactions are less likely to abort the process. The presence of an outsider who is a professional helps keep the family from collapsing into uproar and confusion when these previously unspeakable issues emerge. A therapist can make sure everyone gets a chance to speak and be heard. He or she also can set the tone for the confrontation session by stating that the purpose of the meeting is healing for everyone, not attack, blame, and more destructiveness. Including a therapist also opens the door for the rest of the family to become involved in the therapeutic process, individually and in family sessions. The goal is to assist everyone in facing what must be faced so that the person who was abused no longer bears the burden of trying to protect everyone else from the reality of her painful experiences.

In truth, everyone in the family is affected by unacknowledged sexual abuse. Consciously or unconsciously, each family member has his share in the pain and is affected by it, whether or not he is aware of it and acknowledges it. I wonder how many unacknowledged male abusers have died of painful cancers or suffered through long debilitating illnesses that punish them un-mercifully for their sins buried long ago. How many mothers of sexually abused daughters have retreated into senility to avoid facing their part in their child's suffering? My experiences with my parents may not be atypical. Keeping the abuse secret buried keeps everyone stuck in the pain, especially the abuser whose guilt, whether it is conscious or deeply buried, is overwhelming.

When you confront your family, you acknowledge your love for them, their importance to you, and your respect for them as well. In effect, by taking this step, you state to them that you believe they have the strength to face what must be faced if you are to heal your relationships with them. Rather than hiding behind your perception of them as too weak or too terrifying to face, you honor them, yourself, and your relationship by choosing to be honest. The simple truth is that telling the truth heals. Hiding from the truth creates more and more pain until ultimately the family is destroyed by the effort.

No matter how your parents (or abuser) respond, you will take a giant leap forward toward healing when you face your family with the truth. Remember that you are not responsible for creating the abuse you endured as a child. Your abuser made his choice then. Your choice now is to face him with his responsibility for what he created by abusing you. His reaction to your confrontation is his responsibility. Your responsibility is to communicate honestly, from your center, in an attitude of love and healing, after having done substantial work with forgiveness to prepare yourself for this release.

I believe it is important to let your abuser, especially if he is your parent, know that you are able to see him as the whole person that he is. Let him know that you can acknowledge the positive in him as well as face the negative. Your intention is not to destroy your relationship with him. Rather it is to make it honest and whole at long last. You can let him know what you valued about

him when you were a child as well as what you hated.
You have already had your revenge in fantasy. You are
free now to confront from a position of enlightenment
rather than recrimination.

Ideally, the confrontation should take place in the context of a series of family therapy sessions agreed upon by
everyone in advance. These sessions may include your parents and your siblings or just your parents. Because everyone in your family is affected by the sexual abuse you
experienced (and other siblings may have been abused,
too), I think there are distinct advantages to having everyone in your family present for the confrontation. Though
opening the discussion of sexual abuse in the presence of
your entire family may feel very frightening, it may work
more effectively and be easier for you in the long run. You
may get unexpected support from your siblings or they
may deny what you say. Either way, the fact that everyone
in your family is involved in the process from the beginning will help them come to grips with these issues more
quickly. This approach makes it clear that sexual abuse is a
family issue, not just a private matter between you and
your abuser. It enables everyone in the family to be a part
of the healing process from the beginning and sets the tone
for developing healthy openness and honesty in family
communication patterns.

Another possibility is to have the initial confrontation
with your parents and then schedule whole family sessions
after you have first dealt with them privately. But, if your
siblings are not included at some point in the confrontation process, the sexual abuse may remain a secret from
them. Their exclusion will be a discount to them and to the
family as a whole. It will assist the family in retreating into
denial again, once the initial impact of the confrontation
lessens. Even if your abuser was someone who was not a
member of your immediate family, everyone in your family
needs to know what happened to you and needs an opportunity to deal with the impact of these experiences on you

and on their lives as well.

If your family must travel to join you for the confrontation sessions, or if you decide to travel to them, arrange for at least three to six sessions over a period of a week to ten days to give everyone adequate time to come to grips with facing these issues. If you and your family live in the same locale, ask everyone to agree to come for at least six sessions on a once-or-twice a week basis. If necessary, you may recontract to continue the family work until everyone feels complete with the process. Individual sessions may be advisable also, as well as couples' work for your parents and siblings and their mates.

Careful planning and preparation before confrontation will reap tremendous dividends for everyone involved. You can practice what you want to say in Gestalt work with your therapist and psychodrama or Gestalt work with your therapy group. In Gestalt work, you will experience both your part as well as the parts of the others involved. In psychodrama, you will be able to watch and participate from many different points of view when you ask group members to play the roles of your family members. Their feedback and feelings in the various roles will be helpful to you in preparing yourself. When your actual confrontation takes place, you will be much more at home with the process and aware of different possible reactions from others. You will be less likely to panic or forget what you have to say. Often women do forget what they want to say when actually faced with their parents in the flesh at a confrontation session. Practicing ahead of time will help you remember that your parents are just other adult beings, not still the overwhelmingly powerful arbiters of your fate that they seemed to be when you were a child.

When time for the confrontation comes, be sure everyone involved has adequate space and privacy for dealing with his own individual emotions and reactions. If your parents come from out of town, have them stay in a hotel or a home that provides for separate quarters. Be sure you have a healthy support system for yourself. Have a special friend stand by to be with you if you decide you need companionship and talk. You may choose to have some social time with your family, but do so only if you're satisfied that you really want to and are acting out of your desire, not a need to please or smooth things over. It is important that you do not dilute the impact of the confrontation and pave the way for everyone to retreat into denial again.

THE CONFRONTATION SESSIONS

THE FIRST MEETING: Your therapist will be concerned with establishing rapport with everyone in your family. He or she will convey an attitude of warmth, confidence, and competence that will help people relax and feel hopeful that what is about to take place will be a positive experience. It is essential that the therapist has grown beyond her personal fears of anger, conflict, and strong feelings so she will be able to maintain a centered position throughout the session. Her capacity to stay centered will create a loving energy that will be much stronger than the fears participants will experience. As she is able to hold her centered place in consciousness, others will be better able to keep their balance through the rough places in the path that lies ahead.

Your therapist will take time to get acquainted with everyone present, making sure she establishes both verbal and eye contact with each person and gives each a chance to speak about something that is light and easy to share. I usually ask if this is a first-time therapy experience and comment that people often feel apprehensive about coming to see a therapist for the first time. This gives everyone a chance to share how he is feeling and establishes that it is OK to be human here and tell the truth about what you feel. If there have been prior therapy experiences, I ask about them. If they were positive, I want to know that. If not, I want that to be acknowledged so it will be less likely to interfere with the present encounter.

All this gives everyone time to settle down and gives me time to get a sense about the people who are present. When I feel that I have established adequate rapport to move into the business at hand, I make my opening statement, setting an intention for the experience we are about to begin. I state that my client has done lots of good work in therapy and that at this point in her healing process, it is important for her to talk with her whole family. I acknowledge my appreciation that they are willing to participate and share that our intention is to create new positive possibilities for everyone present through talking honestly about experiences from the past that were difficult for everyone involved. I also state that I know strong feelings will emerge and that that is a healthy part of the healing process. I emphasize that our intention is healing and release for everyone, not attack, blame, or alienation. I then ask my client to share with her family what she wants to accomplish through the meetings we have scheduled. This statement by the person who is the confronter should include these goals:

1) To talk about what happened in the past.

2) To tell her family how these events affected her.

3) To hear her family's responses to what she shares.

4) To face and express the feelings everyone has about what happened and about talking about it now.

5) To release and forgive the old situation and create within her family, a new loving reality, based on honesty and mutual respect.

Once the confronter has set her intention, I ask her to share with her family exactly what happened in the past that was so difficult for her. When she brings up sexual abuse and actually speaks the previously unspeakable words, reactions usually will come quickly. Obviously, there is no way to predict exactly what responses your family will have, but chances are good that some form of denial will be their initial reaction.

You may hear calm and complete denial. "This couldn't possibly have happened. We have excellent memory and we don't remember anything like this. We're not the sort of people who do things like that. You always were excitable and so imaginative. Maybe you need to think something like this to help you get better, but certainly it could never have really happened."

You may encounter outraged, furious denial. "How dare you even suggest such a thing! You ungrateful little bitch, how could you possibly have the audacity to accuse your poor, hardworking father of laying a hand on you! You're a crazy, dangerous no-good, sorry excuse for a daughter. We don't have to take this. We won't sit here and be insulted like this. This lousy therapist has been putting nasty ideas in your head."

Whether you encounter one of these extremes or some middle ground, the likelihood is that you will have to contend with some form of denial that is based on the premise that one way or another, you're nuts. This is when you will be grateful for all the work you've done before reaching this point in the process. You have already dealt with your rage and sadness. Though your family's responses will trigger anger and sorrow in you, you won't be overwhelmed by these feelings as you might have been if you hadn't worked through your old pain. You have dealt with your self-doubt and denial. You know what happened and you are clear about it. Staying clear with yourself, believing yourself, and sticking to your point through your family's denial and counterattack phase are crucial. You can make statements like:

> I know what happened to me.
> I know what I remember.
> I'm not crazy. I never have been. It's crazy to pretend

*that what did happen didn't. I'm not willing to support
that denial any longer.*

*I simply want to be honest about what we've avoided
talking about for all these years so we can have a healthy
relationship now. I'm not willing to continue pretending. It
is something we can face and work through.*

In your first family session, it is unlikely that you will
get much beyond confrontation, denial, counterattack, and
maintaining your position. Your therapist can bring the
session to a close by stepping in to comment that obviously
everyone is filled with many strong feelings in the face of
the issues that have been raised. She may ask each person
to share what he is aware of at the moment, making sure
that each person gets a turn without being interrupted by
someone else who may be trying to escalate into uproar or
retreat into more denial. Once everyone has said what they
need to say before leaving, she can invite each person to
release what has just been experienced, to be kind to himself between now and the next scheduled session, and to
be open to recording any dreams that occur and writing
about the feelings that emerge in response to what has
been discussed. She may also reaffirm the intention for
healing for the family and thank each person for his
willingness to participate.

Between sessions, everyone will need some private time
to assimilate what has occurred and to face his own feelings
about the sexual abuse. You will appreciate your prior
planning for separate accommodations. When the family
gathers again for the second session, everyone will have
had an opportunity to begin grappling with what you have
been working through for months. Hopefully, you will be
patient with them as you have learned to be with yourself.
Don't expect miracles overnight.

SECOND SESSION: Your therapist may begin the
second session by asking each person to share what he is
most aware of now, after time to assimilate the last session.
Hopefully the family will be ready to move to a deeper

level of sharing now, with each person telling how he is affected by the abuse issue. But, denial may still be strong, and during this session you may feel that resolution and healing are a hopeless dream. The second session of any kind of therapy is often a frustrating one. Hopes run high after a first encounter. In the second, as you begin to get down to the tough issues at hand, defenses will be strong, anger will flare, and participants will test the therapist's confidence, competence, and strength. It is essential that she stay centered and hold that balanced energy during this stage of the process.

The objective now is not that everyone agree and accept that sexual abuse occurred. Rather it is that each person speak honestly so his point of view and feelings are clear and can be understood by the others. It is not necessary for the abuser (if he is a family member who is present) to acknowledge his responsibility for his actions. He may eventually do so when he realizes that no one is out to ostracize or crucify him. What is important at this stage is to demonstrate to everyone that this family can face and talk about this emotionally loaded subject even though they may not yet acknowledge its reality.

Hopefully, there will be lots of anger expressed in this second session. If your father is your abuser, your mother will be torn by many powerful emotions. Your therapist will want to note how this revelation affects her and invite her to verbalize the conflict she feels between her loyalty to her mate and her concern for you, her child. She needs to express her anger with both of you and acknowledge the competitive, jealous feelings she is contending with as she realizes that her husband has been unfaithful to her sexually and that her daughter is the "other woman."

If you have siblings present, they may be wondering if they, too, may have been abused and blocked the memory. Or, if they are clear that they were not abused, they may wonder why you were the one who was singled out for this distorted attention from father (if he is the abuser). Either way, they are angry that this issue has come up and that they have to face it, too. Their previous perceptions of their parents and their family are shaken. They may feel guilty that they escaped the sexual abuse and angry that you had to endure it. Or, they may be angry because they, too, were victims and have not faced that reality yet.

If the abuser is your father, he is terrified of facing what he has hidden and denied all his life. He will rely on his defenses to maintain his innocence. He may become defiantly angry and blaming, attempting to project his responsibility onto you. He may adopt a superreasonable position, calmly adopting the position that this couldn't possibly have happened and expressing his dismay at your having taken leave of your senses. He may become a pleaser, trying to smooth over the conflict while denying his role in it and expressing his concern for the depth of your pathology. He may adopt the position of the martyred victim, accused of an impossible crime after all the love and devotion he has showered on you for all these years. How could you possibly do this to someone who loves you so? He may pull health threats, claiming that this is too upsetting for him to talk about and is about to throw him into a heart attack, a stroke, or some other physical calamity. Mother may support him in this escalation, begging you not to upset your father and endanger his life. Or, she may retreat into illness herself if that is her pattern. If she gets sick, she takes the focus off father and helps everyone slip back into denial while directing their concern to her.

The variations and possible responses are numerous. The key for you is to stay clear about what you know and what you have worked through, keeping in mind that the rest of your family is at the very beginning of a process you have been involved with for months. Though you may feel frightened, guilty, angry, and sad as you watch these people you love grappling with what has already been so painful for you, remember that they, like you, have the strength to deal with what has to be faced. Probably the most potent manipulation that might surface is the threat of someone dying because you have raised this monster. Tough as this one is, you know that each person present is choosing his response and is responsible for the choice he makes. If he should choose to die rather than face the consequences of his own actions, that is a choice you cannot control. He has many other possible responses available to him. You are not attacking or blaming anyone. You are insisting that everyone else take his share of the responsibility for the burden you have carried alone for all these years. If you are strong enough to face it alone, they are strong enough also to take their share of the load, deal with their feelings about it, and release it with forgiveness, too. But, your life-long stance as victim and guilty one may make it difficult for you to withstand this kind of lethal manipulation calculated to hold you responsible for someone else's life and death. Stay clear that love is stronger than the fear that is behind such a threat and let the one who escalates illness know that you are confident that he can survive honesty and experience much relief and better health in the future because of it. Your therapist also can intervene with calm reassurances and an invitation for everyone to take time out to breathe, relax, and get centered again.

The second session, filled as it is with strong emotions, may end without a sense of resolution. But, be aware that lots is accomplished in such an encounter. Everyone discovers that the family can survive honesty and strong feelings. They learn that it is possible to disagree and face conflict. They experience that love is stronger than these long-buried, emotional monsters. And, after venting their feelings, they may begin to experience some relief.

As your therapist concludes this second session, she can emphasize the importance of releasing strong feelings once they have been acknowledged and expressed. She might take your family through a short meditative process, helping each person center himself and let go of all the negativity and fear he needs to discharge. In such a meditation, she can suggest that each person take responsibility for his part in the current process while respecting everyone else's responsibility for what belongs to them.

One of the key issues the family is facing is establishing, for the first time, healthy boundaries within the family between family members. Incest/sexual abuse is a profound violation of boundaries. Keeping the abuse secret is also a violation of boundaries. Letting go of the secret acknowledges the boundaries that separate your life from the lives of other members of your family. In effect, you state that you will no longer protect them at the expense of your well-being. Their denial and angry manipulations are efforts to get you to change back to your old position as protector and keeper of the family secret. Your maintaining your boundaries and refusing to change back require others to find their boundaries, too. Your therapist will make these boundaries clear and explicit in the ways she interacts with family members and insists that each person take responsibility for his own feelings, needs, opinions, and defenses. In this meditative process, she reinforces the necessity for developing strong, healthy boundaries within the family structure.

After the meditation, she may suggest again that each person write about their feelings as a way of clarifying them and getting further release. She also can encourage them to record their dreams and take plenty of time to relax and nurture themselves generously. As preparation for the third session, she might suggest that each person think about the vision they have for how this family can be once the sexual abuse issue has been dealt with, released, and forgiven. How would each person present like to see this family system change and grow and heal?

THIRD SESSION: The third session can begin with another opportunity for each person to share his present experience. Your therapist may ask about thoughts, feelings, dreams, and individual responses to the previous sessions. She also may ask about how the family has been coping with this new reality outside the therapy sessions. What has been happening between diads within the family? Have there been any activities that included everyone? How were these experiences for everyone involved?

After exploring the current reality, she may recognize that this process of assimilating a new family reality will take time. You, the confronter, have been working with these issues for months. There must be time now for others to do their work, too. At this point, she may move into creating a therapeutic structure to assist the family in completing its healing process. She can ask each person to share his vision of how he would like the family to change, to grow, to heal, and to become healthy. How can these goals best be accomplished? What sort of treatment plan will work best for everyone involved? If everyone in the family lives in the area, they may agree to continue with a combination of individual and family sessions, building upon the work they have begun with the current therapist. If family members live in different cities, they can develop a therapy plan for each person in the place where he lives. Hopefully, your therapist can provide good referral sources where they are needed. If distance is involved and referrals are necessary, the family may choose to set a time to meet again with the current therapist in three to six months for a follow-up session that includes everyone who is present now. Ideally, everyone would agree to continue in therapy for at least a year to give themselves adequate time to complete their personal healing process.

If your family gets off the track during these initial confrontation sessions and one or more people refuse to continue to meet with the therapist, urge the others to remain and continue the treatment process. If they do so, the ones who left may eventually rejoin the rest of the family as they see clearly that the others refuse to join them in their denial stance and their change-back reaction. If they are successful in leading the rest of your family out of the therapeutic process, and everyone refuses to continue, your therapist can provide them with her card and with names of other therapists they can contact at a later date if they decide they want to do so.

It is crucially important that you continue your own therapy process after your confrontation sessions are done. You want to complete your forgiveness process and move beyond your sexual abuse experience into transforming your life. You owe it to yourself to stay with your commitment to make yourself whole so you reap the full dividends of all the work you have done to this point. Yet, be aware that you may feel a strong temptation to quit your therapy after the confrontation. The pressures from your family may be so strong that your Saboteur is empowered by the stress you experience and becomes vigorously active in its efforts to abort your complete healing. It may distort your feelings in response to the confrontation sessions, especially if you are blocking your anger and sadness over how your family handled your revelation. You may find yourself focusing your anger and possible disappointment on your therapist rather than keeping clear about where these emotions belong. You must acknowledge those feelings, express them, and release them so you can move on beyond confrontation into transformation. If you buy into your Saboteur's suggestions that you stop your therapy now, you will accommodate to your family's change-back manipulations and join them in more denial and self-destructive behavior. Though you may be strongly tempted to try to smooth things over short of resolving the issues, stay aware of your Saboteur and set limits with it and with your family as well.

The period after your confrontation is critical. Your family may make intensive efforts to get you to change back to your old position where you protected everyone else from the reality of your abuse. If you maintain your clarity and your position of honesty while resisting these manipulations, they will have to change their position in order to bring the family system back into balance at a new and higher level of understanding and communication. This is the time when you need the support of your therapist and your therapy group to help you withstand these change-back pressures and stay with your position long enough to ensure the desired changes within your family system.

Even if you stay in therapy, you may be tempted to retreat into denial to smooth things over with your family. This is where Gayle got stuck, allowing her Saboteur to convince her that more intensive work on herself was too much to ask of herself after taking the risk of confronting her father and mother. She went along with her family's response to her confrontation by joining them in acting as if nothing much had happened. Though some significant changes occurred in her relationships with them and she became much more independent than she was previously, the family as a whole has not come to grips with what she shared. Only one of her siblings has been told about her sexual abuse while the other is still protected from knowing. Her family continues to function in secrecy while Gayle has slowed down her own recovery process. Yet, she still attends group and maintains her commitment to complete her healing at the pace she sets for herself. It is important to respect her desire to be in charge of the pace she sets, realizing that her path is her path and that she cannot go faster than she chooses to go. At the same time, the group confronts her Saboteur's activities and encourages her to move ahead.

Gayle's experiences teach us again that healing is not a linear process that proceeds in a straightforward orderly progression from start to finish. In dealing with ourselves as the unique beings that each of us are, we must be aware that patience, understanding, and encouragement are essential, even when we may be stuck at a particular point in the process for longer than we like or longer than other people seem to take. Each person who faces the challenge of healing her life after sexual abuse is an absolutely individual being with her own unique history and her own patterns for growth and change. The healing model I present here is a broad, general structure that includes what I believe are the essential steps along the way. How you make your own journey beyond sexual abuse victim to creator of a new reality in your life will depend upon the path you choose for yourself. You may make side trips that seem to others to be a waste of time but may be essential for you. The key is keeping the commitment you make to yourself when you begin so you stay on the road until you reach your destination and know you have truly transformed your life.

CHAPTER XVI

TRANSFORMATION

STAGE V: TRANSFORMATION

STEP ONE: Changing your image of yourself so you tune out victim consciousness promoted by your Internal Saboteur and tune into active creator counsciousness supported by your Nurturing-Enabling Self.

STEP TWO Taking responsibility for your experience of sexual abuse and for how you deal with it as an adult.

STEP THREE: Accepting the place of your sexual abuse experiences in the context of your whole life; appreciating the value of living through and working through these experiences for your spiritual growth and evolution; taking responsibility for having chosen your family and chosen these experiences for your soul's growth in this particular lifetime (If this perspective fits for you).

STEP FOUR: Transforming these painful experiences into creative purposes and goals for your life.

STEP FIVE: Letting go; accepting the moment by moment discipline of forgiving and releasing the past completely and living successfully in the present.

STEP SIX: Trusting yourself and your capacity to nurture yourself successfully; celebrating the joyous future you are creating with every loving choice you make in the present.

Transformation sounds like a formidable challenge, yet it is an integral aspect of life. Transformations happen with such frequency and predictability, that we take them for granted and forget to notice these miracles of change we witness constantly. Day becomes night, and one season follows another. Tadpoles grow into frogs, and caterpillars become cocoons from which magnificent butterflies emerge. Babies become children who turn into teenagers who soon are adults. Adults grow older, and become wiser and more radiant, or depressed, weary, and disillusioned. Good health is interrupted by illness until wellness is established again. Pain changes to pleasure when we relax and remember to breathe. Conflict opens the door to intimacy when we aren't afraid to be loving and honest. Death is birth, our transformation from physical to nonphysical form.

These transformations are so commonplace that it's easy not to recognize them for the miracles that they are. When we do allow them to teach us, we see that wondrous changes are a natural part of the flow of life. The physical transformations that we observe can help us notice more subtle transformations that are emotional and spiritual in nature. These personal transformations are characterized by leaps in consciousness from a limited self-perception to an expanded version of being that is more nearly congruent with our full potential. They flow from our own direct experience of connection with our Higher Self and with God/Goddess/All That Is.

All the steps in the healing process help you shed your old "victim" consciousness and transform your perception of yourself. Your image of yourself determines what you allow yourself to enjoy as well as how you stop yourself from succeeding. If you think you are still a caterpillar after you've become a butterfly, you will spend your time crawling though you're ready and able to fly. As you grow and change, so must your image of yourself expand to fit the new person you are becoming. Otherwise, if you hang onto your old perception of yourself as a victim of abuse, you will not be able to create the successful new realities you are capable of enjoying in the present and the future. Instead, you will slip back into failure and frustration again and again, precisely because you do not yet believe that you, as you perceive yourself to be, can have the love, happiness, success, and prosperity you seek. Transforming your self-image so it fits your current level of wisdom and development opens the way for you to realize the fruits of your growth process.

Your old image of yourself as victim allowed you only a narrow range of possibilities for pleasure and success. Though there may have been parts of your life where you felt powerful and functioned as an active creator, in most areas, you unconsciously sabotaged your success in order to maintain your victim position. In order to transform your life, you must change that image.

Your Internal Saboteur is devoted to preserving your old self-image which is characterized by Victim Consciousness. It seizes every opportunity to criticize and frighten you when you take healthy steps toward love, success, and pleasure in living. Your Saboteur's basic message is that you are a victim. You are helpless and doomed to pain, failure, frustration, and despair. Ultimately it asks, "Why live at all? Why bother when nothing you do really matters? Sooner or later death will be the end of you."

Your Nurturing-Enabling Self supports your transformed self-image which is characterized by Active Creator Consciousness. Your Nurturing-Enabling Self says you are responsible and powerful, the creator and arbiter of your past, present, and future. You can be as joyous, happy, loving, and successful as you allow yourself to be. Health is your natural state of being. Death is your choice when you are ready to release your physical form; it is another transformation to new life and new consciousness. Your NES (Nurturing-Enabling Self) links you with your Higher Self and helps to align you with your spiritual nature.

In order to move beyond victim to Active Creator Consciousness, you must continue to recognize your Internal

Saboteur, set limits with it, and separate yourself from it. You must also firmly establish and continually strengthen your Nurturing-Enabling Self so it becomes a more and more powerful dimension of your consciousness that is always available when you decide to tune into it. Tuning out your Saboteur and tuning into your NES is like learning to switch channels on your TV set when you don't like the program that is running. Let's contrast the messages your Saboteur broadcasts on its frequency with the programming your NES creates on its channel.

CHAIRMAN OF YOUR INTERNAL BOARD OF DIRECTORS CHOOSES YOUR CHANNEL

VICTIM CONSCIOUSNESS presents *A DEADLY DEAL* script developed by YOUR INTERNAL SABOTEUR	CREATOR CONSCIOUSNESS presents *THIS IS YOUR LIFE!* script developed by YOUR NURTURING-ENABLING SELF
1) Cling to the past. Hold onto your hurts. Repress your feelings. The past always repeats itself.	1) Release the past. Express your feelings. Let go of your hurts. Genuine honesty and forgiveness heal everything.
2) Avoid conflict. Protect others at your expense. Keep the peace.	2) Tell the truth in the spirit of love. The truth heals.
3) Blame others for your problems. Keep yourself helpless. Try to get them to make you happy.	3) Take responsibility for the reality you create. Be aware of your boundaries and keep them strong and healthy.
4) Never ask for help; you don't need it. Strong people solve their problems alone.	4) You are wise to seek help in solving the problems you face. Sharing honestly with

others allows them to
know you and love you.

5) Judge yourself and others
with harsh criticism and
devastating comparisons.

5) Make no comparisons.
Make no judgments.

6) Spend your energy trying
to figure things out.
Confuse yourself and torture
yourself with your need to
understand and apply logic to
your life.

6) Delete your *need* to
understand.

7) Listen to my lies. Believe
whatever I tell you.

7) Love is all there is.
It is the truth. Fear
is an illusion.

8) Life is fearful, over-
whelming, difficult, and
too painful. You'll never
be successful at it, so why
bother?

8) Life is love. You have
all the strength and
resources you need to
be as successful,
happy, and prosperous
as you choose to be.

9) You are a victim. You are
helpless, doomed to pain,
failure, and hopeless
despair.

9) You create your
reality. You can make
it joyous, abundant,
and beautifully
fulfilling.

10) You are guilty, bad, and
impossible. You're not
perfect and you never will
be. Look at the terrible
mistakes you've made. How
awful you are!

10) You are an innocent,
beautiful, totally
deserving human being.
No one is perfect. You
are here to learn from
your mistakes.

11) You can't trust anyone.
They are all out to get you.

11) Learn to love yourself
and trust yourself and
you will be able to
love and trust others
as well.

12) People don't really love
you; they use you.

12) There is an abundance
of love waiting for you
when you let go of fear
and allow yourself to
be loved.

13) You deserve little pleasures like overeating, smoking and abusing drugs, or being sexually promiscuous or compulsive. After all, you work so hard and don't get much in return. You've earned a treat!

13) You can recognize cons like this and say "no." You can set limits with yourself and others.

14) You'll never have enough love, money, security, peace, etc., etc., etc.

14) There are ever expanding resources of love, money, security, and peace when you are open to allowing them.

15) Nothing matters anyway. In the end, you die and death will be the end of you. You're just dust.

15) You count and every choice you make counts. You are part of God. Death is your transformation from this physical reality to the joy of a non-physical reality.

Switching channels from the Saboteur's program to Creator Consciousness is shifting out of the energy of fear into the energy of love. It means letting go of scarcity as a guiding principle and opening to the truth of abundance. This transformation requires that you take full responsibility for yourself and for the choices you make, whether they are conscious or unconscious. It means that you own your power and acknowledge your constant creativity.

When you are centered in Creator Consciousness, you accept your humanness and ask for help when you need it. You aren't afraid to take risks, make and acknowledge mistakes, and learn from them. You are discerning and know when to say "no," but you are not harshly critical and judgmental of yourself and of others. You are a master of the art of letting go. You acknowledge, express appropriately, and release your feelings. You move from one experience to another without holding onto what is past. You forgive honestly and completely. You embrace life joyously and allow yourself to be a channel for the energy of love.

At the most basic level, transformation is letting love in your life by letting down your barriers of fear. It is letting love flow through your being and letting yourself express it through your expanding creativity. It is letting your challenges become your opportunities for growing and giving.

Transforming the experience of sexual abuse from a victim's burden to a Creator's Challenge is the essence of healing. When you make this transformation, you take responsibility for your life and for all it includes. This means that you also take responsibility for your experience of sexual abuse.

Remember that responsibility is not blame. You did not cause your abuser's destructive behavior and are not to blame for it. As a child, you were and are innocent. Yet, as an adult, you are responsible for what you do now with what you experienced then. You can choose to allow sexual abuse to destroy your life. You can choose to carry it about with you as a terrible burden that you cling to because it fits a martyred victim's life script. Or, you can choose to work through it and allow it to be a springboard for you into genuine health and joyous living.

As a child, you handled the abuse as best you could, given the resources and choices that were available to you then. As an adult, you now have many more options open to you. Though you may say to yourself, "Why Me?", ultimately you must accept that, for whatever reason, it was you. This did happen to you. Would you really want to give up on yourself and give up on your life because your parents and/or your abuser were destructive, disturbed people who were unable to control their impulses and unwilling to consider the impact of their behavior on you? Surely, to give up and allow their misguided choices to destroy you would be to accord them far too much power over you.

If the hand dealt you in this life contains the abuse card,

you can still play the game successfully. The key is becoming a skilled player and not allowing that one card to keep you from noticing and using the strength of the rest of your hand. Though you have to take the abuse card into account as you play your hand, you don't have to allow it to spell certain defeat. Instead, you can turn it into an advantage if you use your creativity instead of allowing fear to paralyze you.

The spiritual dimension of consciousness lies beyond what we perceive through the mechanisms of the conscious mind and the physical body. I think it is imperative that you take the spiritual dimension of your being into account in coming to terms with sexual abuse. What fits for you may be different from what feels clear and right for me. Make your own search and find the spiritual truths that help you come to terms with your abuse experiences.

Through my spiritual journey and exploration, I have come to believe that we live many lifetimes, each like a grade in school, where we set special tasks and challenges for ourselves to master. In the context of this understanding of life as a progression of choices, opportunities, and issues to face, I see the incest I experienced as a challenge I chose to accept. I believe that I chose this lifetime, my parents, and what we lived out with each other for my soul's growth and development in order to accomplish the life purpose I set for myself before I came into this lifetime. I also believe that at soul level, my parents and I agreed to live through these experiences together in order ultimately to realize a higher good for all of us. Through meditation, I have felt their support and encouragement through the long process of healing my life and developing this model for resolving sexual abuse.

My inner peace has deepened through writing this book. I am convinced that honoring and exploring your creative resources are crucial to transforming a sexual abuse experience into full recovery and joy in living. When you unblock your long-buried feelings and express and release them, you unlock your creative power. This creative power cannot flow freely when your energy is consumed by the effort required to keep your pain, rage, and sorrow suppressed. Releasing your creativity enables you to find your unique way of transforming your sexual abuse experiences. Through the various forms of self-expression that are appealing to you, you will find deeper and deeper levels of integration and meaningful sharing with others.

Expressing your creativity allows the creative energy of God/Goddess/All That Is to flow through you. Through creative self-expression, you take responsibility for being the agent that you are for manifesting love in the world. Instead of letting yourself remain stuck in Victim Consciousness, feeling depressed and helpless, and expressing fear, you cut the umbilical cord that ties you to your painful past. The new breath you draw after this rebirth is your inspiration. You are filled with the breath of life, inspired to be and express all of who you are. Your newborn creativity thrives in the atmosphere of love you allow in your life. It flows through you, reforming your existence.

Transformation requires that the old be de-formed or dismantled so a new reality can be re-formed. By acknowledging, expressing, and releasing your painful feelings and then confronting your abuser and your family, you have de-formed your old reality. These are essential steps that prepare you for transformation, the re-forming of your reality. You de-form your old victim gestalt in order to re-form into your new Creator Image and Consciousness. Transformation is death and rebirth. There must be death and letting go of victim so there can be rebirth of your Creator-Self. Transformation requires a conscious choice to change and a lasting commitment to that choice. Your rebirth beings you into alignment with the higher aspects of your being. It is growing up and into the fullness of all that you are.

The child's way of dealing with problems is to smooth them over and pretend they don't exist. The adolescent's way is to blame others for what he doesn't like and doesn't take responsibility for in his life. The adult's way is to acknowledge the power he possesses and the reality he creates. The path we have traced through the steps of the healing process follows this evolution from child to adult. We begin with the issue of sexual abuse smoothed over so we can pretend it does not exist. Once we acknowledge that it does exist and has a powerful impact on our lives, we face the depth of our rage and sorrow. In this experience, the adolescent in us feels helpless and blames our abuser and the universe for all our misery. As we take responsibility for our feelings and ultimately exhaust our rage, we grow into adulthood where we are willing to forgive and release. We realize that we choose how we handle the abuse card we drew in this lifetime. We know we can cling to the victim's posture or we can release victim, discard the abuse card, and move into the fullness of our adult power to create the joyous reality we desire and deserve. This is the transformation we seek; we grow-up, stop self-abuse, and create a new past and a new future for ourselves.

To claim transformation we must be clear that we deserve it. This means giving up guilt and embracing forgiveness. It also means allowing ourselves to receive love, knowing that love is not the dangerous, hurtful experience we were told it was by those who confused it with abuse. Love is the energy of life, the healing, joyful experience of being at one with ourselves and the universe. We feel it when we open our hearts to receive the unlimited loving energy that is within us and all around us. This opening is like letting down the walls and barriers we have erected because we learned not to trust. As we let love in, we know we are able to care for ourselves and protect ourselves with the healthy limits and boundaries we need for successful living. We can trust ourselves and God/Goddess/All That Is.

Transformation rests upon awareness, the process of paying attention to the energy patterns that operate within

us and the choices we make moment by moment to identify or stay separate from them. Transformation does not
mean that the Internal Saboteur and its cohorts (the
Pusher, Pleaser, Worrier, Critic, Martyr, and Victim) go
away. Rather, it means we are responsible for the choices
we make to listen or not to listen to what they have to say.
It also means we take responsibility for strengthening our
Nurturing-Enabling Self so it provides a loving environment for the Child parts within us. The better able we are
to nurture ourselves successfully, the less we are troubled
by the Saboteur and its destructive suggestions. Gradually,
it comes to respect us and our authority over our lives. As
we set limits with the Saboteur, its creative, determined,
clever, and persistent energies become available to us to
channel in constructive ways. But, we must never forget
that the Saboteur exists. It is a potential within us; it can be
subtle or blatant in its attacks. It swings into action when
we are stressed and challenged. If we fail to take it into
account, we empower it and leave ourselves vulnerable to
self-sabotage. We must acknowledge the Saboteur's presence and respect its potential if we are to stay in charge of
our lives.

When you transform your life, you are present and
active; willing to communicate and take a stand that
honors yourself and others in equal proportion. You tell
the truth without blame or judgment. You pay attention
and listen with awareness to your inner and outer experiences. You feed your body and your mind a diet that is
nourishing. Music, dance, and exercise are important
dimensions of your daily life. You create a beautiful home
for yourself. You enjoy the outdoors and spend some time
each day connecting with the planet that sustains you. You
have a life purpose and use your creativity to accomplish
that purpose. You are attuned to the spiritual dimension of
your being. You enjoy silence. You tell wonderful stories.
You are not attached to outcomes, but you are open to
what evolves in your life.

When you move beyond victim and transform your life after incest/sexual abuse, you know your strength and you know your vulnerability. You have a profound respect for the impact such a challenge has in a human being's life. You also know that healing is possible for anyone who keeps her commitment to attain it. You know, beyond the shadow of a doubt, that you are responsible for what you create. Mastering the challenge of sexual abuse, you know you can face whatever additional challenges life brings you.

Love heals and there is an abundant supply. Open your heart and take a deep breath! Release all that you need to release. Find your life's mission and set out on your adventure, knowing you will leave this world more healed than you found it. Create the joy you deserve. Your challenge is now. Claim it!

READERS' PERCEPTION OF INTERNAL SELVES

VULNERABLE INNER CHILD

NURTURING,
ENABLING SELF

SABOTEUR

318

VULNERABLE INNER CHILD

HAPPY INNER CHILD

SABOTEUR

NURTURING, ENABLING SELF

BIBLIOGRAPHY
THE PHYSICAL DIMENSION

THE INDIVIDUAL

Barbach, Lonnie, Ph.D. *For Each Other, Sharing Sexual Intimacy.* Garden City, NY: Anchor Books/Doubleday, 1983.

Barbach, Lonnie Garfield. *For Yourself, the Fulfillment of Female Sexuality.* New York: Anchor Books/Doubleday, 1976.

Gach, Michael Reed with Carolyn Marco. *Acu-Yoga, Designed to Relieve Stress and Tension.* Tokyo: Japan Publications, Inc., 1981.

Hay, Louise L. *You Can Heal Your Life.* Farmingdale, NY: Coleman Publishing, 1984.

Hittleman, Richard. *Richard Hittleman's Yoga: 28-Day Exercise Plan.* New York: Bantam Books, 1973.

Ponder, Catherine. *The Dynamic Laws of Healing.* Marina del Rey, CA: DeVorss & Company, 1972.

Ponder, Catherine. *The Healing Secrets of the Ages.* Marina del Rey, CA: DeVorss & Company, 1967.

Siegel, Bernie S., M.D. *Love, Medicine & Miracles.* New York: Harper & Row, 1986.

Simonton, O. Carl, M.D., Stephanie Matthews-Simonton, and James Creighton. *Getting Well Again.* Los Angeles: J. P. Tarcher, 1978.

FAMILIES AND RELATIONSHIPS

Cameron-Bandler, Leslie. *Solutions, Practical and Effective Antidotes for Sexual and Relationship Problems.* San Rafael, CA: FuturePace, Inc., 1985.

Lillibridge, E. Michael, Ph.D. *The Love Book for Couples Building A Healthy Relationship.* Atlanta, GA: Humanics Ltd., 1984.

McClendon, Ruth and Leslie B. Kadis. *Chocolate Pudding and Other Approaches to Intensive Multiple-Family Therapy.* Palo Alto, CA: Science and Behavior Books, Inc., 1983.

Satir, Virginia. *Conjoint Family Therapy.* Palo Alto, CA: Science and Behavior Books, Inc., 1967.

Satir, Virginia. *Making Contact.* Millbrae, CA: Celestial Arts, 1976.

Satir, Virginia. *Peoplemaking.* Palo Alto, CA: Science and Behavior Books, Inc., 1983.

THE WORLD WE SHARE

Ferguson, Marilyn. *The Aquarian Conspiracy.* Los Angeles: J. P. Tarcher, Inc., 1980.

Naisbitt, John. *Megatrends.* New York: Warner Books, 1982.

THE EMOTIONAL DIMENSION

Bass, Ellen and Louise Thornton. *I Never Told Anyone, Writings by Women Survivors of Child Sexual Abuse.* New York: Harper & Row, 1983.

Bolen, Jean Sninoda, M.D. *Goddesses In Everywoman.* San Francisco: Harper & Row, Inc., 1984.

Branden, Nathaniel. *The Psychology of Romantic Love.* Los Angeles: J. P. Tarcher, Inc., 1980.

Branden, Nathaniel. *The Psychology of Self-Esteem.* New York: Bantam Books, 1969.

Butler, Sandra. *Conspiracy of Silence: The Trauma of Incest.* San Francisco: Volcano Press, 1980.

Carter, Steven and Julia Sokol. *Men Who Can't Love.* New York: M. Evans and Company, Inc., 1987.

Cowan, Connell and Melvyn Kinder. *Smart Women, Foolish Choices.* New York: Crown, 1985.

Forward, Dr. Susan and Joan Torres. *Men Who Hate Women & The Women Who Love Them.* Toronto: Bantam Books, 1986.

Friday, Nancy. *My Mother My Self.* New York: Delacourte Press. 1977.

Haley, Jay. *Uncommon Therapy, The Psychiatric Techniques of Milton H. Erickson, M.D.* New York: W.W. Norton, 1973.

Herman, Judith Lewis. *Father-Daughter Incest.* Cambridge, MA: Harvard University Press, 1981.

Leonard, Linda Schierse. *On The Way To The Wedding, Transforming the Love Relationship.* Boston: Shambhala, 1986.

Leonard, Linda Schierse. *The Wounded Woman, Healing the Father-Daughter Relationship.* Athens, OH: Swallow Press, 1982.

Lerner, Harriet Goldhor, Ph.D. *The Dance of Anger, A Woman's Guide to Changing the Patterns of Intimate Relationships.* New York: Harper & Row, 1985.

Miller, Alice. *For Your Own Good: Hidden Cruelty In Child Rearing And The Roots Of Violence.* Translated from German by Hildegard and Hunter Hannum, New York: Farrar, Straus, Giroux, 1983.

Miller, Alice. *The Drama Of The Gifted Child.* Translated from German by Ruth Ward, New York: Basic Books, 1981.

Miller, Alice. *Thou Shalt Not Be Aware.* Translated from German by Hildegard and Hunter Hannum, New York: Farrar, Staus, Giroux, 1984.

Norwood, Robin. *Women Who Love Too Much.* Los Angeles: J.P. Tarcher, Inc., 1985.

Shainess, Natalie, M.D. *Sweet Suffering, Woman As Victim.* Indianapolis: The Bobbs-Merrill Co., Inc., 1984.

Woodman, Marion. *Addiction to Perfection.* Toronto: Inner City Books, 1982.

GESTALT THERAPY

Fagan, Joen and Irma Lee Shepherd. *Gestalt Therapy Now.* New York: Harper Colophon Books, Harper & Row, 1970.

Latner, Joel, Ph.D. *The Gestalt Therapy Book*. New York: The Julian Press, Inc., 1973.

Perls, Frederick S., M.D., Ph.D. *Gestalt Therapy Verbatim*. Lafayette, CA: Real People Press, 1969.

Perls, Frederick S., M.D., Ph.D. *In and Out the Garbage Pail*. Lafayette, CA: Real People Press, 1969.

Polster, Erving and Miriam Polster. *Gestalt Therapy Integrated*. New York: Brunner/Mazel, 1973.

Rosenblatt, Daniel. *Opening Doors, What Happens In Gestalt Therapy*. New York: Harper & Row, 1975.

Stevens, John O., (ed.) *Gestalt Is*. Moab, UT: Real People Press, 1975.

Zinker, Joseph. *Creative Process In Gestalt Therapy*. New York: Vintage Books, 1978.

TRANSACTIONAL ANALYSIS

Berne, Eric. *Beyond Games And Scripts*. New York: Grove Press, Inc., 1976.

Berne, Eric, M.D. *Transactional Analysis In Psychotherapy*. New York: Grove Press, Inc., 1961.

Berne, Eric, M.D. *What Do You Say After You Say Hello?* New York: Grove Press, Inc., 1972.

Goulding, Mary McClure and Robert L. Goudling. *Changing Lives Through Redecision Therapy*. New York: Brunner/Mazel, 1979.

James, Muriel. *Breaking Free, Self-Reparenting For A New Life*. Reading, MA: Addison-Wesley, 1981.

James, Muriel and Dorothy Jongeward. *Born to Win*. Reading, MA: Addison-Wesley, 1981.

Schiff, Jacqui. *Cathexis Reader, Transactional Analysis, Treatment of Psychosis*. New York: Harper & Row, Inc., 1975.

Steiner, Claude, Ph.D. *Games Alcoholics Play: The Analysis of Life Scripts*. New York: Grove Press, 1971.

THE MENTAL DIMENSION

PROSPERITY CONSCIOUSNESS

Cole-Whittaker, Terry. *How To Have More In A Have-Not World.* New York: Fawcett Crest, 1983.

Laut, Phil. *Money Is My Friend.* Hollywood, CA: Trinity Publications, 1978.

Leonard, Jim and Phil Laut. *Rebirthing: The Science of Enjoying All of Your Life.* Hollywood, CA: Trinity Publications, 1983.

Maltz, Maxwell, M.D., F.I.C.S. *Psycho-Cybernetics.* New York: Simon & Schuster, 1960.

Mandel, Bob. *Open Heart Therapy.* Berkeley, CA: Celestial Arts, 1984.

Orr, Leonard and Sondra Ray. *Rebirthing In The New Age.* Berkeley, Ca: Celestial Arts, 1977 and 1983.

Patent, Arnold M. *You Can Have It All.* Piermont, New York: Money Mastery Publishing, 1984.

Ponder, Catherine. *The Dynamic Laws of Prosperity.* Marina del Rey, CA: DeVorss & Company, 1962.

Ponder, Catherine. *The Prospering Power of Love.* Marina del Rey, CA: DeVorss and Company, 1966.

Ray, Sondra. *Celebration of Breath.* Berkeley, CA: Celestial Arts, 1983.

Ray, Sondra, *I Deserve Love.* Millbrae, CA: Les Femmes, 1976.

Ray, Sondra. *Loving Relationships.* Berkeley, CA: Celestial Arts, 1980.

Ray, Sondra. *The Only Diet There Is.* Berkeley, CA: Celestial Arts, 1981.

Ross, Ruth, Ph.D. *Prospering Woman.* Mill Valley, CA: Whatever Publishing, Inc., 1982.

Sher, Barbara with Annie Gottlieb. *Wishcraft, How To Get What You Really Want.* New York: Ballantine Books, 1979.

Waitley, Denis. 10 Seeds of Greatness. Old Tappan, NJ: Fleming H. Revell Company, 1983.

THE SPIRITUAL DIMENSION

Adler, Vera Stanley. From The Mundane To The Magnificent. York Beach, ME: Samuel Weiser, Inc., 1979.

Adler, Vera Stanley. The Finding Of The Third Eye. New York: Samuel Weiser, Inc., 1983.

Assagioli, Roberto, M.D. Psychosynthesis. New York; Penguin Books, 1965.

Capra, Fritjof. The Tao of Physics. Toronto: Bantam Books, 1976.

Capra, Fritjof. The Turning Point. New York: Simon and Schuster, 1982.

Easwaran, Eknath. Dialogue With Death. Nilgiri Press, 1981.

Fankhauser, Jerry, M.S.W. From A Chicken To An Eagle. Farmingdale, NY: Coleman Graphics, 1980.

Fankhauser, Jerry, M.S.W. The Way of the Eagle. Sugarland, Texas: Miracle Publishing Company, Inc., 1986.

Faraday, Dr. Ann. Dream Power. Berkeley, CA: Berkeley Publishing Corporation, 1972.

Faraday, Ann. The Dream Game. New York: Harper & Row, 1974.

Garfield, Patricia L., Ph.D. Creative Dreaming. New York: Ballantine Books, 1974.

Jampolsky, Gerald G. Goodbye To Guilt, Releasing Fear Through Forgiveness. Toronto: Bantam Books, 1985.

Jampolsky, Gerald G. Love Is Letting Go Of Fear. Berkeley, CA: Celestial Arts, 1979.

Jampolsky, Gerald G. Teach Only Love, The Seven Principles of Attitudinal Healing. Toronto: Bantam Books, 1983.

Joy, W. Brugh, M.D. Joy's Way, A Map For The Transformational Journey. Los Angeles: J. P. Tarcher, 1979.

McDonald, Phoebe. *Dreams, Night Language of the Soul*. Baton Rouge: Mosaic Books, 1985.

Moss, Richard, M.D. *The I That Is We*. Millbrae: CA: Celestial Arts, 1981.

Nelson, Ruby. *The Door Of Everything*. Marina del Rey, CA: DeVorss & Company, 1963.

Probstein, Bobbie. *Return To Center*. Marina del Rey, CA: DeVorss & Company, 1985.

Rodegast, Pat and Judith Stanton. *Emmanuel's Book*. New York: Some Friends of Emmanuel, 1985.

Roman, Sanaya. *Living with Joy*. Tiburon, CA: H.J. Kramer, Inc., 1985.

Small, Jacquelyn. *Transformers, The Therapists of the Future*. Marina del Rey, CA: DeVorss & Company, 1982.

Stone, Hal, Ph.D. *Embracing Heaven and Earth, A Personal Odessy*. Marina del Rey, CA: DeVorss & Company, 1985.

Stone, Hal, Ph.D. and Sidra Winkelman, Ph.D. *Embracing Our Selves*. Marina del Rey, CA: DeVorss & Company, 1985.

Talbot, Michael. *Beyond the Quantum*. New York: Macmillan Publishing Company, 1986.

Vaughn, Frances. *The Inward Arc*. Boston: Shambhala, 1986.

ORDER INFORMATION

Audio Tapes of the Meditations from this book are available from
Rainbow Books, P. O. Box 1069, Moore Haven, FL 33471, (813)
946-0293.

Tape 1: Side A: Centering and Changing Old Beliefs
Side B: Creating A New Past Reality for your
Child-Self

Tape II: Side A: Changing Troublesome Behavior Patterns
Side B: Forgiveness

Cassette tapes sell for $12.95 each or two for $19.95. Postage and
handling $1.50.

Books

Nurture Yourself To Success $9.95 each plus $1.50 postage and handling.
Beyond Victim $16.95 each plus $2.50 postage and handling.

If you are interested in being in touch with Martha Baldwin, you
can write or call her at:
OPTIONS NOW, INC.
901 N. W. 62nd Street
Oklahoma City, Oklahoma 73118
405-843-5258